BRI BEAUDOIN, creator of the popular blog *Evergreen Kitchen*, has been captivating her fans with delicious and healthy vegetarian recipes for years. While we all know that a home-cooked meal is the best for our budgets and our health, the idea of cooking dinner on weeknights can feel like a chore. With many of us eating more veggie-forward meals, it's no wonder busy home cooks are craving tasty vegetarian recipes that *everyone* at the dinner table will love.

Evergreen Kitchen is bursting with beautiful, flavourful recipes—that just so happen to be vegetarian. The recipes provide much-needed inspiration for delicious weeknight mains that are sure to make your taste buds sing, and a sprinkling of simple, yet scrumptious, desserts for those who like to end their meal with something sweet. Whether you want to cook a vegetarian meal one night a week—or every night—*Evergreen Kitchen* is packed with over 110 recipes to make it happen with dishes that satisfy the heartiest of appetites like Veggie Skillet Pot Pie and Cheesy Chipotle Quinoa Bake to Spicy Miso Ramen and Sheet-Pan Veggie Fajitas.

Throughout the book, there is something for everyone: salads that eat like a meal, easy one pot and sheet-pan recipes, crowd-pleasing noodles, nostalgic comfort foods, healthy bowls, hearty soups, delicious desserts, and so much more. Many of the recipes feature make-ahead options, easy substitutions, and modifications to make them vegan and/or gluten-free (if they aren't already). In addition, learn how to stock your pantry with the essentials, the small handful of kitchen tools that are actually worth having, and tips and tricks to make vegetarian meals craveable. Filled with gorgeous photography and plenty of step-by-step images throughout the book to illustrate exactly how to get things done, *Evergreen Kitchen* brings weeknight vegetarian dinners to life.

Evergreen Kitchen

Weeknight Vegetarian Dinners for Everyone

BRI BEAUDOIN

PHOTOGRAPHY BY ANGUEL DIMOV

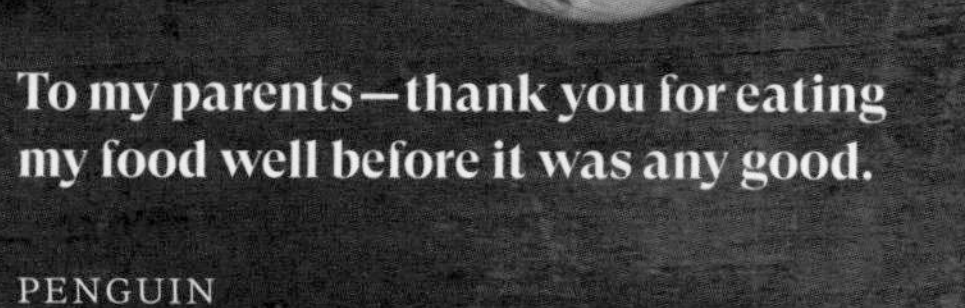

To my parents—thank you for eating my food well before it was any good.

PENGUIN
an imprint of Penguin Canada, a division of Penguin Random House Canada Limited
Canada • USA • UK • Ireland • Australia • New Zealand • India • South Africa • China

First published 2022

www.penguinrandomhouse.ca

Library and Archives Canada Cataloguing in Publication

Title: Evergreen Kitchen : weeknight vegetarian dinners for everyone / Bri Beaudoin.
Names: Beaudoin, Bri, author.
Identifiers: Canadiana (print) 20210394927 | Canadiana (ebook) 20210394943 | ISBN 9780735241923 (hardcover) | ISBN 9780735241930 (EPUB)
Subjects: LCSH: Vegetarian cooking. | LCGFT: Cookbooks.
Classification: LCC TX837 .B43 2022 | DDC 641.5/636—dc23

Cover and interior design by Kate Sinclair
Cover and interior photography by Anguel Dimov
Food and prop styling by Bri Beaudoin

Printed and bound in China

10 9 8 7 6 5 4 3 2 1

Penguin Random House
PENGUIN CANADA

CONTENTS

1 Introduction
4 How to Make Vegetarian Food Taste Better
10 Techniques for Cooking Smart
22 Kitchen Pantry
28 Kitchen Tools
33 Recipe Ideas for Occasions
34 Recipe Ideas for Meal Planning

Sheet Pans, Skillets & One-Pot Bakes

39 Baked Rice Pilaf with Feta and Roasted Tomatoes
40 Hot Honey Roasted Carrots and Lentils
43 Asparagus, Pea, and Whipped Feta Tart
44 Cheesy Chipotle Quinoa Bake
47 Firecracker Tofu with Broccolini and Chili Garlic Oil
48 Flatbread with Orange Arugula Salad
51 Lemongrass Coconut Rice with Roasted Eggplant
54 Miso Ginger Glazed Squash
57 Roasted Vegetables with Balsamic Glaze
58 Crispy Eggplant Roll-Ups
61 Sheet-Pan Veggie Fajitas
62 Harissa-Roasted Vegetables with Couscous
65 Pesto and Greens Frittata
66 Braised Vegetables with Parmesan Croutons

Noodles

71 Pesto Pantry Pasta
72 Mushroom Stroganoff
75 Spinach, Pea, and Pesto Pasta
76 Spicy Sesame Almond Noodles
79 Seared Mushroom and Creamy Garlic Pasta
80 Creamy Roasted Red Pepper Pasta
83 Lemon and Dill Orzo Salad
87 Spinach and Artichoke Pasta
88 Veggie Pad Thai
91 Roasted Cauliflower, Smashed Olive, and Lemon Pasta
92 Miso Brown Butter Pasta
95 Ginger Soy Soba Salad with Spicy Peanut Sauce
96 Roasted Butternut Squash Pasta with Toasted Hazelnuts
99 Coconut Green Curry Pasta

Classic-ish Comfort Foods

103 Meatless Meatballs with Garlic Bread
106 Veggie Skillet Pot Pie
109 Barbecue Pulled Mushroom Sandwiches
113 Healthier Macaroni and Cheese
114 Vegetable Ragu
117 Mediterranean Pesto Pizza
118 Shepherd's Pie
121 Actually Good Fried Rice
122 Vegetable Bourguignon
125 Pea Fritters and Fries with Tartar Sauce
126 Smoky Gouda Mushroom Melts
129 Crispy Veggie Potstickers
133 Buffalo-Sauced Cauliflower with Ranch Celery Salad
137 Savoury Cheddar Apple Hand Pies

Bowl Food

143 Pesto Grain Bowls with Jammy Eggs
144 Bibimbap with Crispy Rice
147 Polenta with Roasted Tomatoes and Basil Oil
148 Charred Sweet Potatoes with Tomato Chili Jam
151 Shortcut Brothy Beans
154 Falafel Bowls
157 Peanut-Glazed Tofu Rice Bowls
158 Smashed Potatoes and Roasted Cauliflower Bowls
161 Burrito Bowls with Smoky Sofritas
162 Orange Ginger and Sesame Meatballs

Handhelds

167 Shawarma-Spiced Mushroom Pita
168 Grilled Halloumi Skewers with Thai Basil and Lime Vinaigrette

171 Crispy Tofu Banh Mi
174 Chipotle Mushroom Tacos with Pineapple Jalapeño Salsa
177 Sweet Potato Black Bean Burgers with Chipotle Mayo
178 Curry Vegetable Fritters
181 Mushroom and Goat Cheese Toasts
182 Caprese Pesto Panini
185 Veggie Sushi with Sriracha Mayo
189 Seared Halloumi Sandwiches with Roasted Red Pepper Spread
190 Cheesy Mushroom Calzones
193 Blistered Tomatoes and Whipped Ricotta Toasts
194 Frico-Style Quesadillas
197 Balsamic Vegetable and Goat Cheese Sandwiches

Soups

201 Roasted Tomato Soup with Cheesy Bread
202 Silky Cauliflower Soup with Cheese and Pepper Crisps
205 Thai Yellow Coconut Curry with Lentils
206 Wild Rice and Mushroom Stew
209 Smoky Jalapeño Corn Chowder
210 Minestrone Soup with Pesto
213 Spicy Miso Ramen
216 Easy Veggie Chili
219 Roasted Butternut Squash Soup with Buttery Sage Croutons
220 Sesame and Smoked Tofu Noodle Soup
223 Potato and Lentil Stew with Crispy Shallots
224 No Cream of Broccoli Soup with Garlicky Breadcrumbs
226 Smoky Red Lentil Soup
229 Veggie Wonton Soup

Salads

235 Santa Fe Salad with Chipotle Lime Vinaigrette
236 Crispy Rice Salad with Smashed Cucumbers
239 Chickpea Salad with Crispy Pita
242 Broccoli Salad with Sticky Harissa Sauce
245 Seared Brussels Sprouts Caesar Salad
246 Green Goddess Salad with Everything Bagel Croutons
249 Vibrant Greens Salad with Sesame Lime Vinaigrette
250 Barley Salad with Mushrooms and Burrata
253 Kale Lentil Salad with Halloumi
254 Roasted Sweet Potatoes with Jalapeño Cilantro Slaw

Desserts

259 Jammy Raspberry Streusel Bars
262 Brown Butter Chocolate Walnut Cookies
265 Cardamom Sugar Knots
268 Chocolate Pudding with Pretzel Crumble
271 Whipped Yogurt Cream with Berries
274 Banana Chocolate Muffins
277 Bottomless Apple Caramel Pie
280 Flourless Chocolate Crackle Cookies
283 Butterscotch Banana Dutch Baby Pancake
284 S'mores No-Churn Ice Cream

Sauces & Extras

289 Quick Pickled Red Onions
290 Fresh Basil Pesto
290 Vegan Pesto
293 Tzatziki
293 Vegan Tzatziki
294 Yogurt Caesar Dressing
294 Vegan Caesar Dressing
297 Quick Pizza Dough
298 Everyday Guacamole
301 Garlic Mashed Potatoes
302 Cooking Rice

307 Acknowledgements
311 Index

INTRODUCTION

Let's get this out of the way now: I will not try to convince you to become a vegetarian. You don't need to be a vegetarian to enjoy vegetables, and you certainly don't need to be a vegetarian to eat a meatless meal once in a while. No matter what you usually eat, as long as you *love to eat*, I think we'll get along great.

We probably all ask ourselves the same question every day: What's for dinner? I'll confess, I've already asked this question twice today. First to Anguel, my husband, over breakfast. It was followed by a blank stare, a long pause, and an obnoxiously long sip of coffee. So I turned this question back to myself.

Not to be dramatic, but I think the idea of "dinner" stresses out a lot of people, myself included. What will I make? What do I need to buy from the store after work? Did Anguel polish off that last piece of bread in the cupboard? And as if the idea of dinner isn't stressful enough, throw a dietary preference into the mix. What the heck can I cook if I want to make a meatless main that isn't a salad?

My hope for this book is that it will help make your dinnertime a bit easier, and even more exciting. I want you to feel confident cooking a meatless meal that everyone at the table will love. Whether you're just looking for veggie-forward meal ideas, trying out Meatless Mondays, or feeding a vegetarian friend or family member, this book is for you. It's stuffed full of 100+ delicious vegetarian dinner recipes. The focus is entirely on main dishes (and a sprinkling of desserts) so there's no need to make a bunch of side dishes, unless you want to.

To cook the recipes in this book, you won't need to hunt down any specialty meat substitutes. All the necessary ingredients should be available at a well-stocked grocery store. Perhaps somewhat selfishly, these recipes reflect how I like to eat and what I like to cook for others. Mostly healthy. Occasionally indulgent. Always full of flavour. And, if you haven't figured it out by now, each recipe just so happens to be vegetarian.

This book is also about helping you become more confident as a home cook. Since we may never get a chance to cook together in *your* kitchen, I've also included some tricks I use in my own—like a speedy hands-free way to grate a chunk of Parmesan cheese, the method for "peeling" carrots that you never knew you needed, and a better way to "pick over" lentils (plus why you should even bother in the first place).

Because photos are often more helpful than words, there are plenty of step-by-step images throughout the book, to illustrate exactly how to get it done. We've got you covered.

The Evergreen Kitchen

After a couple years of dating, Anguel and I (kind of) quit our very intense corporate jobs in Toronto, packed our bags and our kittens, and moved to the Pacific Northwest. When the plane touched down in Vancouver, British Columbia, I was home. This was also the same year that Anguel asked if I wanted to try eating vegetarian with him. Surprisingly, it felt like a much bigger question than when he asked me to marry him a couple years later.

Eating is my favourite thing to do. I *live* to eat. My biggest concern was what would change if we became "those" people. Would friends ever want to come over for dinner again? Would we be signing up for a life of bland food that gets a pass just because it's vegetarian? Despite my fears ~~of commitment~~, the enthusiasm beaming from this very meat-and-potatoes man was hard to deny—we jumped in, taste buds first.

We learned a few things very quickly. Yes, there's a lot of bland food out there (vegetarian and otherwise). Yes, the best way to eat the food *you love* is to make it yourself. And no, it's not as hard as you might think. Over time, we realized our very-not-vegetarian friends and family kept coming over for dinner and what's more, they were asking for the recipes! Our blog *Evergreen Kitchen* was born.

Over the years, *Evergreen Kitchen* (evergreenkitchen.ca) has grown into something bigger than we expected. Now our recipes aren't just for friends and family. Readers are cooking and sharing our recipes around the world! Many of our readers aren't full-fledged vegetarians, and we think that's pretty cool. We're all about cooking food that anyone can enjoy. To make sure of it, most of the amazing recipe testers for this book would consider themselves very-not-vegetarian. Good food is good food, right?

I hope you find inspiration in these pages and discover some reliably tasty vegetarian dinner recipes to turn to. The opportunity to share recipes with you is not something I take lightly. So thank you so much for being here. I hope you love eating what's inside.

Now, let's get cooking!

Bri

HOW TO MAKE VEGETARIAN FOOD TASTE BETTER

People often ask me: "How do I make vegetarian food that *actually* tastes good?" The good news is, making vegetarian food taste better is the same as making *any* kind of food taste better.

Perhaps you were a bit too "free" when you free-styled dinner, or that delicious meal from last night tastes a bit flat today, or maybe your taste buds are just asking for a little *something-something*. If you're faced with some bland food—vegetarian or otherwise—let's fix it! Here are some tips for boosting flavour, including pantry ingredients that can help.

Sprinkle That Salt

Don't skip the salt: Home cooks often under-season. So if your food is tasting a bit bland, ask yourself: Is it seasoned enough? Even an extra pinch can go a long way.

Salt as you cook: Salting *while* cooking, rather than all at the end, gives the salt time to penetrate the food. The result is a well-seasoned and more delicious finished dish.

Salt to suit *your* tastes: Everyone has different tolerance levels for salt. Taste often as you cook and add more as needed. A small dish of extra salt on the table will let others season to their taste if they like things a bit saltier.

Add Some Acid

Vinegar isn't just for salads: I often add a splash of vinegar to soups and sauces after cooking. It's a subtle difference, but it brightens and balances the dish.

Use citrus, usually at the end: Use citrus zest *and* juice for the biggest impact. The flavour of citrus can fade as it sits, so I like to zest and juice just before adding it to the dish. If you're looking to retain the brightest flavour, add the citrus after cooking.

Quick pickles on everything (well, almost everything): I usually have a jar of quick pickled *something* in the fridge. Pickled vegetables add a delicious tangy element to a dish. You can use the quick-pickling technique on a variety of vegetables, such as red onions (page 289), carrots (page 171), and shallots (page 51).

Amp It Up with Umami

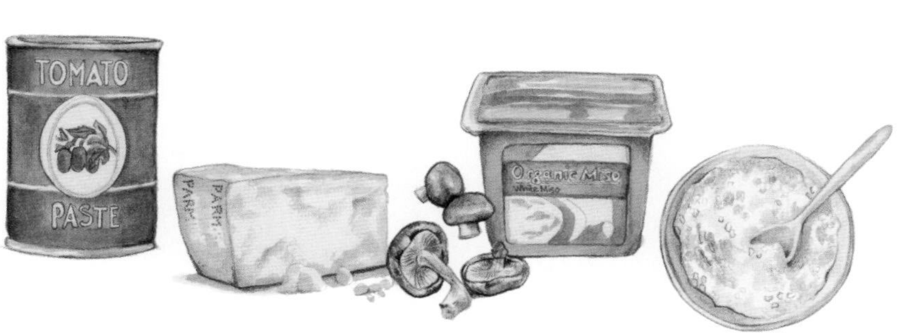

Umami isn't just from meat: Umami, or savouriness, is a rich and meaty element in food. Umami boosters like fish sauce, anchovies, and Worcestershire sauce get a lot of the attention, but there are plenty of vegetarian umami-rich foods too.

Enhance it by cooking or roasting: Our perceptions of umami are heightened in warm foods. Roasting vegetables such as cabbage, broccoli, and asparagus brings out their savoury characteristics more than when they're eaten raw.

Use fermented foods: Fermented foods such as tamari, miso, kimchi, and Parmesan cheese are rich in umami. Try incorporating one (or many) of these ingredients in your cooking.

Don't Forget the Fat

Fat is essential: We are programmed to want fat! Fat not only helps prevent foods from sticking to the pan, but it also facilitates browning, adds flavour, and improves mouthfeel. It's hard to make a dish feel satisfying without a little fat.

Add it yourself: Animal proteins contain fat—and they're usually cooked in it too. With vegetarian foods, you're going to need to add fat. Don't be nervous if it seems like a bit more than you're used to.

Look beyond oil: Some of the most obvious sources of fat are oils, like grapeseed, olive, and sesame oil. But other foods like nuts and seeds, dairy, and avocados are also sources of tasty fat.

Go On, Make It Spicy

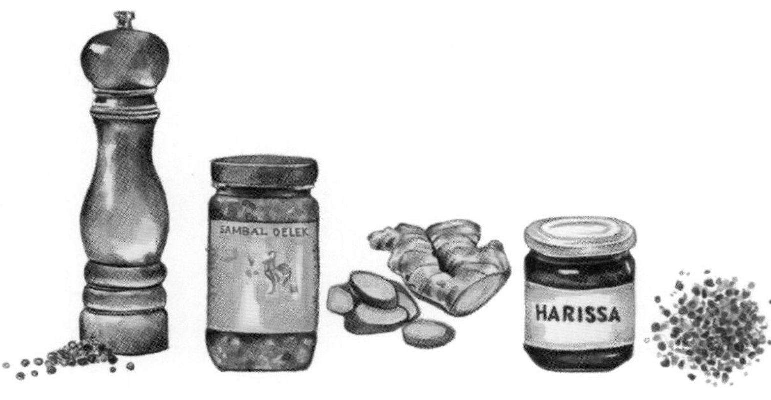

A little heat goes a long way: The sensation of heat can elevate a dish. It doesn't need to be blow-your-head-off spicy, or even register as a "spicy dish." Start small and go from there.

Not just pepper: Black pepper and red pepper flakes are easy ways to add a bit of heat. But there's a whole world of spice out there! Freshly grated ginger, Dijon mustard, and sambal oelek all bring heat in their own ways.

Spicy to you, not to me: We can all handle different amounts of heat. Make it how *you* like it. If you're serving a crowd, you can always go lighter on the heat—and give people the option to add more with hot sauce, red pepper flakes, or sliced fresh chilies on the side.

Layer on That Texture

Crunch factor: Searing, grilling, and roasting create a crispy, caramelized exterior. You can also add crunch through ingredients. Raw veggies such as radishes, carrots, celery, and snap peas add crunch. Or sprinkle on a crunchy topping such as chopped nuts, panko breadcrumbs, or croutons.

Soft and creamy: Creaminess can come from garnishes like a dollop of yogurt or gooey melted cheese. Condiments, sauces, and spreads are often creamy as well—think mayonnaise, tzatziki, or mashed avocado. The jammy yolk in a 6½-minute egg is creamy, as is a vegetable soup that's been blended until silky smooth.

Don't forget chewy: Chewy isn't always bad. Chewy elements, like al dente pasta, squeaky halloumi cheese, and sourdough bread or pizza crust, add varied texture to a dish.

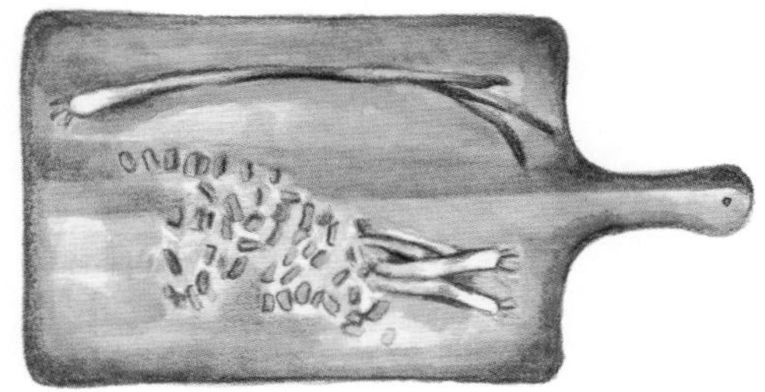

Dress It Up

First, we eat with our eyes: We see a dish before we taste it. Sure, a bit of garnish isn't going to redeem a bad dish, but if your food is looking a bit *meh*, take a second to accessorize.

Throw on some greens: Fresh greens can really liven things up. I often reach for flat-leaf parsley, cilantro, dill, basil, or thyme, depending what suits the dish. Microgreens and sprouts are another pretty (and healthy) way to incorporate some edible greenery.

Get creative: Try a scattering of red pepper flakes, coarsely ground black pepper, nuts and seeds, citrus zest, flaky salt, a spoonful of yogurt, breadcrumbs, a drizzle of olive oil, hot scallion oil, or whatever else looks good to you.

TECHNIQUES FOR COOKING SMART

Dinnertime can be hectic. Here are some time-saving tips for optimizing your time in the kitchen. You likely do some of these already, but perhaps there's a trick or two that's new!

cubed

diced

finely chopped

thinly sliced

matchsticks

finely grated
minced
chopped
shredded cheese
finely grated cheese

Grating Parmesan Cheese

When I need a small amount of grated Parmesan cheese, I usually use a microplane for speed and convenience. But if you need more (which is often the case), there's no shame in chucking it into the blender or food processor to get the job done quickly. Roughly chop the Parmesan, drop it into the blender or food processor, and blend until it is a finely grated, almost powder-like consistency. While you're at it, you can make extra to keep in the fridge for the week.

Finely grated, powdery Parmesan cheese—from a blender, food processor, the small holes on a box grater, or store-bought—typically weighs about 4 oz (113g) per 1 cup. Microplanes yield fluffier shreds of cheese that are twice as light, meaning that same 4 oz (113g) would probably measure closer to 2 cups. For this reason, the recipes in this book call for Parmesan cheese by weight, with approximate volumes provided for finely grated, powdery Parmesan. You can most definitely use a microplane instead, but if you're measuring by volume (cups), double what the recipe calls for.

Picking Over Lentils

Recipes using dried lentils call for "picked over" lentils. Why? Because a small pebble could have accidentally made it into your bag of lentils. It's unlikely, but if/when you find one, you'll be glad you checked. Nobody wants to bite down on a rock, no matter how small! I like to spread the dried lentils out on a parchment-lined baking sheet. That way, when I'm done picking over the lentils, I can use the parchment to make a funnel to transfer the lentils into a sieve for rinsing.

Picking Thyme Leaves

I cook with a lot of fresh thyme. I think it's an underrated herb that complements so many foods. When a recipe calls for "thyme leaves," it's calling for just the soft green leaves. Discard the tough woody stems.

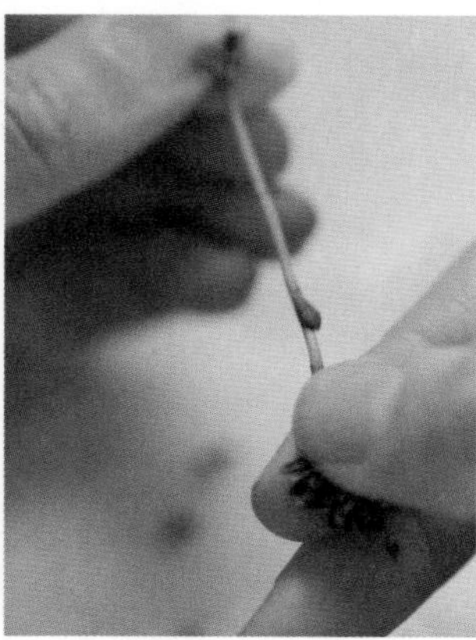

Peeling Vegetables

I look to save as much time as possible, and for me that usually means doing as little peeling as possible. For example, I often use Yukon Gold potatoes, which have a tender skin and so don't need to be peeled. If my ginger is fresh, I don't peel that either. (Nobody has complained, yet!) The recipes in this book will specify when you should peel—otherwise, assume it's fine to skip it (except onions and garlic, of course!). That said, you can always peel your veggies if you prefer—it's your kitchen, after all. Instead of peeling carrots, you can scrub them with a vegetable brush or even a green scrubbing pad. And for ginger, you can use the edge of a spoon to quickly remove the skin.

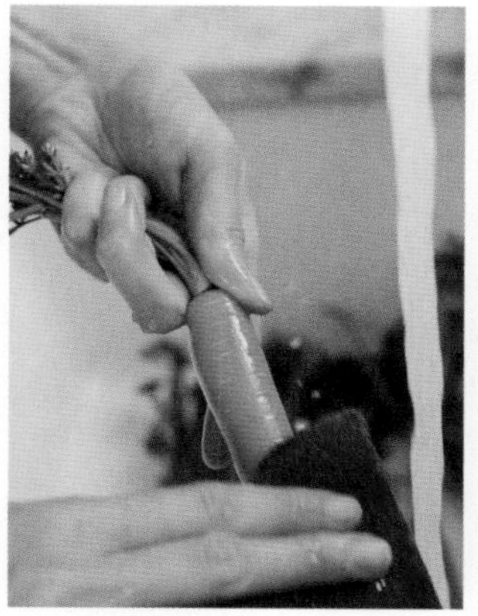

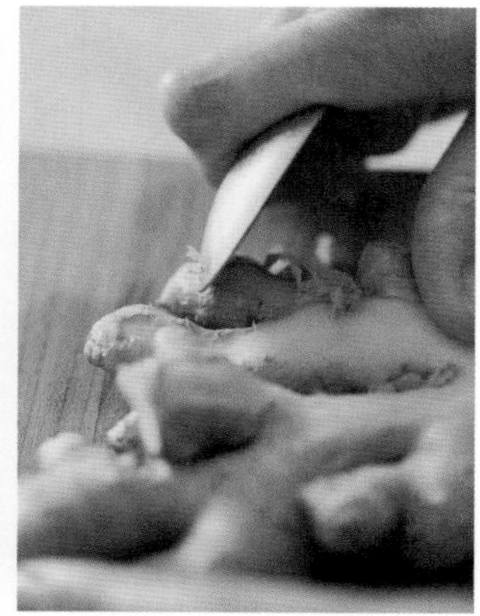

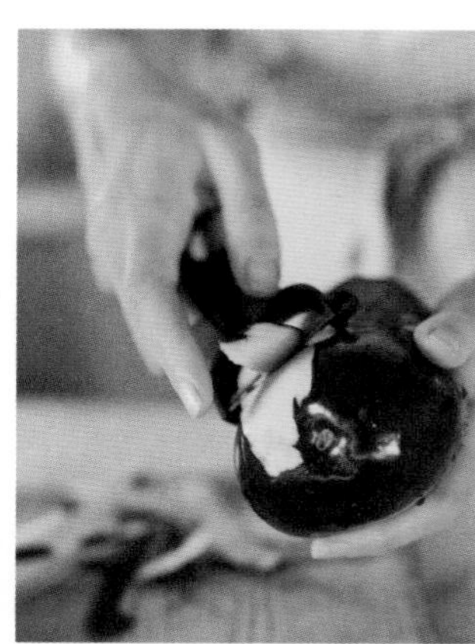

Pulling Mushrooms

Trumpet (aka king oyster) mushrooms can be shredded with a fork so they *almost* resemble pulled meat (especially once coated with sauce). Who would have thought?! Here's how to do it.

Using Shallots

Shallots come in a variety of sizes. In this book, recipes call for either medium or large shallots. One medium shallot yields about ¼ cup minced; one large shallot yields about ½ cup minced. You don't need to remember the approximate yields; those will be stated in the recipe.

Stemming Kale

There are a couple ways to go about this, but here's my favourite way to remove kale stems. Simply hold the base of the stem in one hand, then run your other hand down the stem to separate the leaves. It can be done directly in the colander, before or after rinsing.

Browning Butter

Browned butter has a delicious nutty flavour. To make it, heat up butter in a small saucepan so that the milk solids in the butter fall to the bottom of the pan, where they develop more colour and flavour. Keep a close eye on the butter: it can go from brown to burnt quite quickly. Stop when the butter looks like the picture in the middle; that's what you want for the recipes in this book.

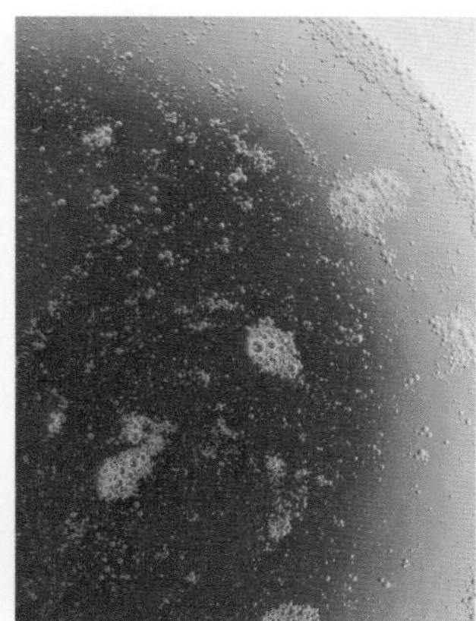

Measuring Flour

I highly recommend a scale so you can skip this step entirely. But if you'll be measuring flour in measuring cups, use the spoon-and-level method. Keep the flour as fluffy as you can. More often than not, too much flour gets packed into a measuring cup.

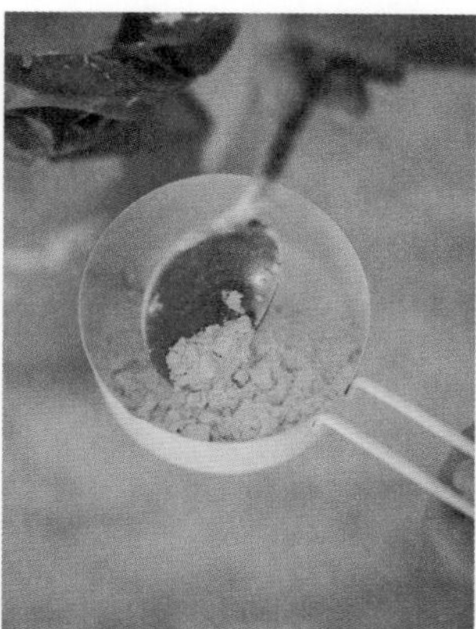

Reviving Stale Bread

We've all been there: that delicious loaf of sourdough has dried up before you finished it. Bring it back to life by quickly rinsing the bottom of the loaf, under the tap, until it's damp but not soggy. Place the loaf directly on a rack in the middle of the oven at 400°F (200°C) until warmed through and crisp on the outside but soft on the inside, about 10 minutes.

Segmenting Citrus

Citrus segments, also known as supremes, have had the bitter pith and tough membranes cut away. This makes them pretty, tastier, and easy to eat. It's like a professionally peeled orange—looking at it, it's all fruit. This might sound complicated, but it's not. Once you get the hang of it, you'll be able to make pretty citrus supremes whenever you want!

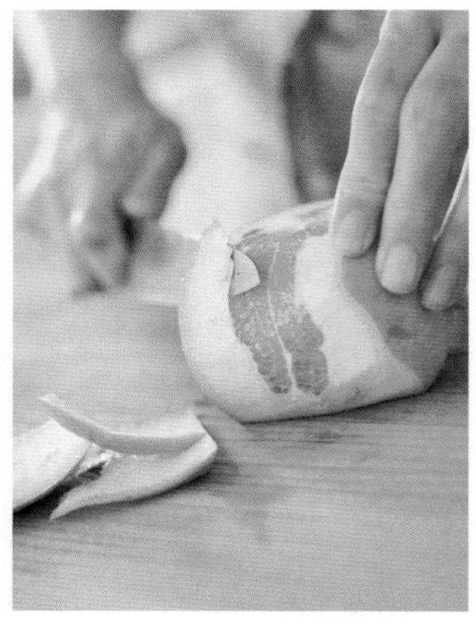

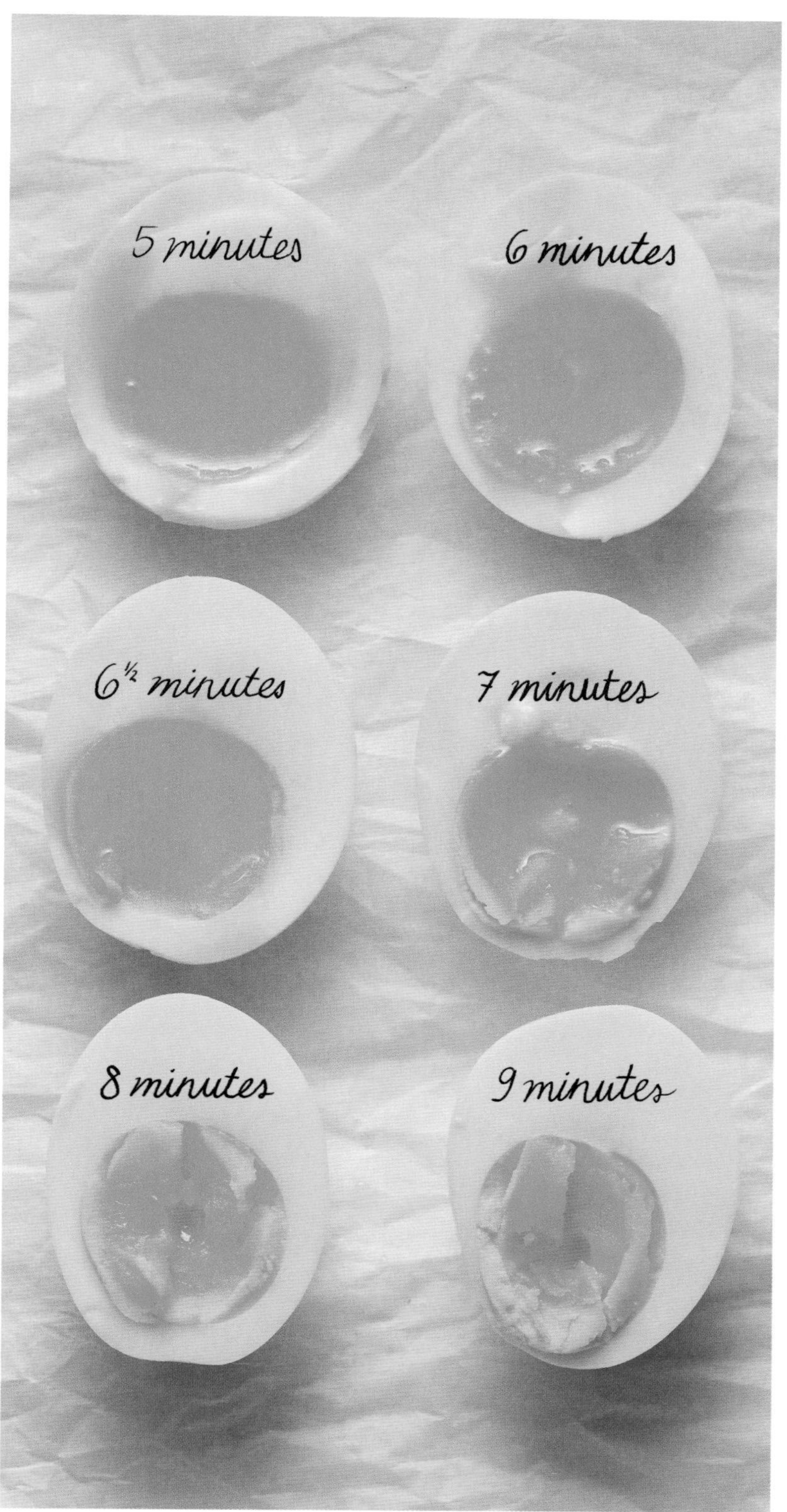

Boiling Eggs

The recipes in this book call for cooking soft-boiled eggs for 6½ minutes (my personal favourite). If you like your eggs cooked less or more, here's a visual guide of cook times. These are the results for large eggs, cooked straight from the refrigerator, and placed in an ice bath after cooking.

Bringing Eggs to Room Temperature

Some dessert recipes call for using room-temperature eggs because they mix more evenly into batter. To warm up cold eggs, submerge the whole eggs in a bowl of warm (but not hot) water for about 10 minutes.

KITCHEN PANTRY

A well-stocked pantry can prepare you for almost anything. But it can also become a black hole of forgotten ingredients that hog precious pantry space. Believe me, I've been there. Your kitchen pantry is *yours*. Stock it with the items that you love *and* will use regularly.

Here are the pantry items that show up often in this book. If you come across a new-to-you ingredient, or need some substitution ideas, check back here. There are also some ideas for ways to use these pantry items, easy substitutes, and tips for buying. These items should be available at a well-stocked grocery store. But if you run into trouble, there's always the internet.

7 Unexpectedly Delightful Pantry Ingredients

Rice vinegar (PAGE 24)

Tamari (PAGE25)

Vegetable stock (bouillon) (PAGE 25)

Miso (PAGE 25)

Canned fire-roasted tomatoes (PAGE 26)

Chipotle peppers in adobo sauce (PAGE 25)

Dried mushrooms (PAGE 26)

Oil and Butter

Grapeseed Oil: My neutral oil of choice. Its high smoke point makes it good for grilling and searing. *Substitute with: another neutral vegetable oil such as sunflower, safflower, or canola.*

Extra-Virgin Olive Oil: A versatile flavoured oil that can be used for cooking or finishing. Different brands of olive oils vary in taste and quality, so see which ones you like best.

Toasted Sesame Oil: A dark, nutty-tasting oil made from toasted sesame seeds. I mostly use it for seasoning after cooking. Toasted sesame oil has a delicious and distinctive flavour, so a little goes a long way.

Butter: For the most control, use unsalted butter and add the salt yourself. All the recipes in this book were tested with unsalted butter. However, if you just have salted butter on hand, don't fret. For any recipe that calls for "butter" you can use salted or unsalted, because it isn't a large enough quantity or a recipe sensitive enough to make a big difference. Where "unsalted butter" is specified, this is what you should use. This will typically be the case for baking recipes that call for higher quantities of butter and where extra salt *could maybe* throw off the science that is baking.

Salt

Fine Sea Salt: A good everyday salt. While I recommend fine sea salt over table salt, you can substitute them 1:1 if needed. All the recipes in this book were tested using fine sea salt. (*See* Kosher Salt.)

Kosher Salt: Kosher salt is what I'd consider a great everyday salt. It has lighter, fluffier crystals, which makes it easier to pinch and evenly sprinkle over food. The big BUT is that there are different kinds of kosher salt, so they cannot be substituted 1:1. You'll need a larger volume of kosher salt compared to fine sea salt. And that amount varies by brand: 1 teaspoon of fine sea salt = 2 teaspoons of Diamond Crystal kosher salt = 1¼ teaspoons of Morton kosher salt. These discrepancies are why the recipes in this book were tested with fine sea salt, for ease of use and so that you don't need to track down a specific brand of salt. But if you'd like to substitute, use a 2× ratio to scale up from fine sea salt to Diamond Crystal and a 1.25× ratio to scale up to Morton.

Flaky Sea Salt: A finishing salt. The large, flaky crystals are not only pretty to look at but also add a bit of crunch. Sprinkle flaky sea salt on top of your food just before eating.

Vinegar

Rice Vinegar: The mildest vinegar in my pantry, which happens to be the one I use most often. Rice vinegar is available "regular" or "seasoned." Choose regular (unseasoned) rice vinegar for the most versatility, because you can always add extra seasoning yourself. Check the package to confirm the rice vinegar is gluten-free, if needed. *Substitute with: apple cider vinegar.*

Apple Cider Vinegar: Since it's made from fermenting apple juice, apple cider vinegar has a mild fruity flavour. Try it in Date Barbecue Sauce (page 109) and Quick Pickled Red Onions (page 289). *Substitute with: rice vinegar.*

White Wine Vinegar: Sharper than apple cider vinegar, but milder than red wine vinegar. I use it when I'm looking for enough acidity to cut through rich dishes without overwhelming them. *Substitute with: red wine vinegar (if its colour isn't an issue)—otherwise rice vinegar.*

Red Wine Vinegar: A punchy vinegar that also adds a pretty pink hue. I use this vinegar when it needs to hold its own amongst other strong flavours, like in Broccoli Salad with Sticky Harissa Sauce (page 242). *Substitute with: white wine vinegar.*

Balsamic Vinegar (+ Balsamic Glaze): An intense, darkly flavoured vinegar. Delicious in vinaigrettes and marinades, like Balsamic Vegetable and Goat Cheese Sandwiches (page 197). Balsamic glaze is made by reducing balsamic vinegar until it's an extra-thick syrup. You can make it yourself, but I usually just buy balsamic glaze from the store. It's great for drizzling onto pizza, sandwiches, and roasted veggies.

Sauces, Spices, and Other Seasonings

Vegetable Stock (Bouillon): Bouillon concentrates are a more efficient way to buy and store vegetable stock. Packaged liquid stock is mostly water—and you can add that part yourself! As much as I don't tend to rely on a single brand for anything, Better Than Bouillon is my go-to bouillon paste. Their Organic Seasoned Vegetable Base makes a good all-around stock. But if you want to branch out, their No Chicken and No Beef varieties work well when you're looking to add a more "meaty" flavour. Dried bouillon cubes work as an alternative.

Tamari: At home, I usually cook with gluten-free tamari. Tamari is a source of umami and salt. I use it often, and even in dishes where you might not expect it, like Meatless Meatballs (page 103), Chipotle Mushroom Tacos (page 174), and Smoky Gouda Mushroom Melts (page 126). Check the package to confirm the tamari is gluten-free, if needed. *Substitute with: soy sauce.*

White Miso: Miso is a fermented soybean paste. There are many varieties of miso, but to keep things simple, all recipes in this book use white (shiro) miso. White miso paste tends to be the most commonly available at grocery stores. It's also the mildest variety: it's slightly sweeter and less salty than other miso pastes such as red (aka) and yellow (shinshu) miso. Check the package to confirm the miso is gluten-free, if needed. *Substitute with: yellow miso.*

Dijon Mustard: Dijon mustard is one versatile condiment! You can spread it directly on sandwiches, use it in vinaigrettes as an emulsifier, or add a spoonful to sauces for extra flavour. I use smooth Dijon mustard most often, but like to keep grainy Dijon on hand too.

Sambal Oelek: A fiery Indonesian chili paste. It adds heat to fried rice, sauces, and noodles. Sambal oelek is usually sold in a clear container with a screw-top lid, and you can often find it on the shelf next to Sriracha sauce. Sambal oelek tastes spicier and less sweet than Sriracha. I also like that it's chunkier, with visible chili seeds. *Substitute with: Sriracha or chili garlic paste.*

Harissa: A spicy chili paste often used in Middle Eastern and North African cuisines. I especially love rose harissa, which has dried rose petals mixed into it. Some brands of harissa are much spicier than others. The recipes in this book typically show a range of measure; start with the smaller amount and add more to taste. Harissa can be found in well-stocked grocery stores, in Middle Eastern grocery stores, and online.

Thai Curry Paste: Pre-made Thai curry paste has saved me on many occasions. Sure, it isn't as flavourful as if you made it fresh with a mortar and pestle, but on a weeknight, the convenience factor makes it worth it for me. Curry pastes often contain shrimp, so check the label to confirm if it's vegetarian.

Nutritional Yeast: Nutritional yeast is a source of umami, so it adds an extra depth of flavour in cooking. It has a slight cheesy taste, which makes it well suited for many plant-based dishes. Nutritional yeast also tastes amazing on popcorn, just saying. Often found in the health food aisle or baking section of grocery stores.

Dried Spices: Dried spices lose their potency over time, so buy small quantities if you can—ideally from grocers that restock their shelves often. The dried spices in these recipes can be found at most grocery stores. "Smoked paprika" refers to smoked sweet paprika, not hot (spicy) paprika. Black pepper should always be freshly ground; it is more flavourful this way.

Cans, Jars, and Dry Goods

Chipotle Peppers in Adobo Sauce: Not only do these peppers pack heat and flavour, but the tangy, smoky, spicy adobo sauce does as well. I usually use a mix of both the peppers and the sauce. If you're sensitive to heat, pick the smallest pepper in the can and use less adobo sauce. Leftovers can be stored in the fridge—or for longer storage (up to 3 months), keep frozen in an ice cube tray or small freezer bag.

Fire-Roasted Tomatoes: As the name implies, these tomatoes have been charred over a fire for subtle smokiness. You can usually buy these tomatoes crushed or diced. I use both—and often.

Tomato Paste: Choose an unseasoned tomato paste for the most versatility. Out of the can (or tube), tomato paste has a pretty intense raw tomato flavour. Caramelizing the tomato paste, by cooking it in oil until it deepens in colour, helps to intensify its flavour. You'll see this method used throughout the book.

Tomato Passata: An uncooked tomato purée that has been strained so that it's completely smooth. It's often sold in tall glass jars, usually located near pasta sauces and canned tomatoes. Passata works well in tomato-based sauces like the Cheesy Chipotle Quinoa Bake (page 44).

Coconut Milk: For the tastiest results, go with full-fat coconut milk. I don't recommend buying low-fat cans: they're a watered-down version, for the same price. If you need, you can always water it down yourself, for free!

Barista-Style Non-Dairy Milk: As a dairy-free alternative to using cream in cooking, I prefer to use barista-style milks or creamers. They often have a slightly higher fat content to replicate the mouthfeel of dairy, and tend to be more neutral in taste. Choose plain, unsweetened non-dairy milk in savoury cooking applications so you don't add an unexpected flavour or sweetness to the dish.

Roasted Red Peppers: Blend them into sauce, chop them up for pasta, or add them to sandwiches. I prefer to buy the jars with whole peppers rather than sliced ones. I find it faster to pull out a whole pepper rather than trying to fish out a bunch of little pieces.

Sun-Dried Tomatoes (Oil-Packed): I always buy oil-packed sun-dried tomatoes for the most flavour—and for convenience. Dry-packed sun-dried tomatoes often require the extra step of rehydrating them in liquid. All recipes in this book were tested with oil-packed varieties.

Dried Mushrooms: Dried mushrooms add depth to meatless cooking. I mostly use dried shiitakes and porcini. You can grind them into powder or rehydrate them in liquid. Porcini and shiitake aren't often a 1:1 swap because their flavour and intensity vary. Generally, dried porcini can more quickly overpower a dish, so use a lighter hand. In recipes where swaps are possible, the amounts are listed.

Noodles: Dried pasta and other noodles (such as soba and rice noodles) are incredibly convenient. Try to keep a couple packages on hand for fast, comforting meals.

Rice: While there are a lot of different amazing rice varieties out there, this book primarily calls for jasmine rice, medium-grain white rice, long-grain white rice, and short-grain brown rice. If you cook a lot of rice, a rice cooker can be a good investment. For stovetop cooking instructions, see page 302.

Proteins

Canned Beans: The convenience of canned beans is undeniable. Before using, drain and rinse the beans to remove excess salt and cooking liquid. *Substitute with: For 1 regular-sized can (14 fl oz / 398 ml) of beans, use 1½ cups of home-cooked beans.*

Canned and Dried Lentils: Generally speaking, dried lentils are fairly quick cooking, but some varieties do take longer than others. I use both canned and dried lentils, depending on the dish—and how much time I have. *Substitute with: For 1 regular-sized can (14 fl oz / 398 ml) of lentils, use 1½ cups of home-cooked lentils.*

Tofu (including Smoked Tofu): Tofu gets a bad rap, and I don't think that's fair! Tofu has a lot of potential—when seasoned and cooked well, it is satisfying, filling, and delicious. But I totally respect if tofu's not your thing. I grew up eating tofu and I love it, so you'll see it show up in some of my recipes. Tofu is usually labelled by firmness—I often use extra-firm or firm varieties. Smoked tofu is precooked tofu that's been smoked to infuse it with extra flavour. It's quite firm out of the package, so you can just chop it up and add it to the dish.

Nuts and Nut Butters: Nuts are an amazing way to add crunch and flavour—and they can also be used to make a variety of creamy sauces. Some of my recipes use either peanut butter or almond butter, and they're often interchangeable. I opt for an all-natural roasted smooth variety. When it comes to nuts, they're prone to rancidity, so buy them in small quantities, eat them quickly, and store them in the fridge or freezer to maximize freshness.

Greek Yogurt: I use plain Greek yogurt in both sweet and savoury dishes. It can often be used in place of mayonnaise, sour cream, or even buttermilk. For the best flavour, choose a full-fat variety.

A Note on Vegetarian Ingredients

There are some foods you might expect to be vegetarian but are surprisingly not, at least not *technically*. For many people, this isn't a concern. And that's totally cool—just skip this section. Everyone's stance on this topic is different: even vegetarians seem to draw different lines in the sand. If it matters to you, or you're feeding someone where this nuance would be important, here are some things to look out for throughout the book.

Cheese: Rennet, an animal-derived enzyme, is often used to coagulate the milk when making cheese. It's not used in all cheeses, but often in imported Parmesan and Gruyère, among others. A growing number of producers are using vegetarian-friendly enzymes instead. Check to see if the cheese is labelled "vegetarian-friendly"—or if it lists "microbial enzymes" (instead of rennet) in the ingredients list. If you're looking for a vegetarian Parmesan but can't find it, use Asiago instead.

Pesto Sauce: Most store-bought pesto sauces contain Parmesan cheese. It may not be obvious if that cheese contains rennet. If this is something that concerns you, your best bet is to make your own pesto. You can use vegetarian-friendly Parmesan or Asiago cheese in the Fresh Basil Pesto (page 290). Or, skip the cheese entirely and make the Vegan Pesto (page 290).

Thai Curry Paste: Curry pastes can contain shrimp. Check the label to confirm. There are a number of vegetarian curry pastes to choose from, including the widely available Thai Kitchen brand.

Red Wine: Animal products are sometimes used in producing wine. If this is something you want to avoid, check the labels for a vegetarian symbol or ask the retailer for assistance.

Marshmallows: Most marshmallows contain gelatin, which is commonly derived from animal collagen. Look for a vegetarian/vegan-friendly brand (such as Dandies), if needed.

Note: This isn't intended to be a comprehensive list. If you're ever unsure, just check the ingredient label.

Vegan and Gluten-Free

Many of the recipes in this book are either vegan and/or gluten-free—or can be easily made so based on the modification notes at the bottom of the page. Look for these symbols:

If you see a recipe with one of these symbols, but no modification notes at the bottom of the page, then it is already vegan and/or gluten-free. Otherwise, follow the modification suggestions to make it so.

To avoid repetition in this book, all miso paste, tamari, and rice vinegar listed in the recipes are assumed to be gluten-free, if that's something you need. If you have a dietary restriction, always read the labels to confirm because ingredients vary by brand.

While I have included my suggestions for vegan and gluten-free alternatives, there are more and more amazing options coming onto the market each day. Feel free to use the substitutes you love best and make adaptations as you need.

KITCHEN TOOLS

No one wants to hack their way through a tomato with a dull knife or always be googling "how much does an [insert ingredient] weigh." That's why investing in a good set of tools can make cooking easier and more enjoyable. Here's the list of tools I love, how to use them, and what to look for if you're inspired to get one. With that said, you do *not* need to rush out and get the items you don't have. Add them over time, and give priority to the tools you'll actually use.

7 Kitchen Tools You'll Reach for Over and Over Again

Chef's knife (*that's actually sharp*) (PAGE 30)

Digital kitchen scale (PAGE 31)

Microplane (rasp grater) (PAGE 31)

Kitchen timer (PAGE 31)

Flexible (Fish) spatula (PAGE 30)

Offset spatula (PAGE 31)

Enamelled Dutch oven (PAGE 30)

Microplane
BLADE MADE IN USA
OXO
clock
T1
T2
T3
1
2
3
4
5
6
7
8
9
clear/ memory
0
stop/ start
Winco
STAINLESS
UNIT

Cookware

Raw Cast-Iron Skillet: Great for high-heat cooking. I recommend a 12-inch (30 cm) skillet, but a 10-inch (25 cm) works too. Even better if you can get one of each. You will need to season them regularly to achieve an *almost* nonstick finish. Raw cast iron can be sensitive to highly acidic foods like tomatoes. If you're planning to simmer a tomato sauce for a while, play it safe and grab a different pan (like enamelled cast iron or stainless steel). Otherwise, a quick splash of acid at the end of cooking shouldn't be an issue if your pan is well seasoned. *(Visit evergreenkitchen.ca for instructions on how to season and care for your cast iron.)*

Large Dutch Oven: A Dutch oven is a heavy pot with a tight-fitting lid. For me, these are workhorses in the kitchen, used for soups and stews and all sorts of cooking. I use enamelled cast iron. Enamelled cookware usually performs best at medium heat, rather than medium-high. If you struggle with food sticking to the bottom, reduce the heat. Because of cast iron's heat retention, the Dutch oven will still be plenty hot. A 5½ to 6-quart (5.5 to 6 L) capacity (large) is typically good for everyday cooking. These pots can be a bit pricy if you choose one of the traditional brands, but there are increasingly more affordable options available, so do your research and buy the best quality you can afford. You might just have it for your lifetime. If you don't have a Dutch oven, use a large pot instead.

Large Nonstick Skillet: There are some situations where I'll reach for my nonstick pan over my well-seasoned cast iron. Crisping up rice and frying eggs for the Bibimbap with Crispy Rice (page 144) is one of them. Nonsticks allow you to get a golden crust without using a ton of oil. Treat your pan with care and skip the sharp/abrasive utensils so you don't damage the finish. And if the finish does get damaged, don't hesitate to replace the pan. A skillet 10 to 12 inches (25 to 30 cm) wide is plenty.

Small and/or Medium Saucepans: Use these for cooking and warming smaller quantities of food, like leftover soups and sauces. I use a pretty basic stainless steel saucepan with a lid. Depending on how much cooking you do at once, you may want to get a couple of different sizes.

Large Pot: Use for cooking large amounts of food—and, perhaps more importantly, boiling pasta. You want the pot to be deep enough to fit long noodles like spaghetti. A 6 to 8-quart (6 to 8 L) pot usually does the trick.

Braiser or Enamelled Casserole: Think of a braiser as a cross between a skillet and a Dutch oven. It has shallower sides, with a tight-fitting lid. The shallower sides make it great for cooking *and* baking casseroles, so you can skip the step of transferring the mixture into a casserole dish for baking. I use mine a lot more than I initially expected. That said, I'd recommend investing in a Dutch oven first. But if you're looking to expand, consider a braiser next. A 3½ to 4-quart (3.5 to 4 L) braiser has the same capacity as a 13 x 9-inch (3.5 L) casserole dish.

Smallish Things

Chef's Knife: A good sharp knife makes all the difference: invest in one. Everyone has a personal preference when it comes to length, weight, and shape, so pick the one that feels good to *you*. The blade of an average chef's knife is usually around 8 inches (20 cm), but feel free to go up or down from there. And for heaven's sake: keep it sharp! Either learn to sharpen it yourself or take it to a professional who can.

Flexible (Fish) Spatula: I may not eat fish, but I do love this type of spatula. The thin, slotted metal end is flexible enough to manoeuvre into skillets but also sturdy enough to scrape up the brown bits from the bottom of a baking sheet. I prefer one with a wooden handle, so I don't need to worry about plastic melting.

Silicone Spatula: A heatproof silicone spatula can be used to mix cookie batter, stir brown butter, and cook eggs in a nonstick pan. I prefer a silicone spatula with a head that's not too firm, but also not too flimsy. Pick one that feels good in your hand, because you'll be holding it often!

Small Offset Spatula: This five-dollar tool is my Swiss Army knife in the kitchen. It has a flexible blade and rounded edges, which makes it perfect for loosening muffins in baking tins, spreading butter, flipping small items, even stirring ingredients in a pinch.

Microplane (Rasp Grater): This small handheld grater makes quick work of grating hard cheeses like Parmesan—as well as finely grating citrus zest, garlic, and ginger for recipes where mincing won't quite do. Once you get one, it'll be hard to imagine life without it.

Box Grater: You likely already have this, but it's worth a mention. Use this for shredding not-so-hard cheeses like cheddar and mozzarella. Also great for quickly grating vegetables, like for Curry Vegetable Fritters (page 178).

Colander: This humble kitchen tool is one you probably have. Great for straining large volumes of pasta, vegetables, etc., and for anytime you don't have an extra hand to hold a sieve. A basic stainless steel one is all you need.

Fine-Mesh Sieve: Use for rinsing rice and lentils, scooping things out of boiling water, or on the rare occasion you need to sift flour. Look for a sieve with a fairly fine mesh, so that you can use it to catch ingredients that would pass through a colander.

Digital Kitchen Scale: Some ingredients, such as grated cheese, are better measured by weight than volume. For baking, a digital kitchen scale is almost essential. Baked goods are much less forgiving when quantities are off—something that is usually the case with fluffy ingredients like flour and icing (powdered) sugar.

Kitchen Timer: I love my triple timer. It helps me keep track of when different items should be coming out of the oven, and I don't need to worry about fumbling with a timer on my cell phone.

Cookie Dough Scoop: These make it super easy to portion out batter and dough, for anything from falafel to meatballs to cookies (of course). I use a 2-tablespoon scoop (No. 30) most often, but they come in a range of sizes.

Citrus Squeezer: I'm generally not a fan of single-use tools, but the exception is a citrus squeezer. I use a lot of fresh citrus, so this makes sure I get every drop, and none of the seeds. A wooden reamer works too, if you prefer.

Mandoline: Not absolutely necessary if you have a sharp knife, but it does quickly shave vegetables into razor-thin pieces. If you do a lot of veggie prep, or have a thing for pretty vegetables, you might want to consider one. Mandolines can be dangerous, so use the guard to be safe.

Painter's Tape: If you're tired of fishing leftovers out of the fridge and asking yourself "WHAT is this?" then you might just fall in love with painter's tape. Use it to label containers, then simply peel off the tape when you're done.

Bakeware

Large Rimmed Baking Sheets: I recommend getting the largest baking sheets that'll fit in your oven: usually that's a half sheet pan (18 x 13-inch / 45 x 33 cm). The larger the baking sheet, the more space you have for spreading out ingredients. I use uncoated aluminum sheets with rolled edges, because they're durable and inexpensive. I usually get them from restaurant supply stores—nothing fancy! Baking sheets with nonstick coatings are also available, but the coating can scratch over time. Instead, I just line my baking sheets with parchment paper to prevent sticking—and when roasting acidic ingredients like tomatoes.

Casserole Dish: A 13 x 9-inch (33 x 23 cm) casserole dish is a standard size, at 3½ quarts (3.5 L). Not all casserole dishes can go under the broiler—glass, for example, should not be broiled—so look for one that is labelled "broiler-safe." In many recipes a braiser can be used in place of a casserole dish (it also has the benefit of being able to go from stovetop to oven to tabletop).

Square Cake Pans: A cake pan isn't just for cakes. It can be used for bars like Jammy Raspberry Streusel Bars (page 259). I also use a cake pan when I want to squeeze something small into the oven, like when I want to keep beets separate from other veggies. I recommend an 8-inch (20 cm or 2 L) or 9-inch (23 cm or 2.5 L) light-coloured metal pan.

Muffin Pan: I like a light-coloured nonstick muffin pan. Darker pans encourage more browning on the bottoms and sides of the muffin. If you use a dark pan, check the muffins a couple minutes before the recipe prompts you to, just in case.

Oven Thermometer: If you think your oven runs hot or cold, buy an inexpensive oven thermometer to find out. Most ovens are off to some degree, and sometimes the difference is huge! I keep a thermometer in my oven—this way I always know when I'm working at the right temperature.

Kitchen Appliances

High-Speed Blender: These can be expensive, but they do last. When my husband and I started dating, he was appalled by how much my high-speed blender cost. Now, more than a decade later, we still use the same one daily (he has since apologized, to the blender). Check online for refurbished models. High-speed blenders have lids designed for blending hot soups—something many standard blenders do not. So if you're using a standard blender with hot liquids, work in smaller batches and remove the centre cap (so pressure doesn't build up) and cover it with a kitchen towel when blending.

Food Processor: I use a food processor a lot more than I initially expected. Some days I use the food processor more often than the blender. It's great for chunky sauces, quickly chopping vegetables, and for making falafel and veggie burgers. I have an 11-cup (2.6 L) food processor, which has ample capacity but doesn't take up a ridiculous amount of counter space.

Electric Hand Mixer: As cool as a stand mixer is, I actually use my electric hand mixer more often. A hand mixer is small and portable, and cleanup is easy (just toss the beaters into the dishwasher!). Unless you're doing a lot of heavy-duty baking, a hand mixer is more than sufficient.

A Note on Ovens

Rack position: The recipes in this book specify where to position your racks. Sounds kind of fussy, right? Well, hear me out. Things bake differently depending on where they sit in your oven. Most ovens have the heating element at the bottom, with the broiler on top. As you bake, the bottom heating element will turn on and off to try to maintain the oven's target temperature. What this means is that the top of the oven will consistently be the warmest, whereas the bottom will experience more intense bursts of heat. The recipes in this book take this into account and specify the rack position(s). However, keep in mind that every oven is different, so feel free to adjust, as needed, to accomplish similar results. You know your oven best.

Conventional versus convection: The recipes in this book have been developed with the more common conventional oven in mind. Convection ovens cook food more quickly, since they have fans to circulate the hot air. If you're using a convection oven or setting, reduce the oven temperature by 25°F (4°C).

RECIPE IDEAS FOR OCCASIONS

Summer Dinner Alfresco

Asparagus, Pea, and Whipped Feta Tart (PAGE 43)

Blistered Tomatoes and Whipped Ricotta Toasts (PAGE 193)

Sweet Potato Black Bean Burgers with Chipotle Mayo (PAGE 177)

Balsamic Vegetable and Goat Cheese Sandwiches (PAGE 197)

Grilled Halloumi Skewers with Thai Basil and Lime Vinaigrette (PAGE 168)

Crowd-Pleasing Potluck

Green Goddess Salad with Everything Bagel Croutons (PAGE 246)

Cheesy Chipotle Quinoa Bake (PAGE 44)

Hot Honey Roasted Carrots and Lentils (PAGE 40)

Pesto and Greens Frittata (PAGE 65)

Veggie Sushi with Sriracha Mayo (PAGE 185)

Cozy Vibes

Easy Veggie Chili (PAGE 216)

Spicy Miso Ramen (PAGE 213)

Seared Mushroom and Creamy Garlic Pasta (PAGE 79)

Vegetable Ragu (PAGE 114)

Shortcut Brothy Beans (PAGE 151)

Feeding Kids

Healthier Macaroni and Cheese (PAGE 113)

Roasted Tomato Soup with Cheesy Bread (PAGE 201)

Meatless Meatballs with Garlic Bread (PAGE 103)

Veggie Skillet Pot Pie (PAGE 106)

Frico-Style Quesadillas (PAGE 194)

For the Veggie Skeptics

Mushroom Stroganoff (PAGE 72)

Pea Fritters and Fries with Tartar Sauce (PAGE 125)

Caprese Pesto Panini (PAGE 182)

Burrito Bowls with Smoky Sofritas (PAGE 161)

Actually Good Fried Rice (PAGE 121)

Feeling Festive

Seared Brussels Sprouts Caesar Salad (PAGE 245)

Savoury Cheddar Apple Hand Pies (PAGE 137)

Shepherd's Pie (PAGE 118)

Kale Lentil Salad with Halloumi (PAGE 253)

Crispy Eggplant Roll-Ups (PAGE 58)

Work Lunch Friendly

Peanut-Glazed Tofu Rice Bowls (PAGE 157)

Pesto Grain Bowls with Jammy Eggs (PAGE 143)

Falafel Bowls (PAGE 154)

Ginger Soy Soba Salad with Spicy Peanut Sauce (PAGE 95)

Lemon and Dill Orzo Salad (PAGE 83)

Veggie Reset

Sesame and Smoked Tofu Noodle Soup (PAGE 220)

Thai Yellow Coconut Curry with Lentils (PAGE 205)

Smoky Red Lentil Soup (PAGE 226)

Miso Ginger Glazed Squash (PAGE 54)

Vibrant Greens Salad with Sesame Lime Vinaigrette (PAGE 249)

RECIPE IDEAS FOR MEAL PLANNING

I talk a lot about meal planning on our blog, *Evergreen Kitchen* (evergreenkitchen.ca), and certainly won't do it justice here. But if you're interested in giving meal planning a try, here are a few tried-and-true tips.

Start Small

Some people can make a meal plan for the entire week and stick with it. I wish I was one of them, but I am definitely not. If you're new to meal planning (or even if you're not!), I recommend starting small by planning for just a portion of your week. Try planning meals for three days at first. This way, if something comes up (like a serious pizza craving, an invite from friends, a late night at work that requires food that can be prepared and consumed in 10 minutes), then you can easily push your meal plan back by a day without stressing. Meal plans are supposed to make your life easier, not harder.

Shop and Cook Smart

If you can, plan to make recipes that use similar ingredients. This is especially helpful when it comes to cooking with fragile herbs (like dill and cilantro) and bulky ingredients where you may not use the whole item in one recipe (like cauliflower and butternut squash). Batch cook ingredients that take longer to cook, like grains, because you can refrigerate or freeze extras to use in other meals.

Use Your Freezer

You might end up with more leftovers than you feel like eating in a week. Your freezer is your best friend here. Freeze things like soups, wontons, dumplings, and pesto and batch-cooked grains and beans. Next time you're hangry or just short on time, you'll be thrilled you squirrelled these away for another day.

Here are some recipes that share ingredients and prep, making them a good combo to cook in the same week.

Peanut-Glazed Tofu Rice Bowls (PAGE 157)
Crispy Rice Salad (PAGE 236)
Cheesy Chipotle Quinoa Bake (PAGE 44)

Shared Ingredients:
Cilantro, scallions, limes, peanuts, jasmine rice

Shared Prep:
Make a double batch of rice to share across the Peanut-Glazed Tofu Rice Bowls and Crispy Rice Salad.

Spinach, Pea, and Pesto Pasta (PAGE 75)
Pesto and Greens Frittata (PAGE 65)
Savoury Cheddar Apple Hand Pies (PAGE 137)

Shared Ingredients:
Milk, cheddar cheese, eggs, frozen peas, pesto

Shared Prep:
Make a double batch of Fresh Basil Pesto (page 290) to share across the Spinach, Pea, and Pesto Pasta and Pesto and Greens Frittata.

Buffalo-Sauced Cauliflower (PAGE 133)
Lemon and Dill Orzo Salad (PAGE 83)
Healthier Macaroni and Cheese (PAGE 113)

Shared Ingredients:
Cauliflower, panko breadcrumbs, fresh dill, lemons

Shared Prep:
The Buffalo-Sauced Cauliflower doesn't use loose cauliflower florets, so save them for the Healthier Macaroni and Cheese.

Sweet Potato Black Bean Burgers (PAGE 177)
Bibimbap with Crispy Rice (PAGE 144)
Burrito Bowls with Smoky Sofritas (PAGE 161)

Shared Ingredients:
Short-grain brown rice, chipotle peppers in adobo sauce, Quick Pickled Red Onions

Shared Prep:
Make a triple batch of rice for all three recipes (substitute brown rice for white rice in the Bibimbap) and make one batch of Quick Pickled Red Onions (page 289) to share across the Sweet Potato Black Bean Burgers and Burrito Bowls with Smoky Sofritas (and anything else you eat that week!).

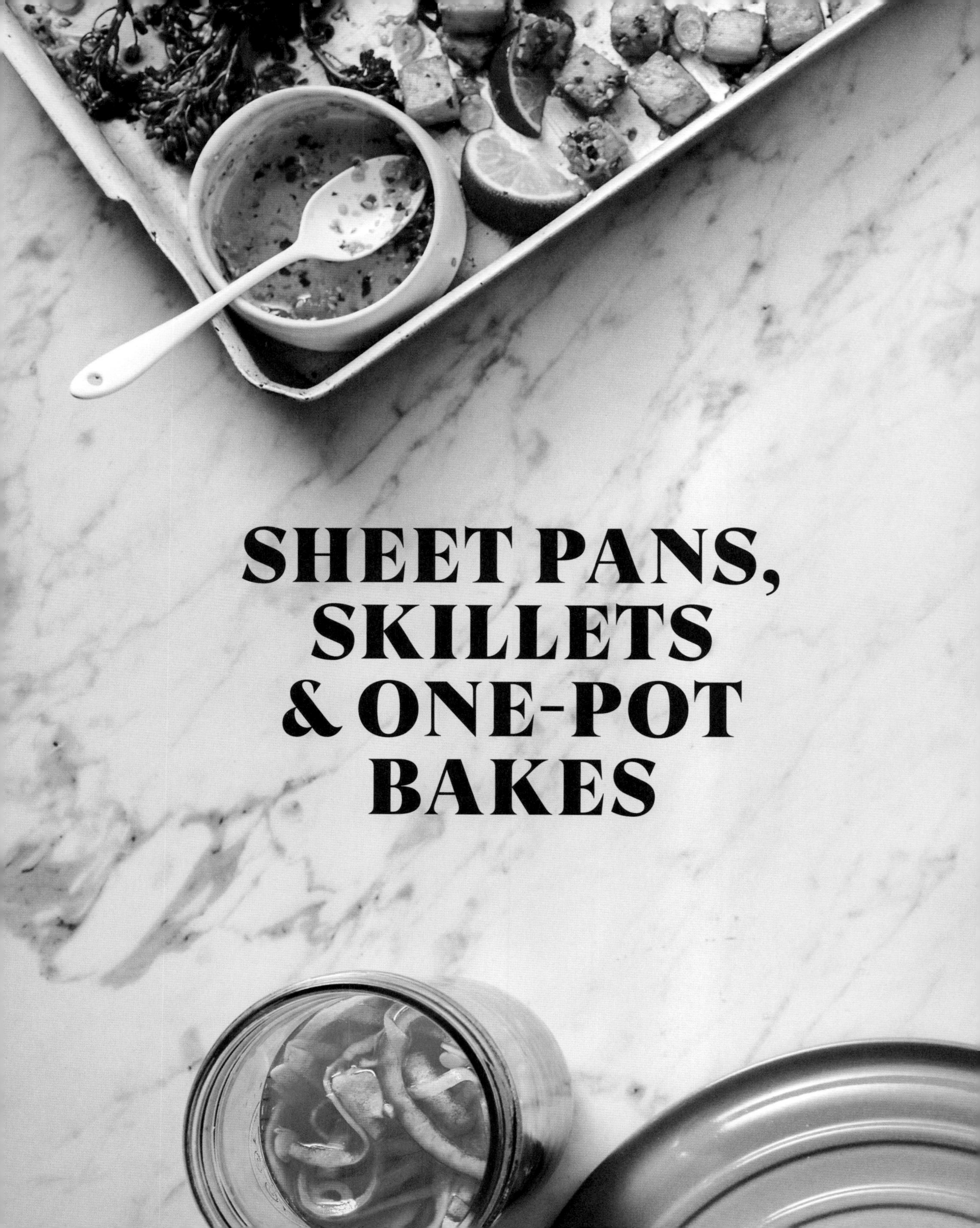

SHEET PANS, SKILLETS & ONE-POT BAKES

ACTIVE TIME: 20 MINUTES • **TOTAL TIME:** 1 HOUR • **SERVES** 4 TO 5

BAKED RICE PILAF WITH FETA AND ROASTED TOMATOES

1½ cups **long-grain white rice**

2½ cups **vegetable stock**

⅔ cup **roasted red peppers** from a jar, diced

4 tablespoons **extra-virgin olive oil**, divided

3 **garlic cloves**, minced

1 tablespoon **dried oregano** ❶

½ teaspoon **fine sea salt**

¼ to ½ teaspoon **red pepper flakes**

¼ cup **fresh lemon juice**

¼ cup drained and minced **sun-dried tomatoes**

1 can (14 fl oz / 398 ml) **cannellini beans**, drained and rinsed

2 cups lightly packed chopped **spinach**

1 oz (28g) finely grated **Parmesan cheese** (¼ cup)

¾ cup crumbled **feta cheese**

10 oz (283g) **cherry tomatoes** on the stem or loose

¼ cup chopped **fresh dill**

This dish is so easy to make, it's almost too easy. But don't question the magic—just grab a fork and dig in. The rice cooks itself in the oven. Your job? Fold in the yummy ingredients—Parmesan, spinach, sun-dried tomatoes, roasted red peppers, and a sprinkle of feta—at the end. The fresh dill garnish really makes the flavours pop. If you don't like dill, you can use flat-leaf parsley instead.

1. **Preheat the oven:** Place an oven rack in the centre position and preheat to 425°F (220°C).

2. **Prep the rice:** Rinse the rice in a sieve under cold running water, while swishing the rice with your fingertips, until the water almost runs clear, about 1 minute. Shake the sieve to remove excess water (too much water will throw off your ratios, so drain well). Transfer the rice to a large braiser or Dutch oven. Add the vegetable stock, roasted red peppers, 3 tablespoons of the olive oil, the garlic, oregano, salt, and red pepper flakes. Stir to combine and cover with the lid.

3. **Bake the rice:** Bake for 35 minutes, or until the liquid has been absorbed and the rice is tender. Remove from the oven and let sit for 5 minutes (keep the lid on), then uncover and fluff the rice with a fork.

4. **Set the oven to broil:** Once the rice is out of the oven, reposition the rack, if needed, so that the top of the pot is 4 to 5 inches (10 to 12 cm) under the broiler. Set the oven to broil.

5. **Finish assembling and broil:** Add the remaining 1 tablespoon olive oil, lemon juice, and sun-dried tomatoes to the pot of rice. Using a silicone spatula, gently stir to mix. Then stir in the cannellini beans, spinach, and Parmesan. Top with the feta and tomatoes. Broil until the feta is golden brown, 4 to 8 minutes. (Watch carefully, as broil times vary.) Sprinkle with the dill. Season with more salt, if needed.

VEGAN: Use vegan grated Parmesan and feta cheese or omit. If omitting the cheese, you may want to season the rice with more salt and double up on the beans.

❶ To help bring out the flavour in dried oregano, rub the dried leaves between your fingers before using.

ACTIVE TIME: 15 MINUTES • TOTAL TIME: 30 MINUTES • SERVES 4

HOT HONEY ROASTED CARROTS AND LENTILS

HOT HONEY

3 tablespoons **honey**

3 tablespoons **butter**

¾ to 1 teaspoon **red pepper flakes**

1 tablespoon **hot sauce** ❶

ROASTED CARROTS AND LENTILS

1 lb (454g) **carrots**, peeled and cut diagonally ½ inch (1 cm) thick

1 can (14 fl oz / 398 ml) **chickpeas**, drained, rinsed, and patted dry

¾ teaspoon **fine sea salt**, divided

2 cans (19 fl oz / 562 ml each) **lentils**, drained and rinsed

2 tablespoons **extra-virgin olive oil**

2 teaspoons **Dijon mustard**

1½ teaspoons **ground cumin**

¼ teaspoon **cinnamon**

¼ cup minced **fresh flat-leaf parsley leaves**

¼ cup sliced **almonds**

Zest and juice of ½ **lemon**

⅓ cup crumbled **feta cheese**

½ cup plain **Greek yogurt**

Roasted carrots get so deliciously sweet and caramelized in the oven, they deserve their promotion from casual side to a main dish. Here they're paired with chickpeas, tossed in a hot honey glaze, and sprinkled with salty feta cheese. Canned lentils get jazzed up with cumin, cinnamon, and fresh herbs, then the whole dish is topped with creamy yogurt and sliced almonds for crunch. This dish can be served hot or cold, so if you manage to save some, you've already got tomorrow's lunch covered.

---

1. **Preheat the oven:** Place an oven rack in the centre position and preheat to 425°F (220°C). Line a large baking sheet with parchment paper.

2. **Make the Hot Honey:** In a small saucepan, stir together the honey, butter, red pepper flakes, and hot sauce over low heat. Once the butter is melted, cook, stirring occasionally, for another 5 minutes to let the flavours infuse.

3. **Start the Roasted Carrots and Lentils—roast the carrots and chickpeas:** Scatter the carrots and chickpeas on the prepared baking sheet. Drizzle with half of the hot honey and toss to coat. Sprinkle with ½ teaspoon of the salt and toss to coat. Roast until the carrots are almost fork-tender but not yet fully cooked, 15 to 20 minutes.

4. **Season the lentils:** In a 13 x 9-inch (3.5 L) casserole dish, combine the lentils, olive oil, Dijon mustard, cumin, cinnamon, and remaining ¼ teaspoon salt. Add the parsley and stir to mix.

5. **Top the lentils and bake:** Pile the carrots and chickpeas on top of the lentils. Drizzle with the remaining hot honey and sprinkle with the almonds. Bake until the lentils are warm, about 5 minutes. Garnish with the lemon zest, lemon juice, feta, and dollops of yogurt.

---

❶ I like to use a red Mexican hot sauce here, like Valentina or Cholula, which are less acidic than vinegar-forward hot sauces like Frank's or Tabasco.

ASPARAGUS, PEA, AND WHIPPED FETA TART

8 oz (227g) **frozen puff pastry** (1 sheet), defrosted in fridge overnight ❶

1 large **egg**, whisked

8 oz (227g) **asparagus**, trimmed ❷

3 teaspoons **extra-virgin olive oil**, divided

Pinch of **fine sea salt**

1 cup crumbled **feta cheese** (4.4 oz / 125g)

3 to 4 tablespoons plain **Greek yogurt**

½ cup **frozen peas**

2 tablespoons thinly sliced **fresh mint leaves**

1 tablespoon **honey**

1 tablespoon chopped **pine nuts**

Freshly ground **black pepper**

Red pepper flakes

Flaky sea salt

This flaky puff pastry tart layers creamy feta, tender asparagus, mint, and peas. By the time the pastry is out of the oven, the other components are ready to go. For the asparagus to be its best, it's roasted separately from the pastry. This gives the pastry enough time to get golden brown all over without overcooking the asparagus in the process. If you're serving a crowd, this recipe is easily doubled. Serve with a side salad or fresh veggies, if you'd like.

---

1. **Preheat the oven:** Place the oven racks in the upper and lower thirds of the oven and preheat to 425°F (220°C). Set aside 2 large baking sheets; line 1 with parchment paper.

2. **Prep and bake the puff pastry:** Place the puff pastry on a lightly floured sheet of parchment paper. Using a lightly dusted rolling pin, gently smooth out any creases. If needed, stretch the dough into a 10-inch (25 cm) square. Using a sharp knife, cut off a ¾-inch-wide (2 cm) strip from each side (you will end up with 4 strips total). Prick the pastry all over with a fork, then brush with the whisked egg. Arrange the 4 strips of puff pastry on top of the outer edges of the pastry square to create a raised border. Trim off any overhang at the corners, then brush the border with the egg. Slide the parchment paper with the pastry onto the unlined baking sheet and bake on the lower rack until the pastry is golden brown and puffed up, 14 to 16 minutes.

3. **Meanwhile, roast the asparagus:** Place the asparagus on the lined baking sheet. Drizzle with 2 teaspoons of the olive oil and toss to coat. Sprinkle with the salt. Roast on the upper rack until the asparagus is fork-tender and bright green, 6 to 10 minutes.

4. **Whip the feta:** In a food processor, combine the feta and 3 tablespoons of the yogurt. Process until smooth, about 2 minutes, scraping down the sides as needed. Add the remaining 1 tablespoon yogurt to thin, if needed.

5. **Prep the peas:** Rinse the peas in a colander under cool running water until defrosted, about 1 minute. Shake to drain, then pour the peas onto a clean kitchen towel to absorb excess water. Transfer the peas to a small bowl and drizzle them with the remaining 1 teaspoon olive oil. Toss to coat, then stir in the mint.

6. **Assemble:** Let the pastry cool slightly, 5 to 10 minutes. Spread the whipped feta over the puff pastry, inside the border. Scatter the asparagus and peas overtop, then drizzle with the honey. Sprinkle with the pine nuts, black pepper, red pepper flakes, and flaky salt. Cut into slices.

---

❶ Most packages of puff pastry include two individually wrapped sheets. Since puff pastry is best fresh, just defrost the one sheet you need. Keep the other sheet in the freezer for another use.

❷ Make sure the asparagus is dry, so it doesn't steam in the oven. After washing it, be sure to pat it dry with a clean kitchen towel.

ACTIVE TIME: 25 MINUTES • **TOTAL TIME:** 45 MINUTES • **SERVES** 6 TO 8

CHEESY CHIPOTLE QUINOA BAKE

2 tablespoons **extra-virgin olive oil**

1 **yellow onion**, finely chopped (2 cups)

4 **garlic cloves**, minced

2 canned **chipotle peppers** in adobo, minced + 1 tablespoon **adobo sauce**

1 tablespoon **ground cumin**

1 jar (23 fl oz / 680 ml) **passata** ❶

½ cup **water**

1 can (14 fl oz / 398 ml) **diced fire-roasted tomatoes**

2 tablespoons **tamari**

1 cup dried **quinoa**, rinsed and drained

1 can (14 fl oz / 398 ml) **pinto beans**, drained and rinsed

1½ cups **frozen corn kernels**

2 cups shredded **aged cheddar cheese** (8 oz / 227g), divided

¾ cup chopped **fresh cilantro leaves**, more for garnish

½ cup **Quick Pickled Red Onions** (page 289) ❷

2 **scallions**, thinly sliced

This cheesy one-pot bake could become your new favourite way to eat quinoa. It channels comfort-food vibes without being overly indulgent. The chipotle and tomato flavoured quinoa is studded with beans and corn, then it's topped with cheddar cheese that melts and bubbles in the oven. Before serving, scatter fresh cilantro and pickled red onions on top—not just for looks but also for a pop of acidity and freshness. Leftovers reheat well, especially when sprinkled with a bit of extra cheese.

1. **Preheat the oven:** Place an oven rack in the centre position and preheat to 425°F (220°C).

2. **Start cooking over the stovetop:** In a large Dutch oven or braiser, heat the olive oil over medium heat. Add the onion and cook, stirring occasionally, until soft and golden brown around the edges, 8 to 10 minutes. Add the garlic, chipotle peppers and adobo sauce, and cumin and cook, stirring frequently, until fragrant, 1 to 2 minutes. Pour in the passata. Use the water to rinse the jar and pour the contents into the pot. Add the fire-roasted tomatoes and tamari, stir, and bring to a simmer over medium heat. Stir in the quinoa.

3. **Bake the chipotle-quinoa mixture:** Cover the pot with a lid and bake for 20 minutes, or until the quinoa is fully cooked.

4. **Set the oven to broil:** Remove the chipotle-quinoa from the oven and reposition the rack, if needed, so that the top of the pot is 4 to 5 inches (10 to 12 cm) under the broiler. Set the oven to broil.

5. **Assemble and broil:** To the pot, stir in the pinto beans, corn, 1 cup of the cheddar, and cilantro. Sprinkle with the remaining 1 cup cheddar. Broil until the cheese is golden brown and bubbling, 4 to 8 minutes. (Watch carefully, as broil times vary.) Remove from the oven and top with pickled red onions, scallions, and more cilantro.

VEGAN: Use your favourite meltable vegan cheddar cheese.

❶ Passata is strained puréed fresh tomatoes. It is typically sold in jars and is sometimes labelled "strained tomatoes." If you must substitute, use an equal amount of whole peeled tomatoes blended until smooth (23 fl oz = 2¾ cups + 2 tablespoons).

❷ If you don't have Quick Pickled Red Onions on hand, make them first so they have time to marinate.

ACTIVE TIME: 20 MINUTES • **TOTAL TIME:** 35 MINUTES • **SERVES** 4

FIRECRACKER TOFU WITH BROCCOLINI AND CHILI GARLIC OIL

16 oz (454g) **extra-firm tofu**, patted dry and cut into ½-inch (1 cm) cubes

2 tablespoons **tamari**

7 tablespoons **grapeseed oil**, divided

4 teaspoons **cornstarch**

6 **garlic cloves**, finely grated

1 tablespoon **toasted sesame seeds**

1 to 2 teaspoons **red pepper flakes** ❶

½ teaspoon **fine sea salt**, divided

2 bunches (1 lb / 454g total) **broccolini**, trimmed

2 **scallions**, thinly sliced, for garnish

Flaky sea salt, for garnish

Cooked jasmine rice (page 302), for serving

Lime wedges

Some of my favourite food memories are of being at my grandma Popo's house. She'd babysit all nine grandkids at once, and I'm pretty sure the only time she'd get a moment of semi-quiet was mealtime. She'd pour sizzling hot oil over bowls of rice—the crackling sounds and intoxicating smell of oil, flavoured with whatever she was into that day, always worked its magic. This recipe uses the heat of the oven to steep the oil with plenty of garlic and red pepper flakes, while the tofu and broccolini bake alongside.

---

1. **Preheat the oven:** Place the oven racks in the upper and lower thirds of the oven and preheat to 425°F (220°C). Line 2 large baking sheets with parchment paper.

2. **Bake the tofu:** Scatter the tofu on one of the prepared baking sheets. Drizzle the tamari over the tofu, and using your fingers, toss until most of the tamari is absorbed. Drizzle 1 tablespoon of the grapeseed oil over the tofu and toss to coat. Sprinkle the cornstarch over the tofu and toss to coat. Spread the tofu in an even layer, then bake on the lower rack for 15 minutes, until the tofu is light golden but not yet crispy.

3. **Mix the chili garlic oil:** In a small oven-safe glass container ❷, combine 5 tablespoons of the grapeseed oil, garlic, sesame seeds, red pepper flakes, and ¼ teaspoon of the salt.

4. **Flip the tofu and heat the oil:** Once the tofu has baked for 15 minutes, flip the cubes. Place the container of chili garlic oil onto the same baking sheet and bake on the lower rack until the tofu is golden brown and crispy around the edges and the oil is lightly bubbling, about 15 minutes.

5. **Meanwhile, bake the broccolini:** Scatter the broccolini on the second baking sheet. Drizzle the remaining 1 tablespoon grapeseed oil over the broccolini and toss to coat. Sprinkle with the remaining ¼ teaspoon salt. Bake on the upper rack until the broccolini is bright green and tender, 8 to 10 minutes.

6. **Assemble:** Drizzle 2 tablespoons of the chili garlic oil over the tofu (careful, the bowl is hot!). Using a flexible spatula, toss the tofu until evenly coated in the oil. Combine the coated tofu and broccolini on a serving platter. Garnish with scallions and flaky salt. Serve with rice, lime wedges, and the remaining chili garlic oil for drizzling.

---

❶ If you like things on the spicier side, use 2 teaspoons of red pepper flakes, or if you prefer a milder spice, reduce it accordingly.

❷ I use a small glass oven-safe food container (Pyrex) for infusing the oil in the oven. If you don't have one, you can combine the ingredients in a small saucepan and heat on the stovetop over low heat until fragrant and small bubbles appear in the oil, 5 to 10 minutes.

ACTIVE TIME: 35 MINUTES • **TOTAL TIME:** 35 MINUTES • **SERVES** 4

FLATBREAD WITH ORANGE ARUGULA SALAD

FLATBREADS

1 batch **Quick Pizza Dough** (page 297) or 1 lb (454g) store-bought, room temperature ❷

2 tablespoons **extra-virgin olive oil**, for brushing

1.3 oz (37g) finely grated **Parmesan cheese** (⅓ cup)

Freshly ground **black pepper**

CREAMY GOAT CHEESE

4 oz (113g) **soft goat cheese**

¼ cup **whole milk**

SALAD

2 **oranges**

2 tablespoons **extra-virgin olive oil**

1 tablespoon **red wine vinegar**

1 teaspoon **Dijon mustard**

¼ teaspoon **fine sea salt**, more to taste

1 medium **shallot**, thinly sliced (¼ cup)

3 cups lightly packed **arugula**

GARNISHES

Chopped **pistachios**

Red pepper flakes (optional)

I'm not sure if this is more of a salad or a flatbread. Either way, it's delicious. Pizza dough makes a quick, hassle-free base. Once stretched, it's brushed with olive oil and sprinkled with Parmesan so it gets crispy in the oven. The orange arugula salad is bright and juicy, and piled on top of the flatbread. If you've never segmented an orange before, don't be intimidated. See the how-to on page 20. Great for a casual dinner, the flatbread is personal-sized, so you won't need to worry about sharing! ❶

---

1. **Preheat the oven:** Place the oven racks in the upper and lower thirds of the oven and preheat to 450°F (230°C). Set aside 2 large baking sheets.

2. **Make the Flatbreads:** Cut the pizza dough into 4 equal portions. Lightly dust the work surface with flour. Using your fingers or a rolling pin, stretch or roll each piece of dough into an 8 x 4-inch (20 x 10 cm) oval about ¼ inch (5 mm) thick. Brush the bottom of each flatbread with olive oil. Place 2 flatbreads oiled side down on each of the baking sheets. Brush the top of the flatbreads with olive oil, then sprinkle with the Parmesan and black pepper. Bake until the flatbreads are golden brown and crisp on the bottom, 12 to 16 minutes, swapping top and bottom positions halfway through.

3. **Meanwhile, make the Creamy Goat Cheese:** In a small bowl, combine the goat cheese and milk. Use a fork to stir vigorously until the goat cheese is spreadable.

4. **Start the Orange Arugula Salad—segment the oranges (page 20):** Using a knife, trim the top and bottom off the oranges so they stand upright on the cutting board. Remove the peel by sliding a sharp knife downwards between the flesh and peel, following the curves of the orange. Then cut out the orange segments by slicing on each side of each membrane until the cuts meet.

5. **Make the salad dressing and combine:** In a medium bowl, whisk together the olive oil, red wine vinegar, Dijon mustard, and salt. Add the shallot and toss to coat. Add the arugula and use your hand to gently toss the salad. Add the oranges and gently toss once more. Season with more salt, if needed.

6. **Assemble:** Spread the creamy goat cheese over the warm flatbreads. Using your hand, grab a handful of salad, shake off any excess dressing into the bowl, then scatter the salad over one of the flatbreads. Repeat for the remaining flatbreads. Garnish with the pistachios and red pepper flakes, if using. Slice individual flatbreads into wedges or serve whole with a knife and fork.

GLUTEN-FREE: Use your favourite gluten-free pizza dough.

---

❶ If you won't be serving all 4 flatbreads at once, refrigerate the extra dough in a lightly oiled airtight container or plastic-covered bowl and bake it fresh the next day. The dressing can be stored in the fridge for up to 2 days, but the arugula and orange segments should be tossed in just before serving.

❷ If the pizza dough is refrigerated, let it sit on the counter to come up to room temperature before rolling.

ACTIVE TIME: 30 MINUTES • **TOTAL TIME:** 1 HOUR • **SERVES** 4

LEMONGRASS COCONUT RICE WITH ROASTED EGGPLANT

BAKED RICE AND EGGPLANT

1¼ cups **jasmine rice**

1 can (14 fl oz / 398 ml) **full-fat coconut milk**

½ cup **water**

2 **lemongrass stalks**

16 oz (454g) **medium-firm tofu**, patted dry

3 **garlic cloves**, minced

½ teaspoon **fine sea salt**, divided

1 lb (454g) **Japanese** or **Chinese eggplants** (2 large), cut into ½-inch (1 cm) rounds

2 tablespoons **grapeseed oil**

1 **lime**, cut into wedges, divided

Fresh cilantro leaves, for garnish

QUICK PICKLED SHALLOTS

⅓ cup **boiling water**

1 tablespoon **granulated sugar**

¼ teaspoon **fine sea salt**

⅓ cup **rice vinegar**

1 large **shallot**, thinly sliced (½ cup)

GINGER SCALLION OIL

4 **scallions**, thinly sliced

1 tablespoon minced **fresh ginger**

¼ teaspoon **fine sea salt**

¼ cup **grapeseed oil**

This comforting dish is made with fragrant coconut- and lemongrass-infused rice, roasted eggplant, steamed tofu, and sizzling scallion oil. The fresh lemongrass does double duty: not only does it add flavour but it also lifts the tofu from the bottom of the pot, so the rice cooks evenly underneath it (page 52). Make sure to drizzle the finished dish with every last drop of the ginger scallion oil—it's liquid gold.

---

1. **Preheat the oven:** Place the oven racks in the centre and lower thirds of the oven and preheat to 425°F (220°C). Line a large baking sheet with parchment paper.

2. **Start the Baked Rice and Eggplant—prep the rice:** Rinse the rice in a sieve under cold running water, while swishing the rice with your fingertips, until the water runs mostly clear, about 1 minute. Shake the sieve to remove excess water (too much water will throw off your ratios, so drain well). Transfer the rice to a large braiser or Dutch oven. Pour in the coconut milk and water and stir to mix.

3. **Add the lemongrass and tofu:** Cut off and discard the bottom 1 inch (2.5 cm) of the lemongrass stalks. Then cut 8 inches (20 cm) up from the bottom and discard the top. Peel away and discard the tough outer layer. Pound each stalk with the back of a knife to release the oils, then cut each stalk in half lengthwise. Nestle the lemongrass pieces side by side in the middle of the rice. Cut the block of tofu crosswise into ¼-inch (5 mm) thick slices. Fan the tofu out on top of the lemongrass, with the pieces overlapping to fit. Sprinkle the garlic and ¼ teaspoon of the salt in between the tofu slices. Cover the pot with the lid. Bake on the centre rack for 35 minutes or until the liquid has been absorbed and the rice is tender. Remove from the oven and let sit for 5 minutes before removing the lid.

4. **Meanwhile, roast the eggplant:** Scatter the eggplant on the prepared baking sheet. Drizzle the eggplant with the grapeseed oil and toss to coat. Spread in an even layer and sprinkle with the remaining ¼ teaspoon salt. Roast on the lower rack until the eggplant is golden brown on both sides, 30 to 35 minutes, flipping halfway through.

5. **Make the Quick Pickled Shallots:** In a small heatproof bowl, combine the boiling water, sugar, and salt. Stir until the sugar and salt are dissolved. Add the rice vinegar and stir to mix. Submerge the shallots in the liquid.

6. **Make the Ginger Scallion Oil:** In a small heatproof jar or glass measuring cup, combine the scallions, ginger, and salt. In a small saucepan, heat the grapeseed oil over medium heat. Once the oil is hot, drop a slice of scallion into it. If it sizzles, it's good to go; if it doesn't, heat the oil longer. Carefully pour the hot oil into the jar and stir to combine.

7. **Combine:** Fluff the rice with a fork. Scatter the eggplant over the rice. Squeeze half of the lime wedges over the dish. Generously spoon the ginger scallion oil on top. Garnish with the pickled shallots and cilantro. Serve with the remaining lime wedges on the side.

MISO GINGER GLAZED SQUASH

VEGETABLES AND BEANS

1¼-lb (567g) **acorn squash**

2 tablespoons **grapeseed oil**, divided

¼ teaspoon **fine sea salt**, divided

7 oz (200g) **savoy cabbage**, torn into bite-size pieces (4 cups) ●

1 can (14 fl oz / 398 ml) **navy beans**, drained and rinsed

3 **scallions**, thinly sliced

1 tablespoon **toasted sesame seeds**

MISO GINGER GLAZE

3 tablespoons **white miso**

3 tablespoons **rice vinegar**

2 tablespoons **toasted sesame oil**

1 tablespoon **tamari**

1 tablespoon **granulated sugar**

2 teaspoons minced **fresh ginger**

Cooked jasmine rice (page 302), for serving

This flavourful sheet-pan bake makes the most of winter vegetables. The acorn squash is roasted until golden brown, then brushed with a delicious miso ginger glaze that caramelizes in the oven. The glaze is sweet, salty, and packed with umami. It's inspired by the mouth-watering glaze that's brushed on one of my favourite Japanese dishes, nasu dengaku (grilled eggplant). The skin of acorn squash is edible, so save yourself the time and don't bother peeling it.

---

1. **Preheat the oven:** Place the oven racks in the upper and lower thirds of the oven and preheat to 450°F (230°C). Set aside 2 large baking sheets.

2. **Start the Vegetables and Beans—roast the squash:** Trim the ends off the squash, then cut in half lengthwise. Use a spoon to scoop out the seeds, then slice into ¼-inch (5 mm) half-moons. Scatter the squash on one of the baking sheets. Drizzle with 1 tablespoon of the grapeseed oil and toss to coat. Sprinkle with ⅛ teaspoon of the salt. Spread the squash in an even layer and roast on the upper rack until fork-tender and golden brown around the edges, 25 to 35 minutes.

3. **Meanwhile, make the Miso Ginger Glaze:** In a small bowl, whisk together the miso, rice vinegar, sesame oil, tamari, sugar, and ginger.

4. **Continue the Vegetables and Beans—prep the cabbage and beans:** Scatter the cabbage and beans on the second baking sheet. Drizzle with the remaining 1 tablespoon grapeseed oil and toss to coat. Drizzle with half of the glaze, sprinkle with the remaining ⅛ teaspoon salt, and toss to coat.

5. **Broil the squash, cabbage, and beans:** Set the oven to broil. Brush the remaining half of the glaze on the roasted squash. Place the sheet of squash on the upper rack and the sheet of cabbage and beans on the lower rack. Broil, until the glaze on the squash is bubbling and golden brown and the cabbage is bright green, 2 to 4 minutes. (Watch carefully, as broil times vary.)

6. **Assemble:** Transfer the roasted squash, cabbage, and beans to a serving platter. Sprinkle with the scallions and sesame seeds. Serve with rice.

● Can be replaced with green cabbage.

ACTIVE TIME: 15 MINUTES • **TOTAL TIME:** 50 MINUTES • **SERVES** 4

ROASTED VEGETABLES WITH BALSAMIC GLAZE

3 **carrots**, peeled, cut into 2-inch (5 cm) pieces, and halved lengthwise

2 **parsnips**, peeled, cut into 2-inch (5 cm) pieces, and halved lengthwise

8 oz (227g) **Brussels sprouts**, trimmed and halved

2 large **shallots**, thinly sliced (1 cup)

1 can (14 oz / 398 ml) **chickpeas**, drained, rinsed, and patted dry

3 tablespoons **extra-virgin olive oil**

1 tablespoon **fresh thyme leaves**

¾ teaspoon **fine sea salt**

½ teaspoon freshly ground **black pepper**

2 cups lightly packed **arugula**

½ cup crumbled **feta cheese**

Red pepper flakes

Balsamic glaze, for drizzling

Cooked rice (page 302) or other grain, for serving (optional)

Need a veggie fix? This sheet-pan delivers. Here, Brussels sprouts, carrots, and parsnips are roasted alongside chickpeas and shallots until golden brown. Then everything gets drizzled with sticky balsamic glaze and sprinkled with feta. Simple and so good. When it comes to crisp veggies, it's worth taking a second to spread everything out as much as possible. You want the vegetables to roast, rather than steam. The carrots and parsnips might take a bit longer to bake, so if that's the case, just pull the other sheet pan out when it's done.

---

1. **Preheat the oven:** Place the oven racks in the upper and lower thirds of the oven and preheat to 425°F (220°C). Line 2 large baking sheets with parchment paper.

2. **Roast the vegetables and chickpeas:** Scatter the carrots and parsnips on one of the prepared baking sheets. Scatter the Brussels sprouts, shallots, and chickpeas on the second baking sheet. Drizzle each baking sheet with half of the olive oil and toss to coat. Sprinkle each baking sheet with half of the thyme, salt, and black pepper. Roast until the vegetables are tender and golden brown around the edges, 35 to 40 minutes, flipping the vegetables and swapping top and bottom positions halfway through.

3. **Serve:** Combine all the roasted vegetables and chickpeas onto 1 baking sheet. Stir in the arugula. Sprinkle the feta and red pepper flakes over top. Season with more black pepper and salt, if needed. Generously drizzle balsamic glaze over everything. Serve with cooked rice or grains, if using.

VEGAN: Use vegan feta cheese or omit.

ACTIVE TIME: 30 MINUTES • TOTAL TIME: 1 HOUR • SERVES 4 TO 5

CRISPY EGGPLANT ROLL-UPS

1½-lb (680g) **globe eggplant** ❶

2 tablespoons + 2 teaspoons **extra-virgin olive oil**, divided

½ teaspoon **fine sea salt**

½ cup raw **walnuts** (optional)

1 cup **full-fat (4%) cottage cheese** (8.8 oz / 250g) ❷

1 large **egg**

2 oz (57g) finely grated **Parmesan cheese** (½ cup), divided

¼ cup chopped **fresh basil leaves** (10g)

¼ teaspoon **red pepper flakes**

¼ cup **panko breadcrumbs**

2½ cups **marinara sauce**, divided

1 can (14 fl oz / 398 ml) **cannellini beans**, drained and rinsed

Focaccia or crusty bread, for serving (optional)

This comforting dish has some lasagna-like flavours, but with a lighter twist. Oven-roasted eggplant is rolled around a cheesy basil filling, then nestled in a bed of tomato sauce. Instead of ricotta, the filling is made from cottage cheese that's been whipped until smooth and fluffy. The creamy cannellini beans, walnuts, and cottage cheese are all great sources of protein to keep you full. Serve with warm bread to scoop up every last drop of sauce.

---

1. **Preheat the oven:** Place the oven racks in the upper and lower thirds of the oven and preheat to 425°F (220°C). Line 2 large baking sheets with parchment paper.

2. **Prep and roast the eggplant:** Trim the stem end off the eggplant, then slice it lengthwise ⅓ inch (8 mm) thick. Evenly arrange the slices on the 2 prepared baking sheets. Brush both sides of the eggplant with 2 tablespoons of the olive oil, then sprinkle with the salt. Roast until the eggplant is golden brown, 25 to 35 minutes, swapping top and bottom positions halfway through.

3. **Meanwhile, pulse the walnuts:** In a food processor, pulse the walnuts (if using) until a fine crumble forms. Transfer to a small bowl.

4. **Pulse the cottage cheese until smooth:** In the food processor, pulse the cottage cheese until completely smooth and creamy. Add the egg and half the Parmesan and pulse to mix. Add the basil and red pepper flakes and pulse just until incorporated.

5. **Toss the panko in oil:** In a small bowl, toss the panko with the remaining 2 teaspoons olive oil.

6. **Prep the baking dish:** Spread 1 cup of the marinara sauce in a 2.5-quart (2.5 L) oval or 9-inch (2.5 L) square baking dish. Scatter the beans evenly on top. Spoon another 1 cup of the marinara sauce over the beans.

7. **Roll the eggplant:** Working with 1 slice of eggplant at a time, with a short end facing you, spread 1 to 2 tablespoons of the cheese mixture over the eggplant. Sprinkle with some of the walnuts. Starting at the end closest to you, gently roll up the eggplant. Nestle the eggplant roll into the sauce, seam side down. Repeat to fill and roll the remaining slices of eggplant.

8. **Top and bake ❸:** Spoon the remaining ½ cup marinara sauce over the eggplant rolls. Sprinkle with the remaining half of the Parmesan and the panko. Bake on the upper rack until the sauce is bubbly and the panko is golden brown, about 20 minutes. Serve with focaccia or crusty bread for dipping, if using.

GLUTEN-FREE: Use gluten-free panko breadcrumbs. Use gluten-free bread or omit.

---

❶ Some people find the skin of eggplant bitter, so peel it if you'd like. I usually roast it skin-on.

❷ Cottage cheese can be replaced with 1 cup ricotta cheese. Season the ricotta with a bit of salt and lemon juice to taste to match the saltiness and tang of cottage cheese.

❸ Make ahead option: Finish rolling the eggplant (step 7), cover the baking dish and refrigerate. Bring to room temperature before baking or cover the top loosely with foil and bake until the eggplant is no longer cool to the touch, about 10 minutes. Then, follow the instructions in step 8.

ACTIVE TIME: 30 MINUTES • TOTAL TIME: 40 MINUTES • SERVES 4

SHEET-PAN VEGGIE FAJITAS

FAJITA SEASONING

1 tablespoon **chili powder**

2 teaspoons **ground cumin**

1½ teaspoons **smoked sweet paprika**

¾ teaspoon **fine sea salt**

½ teaspoon **onion powder**

½ teaspoon **garlic powder**

FILLINGS AND TORTILLA

1 small **red onion**, cut into ¼-inch (5 mm) half-moons

3 **bell peppers** (red, orange, or yellow), cut into ⅓-inch (8 mm) wide strips

3 tablespoons **grapeseed oil**, divided

1 can (14 fl oz / 398 ml) **black beans**, drained and rinsed

12 (6-inch / 15 cm) **corn** or **flour tortillas**

SLAW

3 cups shredded **savoy** or **green cabbage**

½ teaspoon **lime zest**

2 tablespoons **fresh lime juice**

1 tablespoon **grapeseed oil**

Fine sea salt

3 tablespoons chopped **fresh cilantro leaves**

TOPPINGS (OPTIONAL)

Everyday Guacamole (page 298) or store-bought

Lime wedges

Sour cream

Shredded **cheddar cheese**

Hot sauce

Fajitas are a delicious, choose your own meal adventure. Most nights I keep things simple with red onion, bell peppers, and black beans—all tossed in a flavourful seasoning blend, because it wouldn't feel like fajitas without it. While the oven does the work roasting and warming, you're freed up to make a lime cilantro slaw and guacamole (just try not to eat it all before the meal begins!). If you have extra veggies at the end of the meal, save them for quick weekday fajita bowls and just add rice.

1. **Preheat the oven:** Place the oven racks in the upper and lower thirds of the oven and preheat to 425°F (220°C). Line 2 large baking sheets with parchment paper.

2. **Make the Fajita Seasoning:** In a small bowl, combine the chili powder, cumin, smoked paprika, salt, onion powder, and garlic powder. Stir until well mixed.

3. **Start the Fillings—roast the vegetables:** Arrange half of the red onion and half of the bell peppers on each of the 2 prepared baking sheets. Drizzle each baking sheet with 1 tablespoon of the grapeseed oil and 1 tablespoon of the fajita seasoning, then toss to coat. Roast for 10 minutes.

4. **Meanwhile, prep the beans and tortillas:** In a medium bowl, combine the black beans, the remaining 1 tablespoon grapeseed oil, and the remaining fajita seasoning (about 1 scant tablespoon). Toss to coat. Wrap 2 stacks of tortillas (6 per stack) tightly in foil.

5. **Add the beans and tortillas to the baking sheets:** Add the black beans to one of the baking sheets (push some of the vegetables to one side to make space) and the stacks of tortillas to the other baking sheet (if there's no space for the tortillas, place them directly on the oven rack). Return both baking sheets to the oven, swapping the top and bottom positions. Roast until the vegetables are fork-tender and the beans and tortillas are warmed through, 5 to 10 minutes.

6. **Meanwhile, make the Slaw:** In a medium bowl, combine the cabbage, lime zest, lime juice, grapeseed oil, and salt to taste. Sprinkle in the cilantro and toss to mix.

7. **Serve:** Transfer the roasted vegetables and beans to a medium serving dish. Set out the tortillas and toppings of your choice. Let everyone assemble their own fajitas at the table.

VEGAN: Use vegan sour cream and shredded cheese or omit. **GLUTEN-FREE:** Use gluten-free tortillas, such as corn.

ACTIVE TIME: 20 MINUTES • TOTAL TIME: 45 MINUTES • SERVES 4

HARISSA-ROASTED VEGETABLES WITH COUSCOUS

ROASTED VEGETABLES

2 medium **zucchini** (1 lb / 454g), cut into ¾-inch (2 cm) rounds

2 **bell peppers** (red, orange, or yellow), chopped

1 **red onion**, chopped (2 cups)

1 can (14 fl oz / 398 ml) **chickpeas**, drained, rinsed, and patted dry

7 oz (200g) **halloumi cheese**, cut into ¾-inch (2 cm) cubes

2 tablespoons **extra-virgin olive oil**, divided

2 tablespoons **rose harissa paste** ❶

2 teaspoons **smoked sweet paprika**

1 teaspoon **ground cumin**

½ teaspoon **fine sea salt**

YOGURT DIP

1 cup plain **Greek yogurt**

¼ teaspoon **fine sea salt**

Extra-virgin olive oil, for garnish

¼ to ½ teaspoon **za'atar** (optional)

COUSCOUS

1 cup **couscous**

1½ cups **boiling water**

3 tablespoons **fresh lemon juice**

1 tablespoon **extra-virgin olive oil**

¼ teaspoon **fine sea salt**

¼ cup minced **fresh flat-leaf parsley leaves**, more for garnish

FOR SERVING (OPTIONAL)

Pomegranate molasses ❷

Pitas

This colourful feast comes together with minimal effort. The vegetables, chickpeas, and halloumi cheese are coated in spicy harissa paste and fragrant spices, then roasted in the oven. The cooling yogurt dip is perfect for spooning over the vegetables and dipping pita into. A lemon-and-herb couscous rounds out the meal. Making couscous couldn't be easier: pour boiling water overtop, and 5 minutes later it's ready to serve.

---

1. **Preheat the oven:** Place the oven racks in the upper and lower thirds of the oven and preheat to 425°F (220°C). Line 2 large baking sheets with parchment paper.

2. **Make the Roasted Vegetables:** Scatter the zucchini and bell peppers on one of the prepared baking sheets. Scatter the red onion, chickpeas, and halloumi on the second baking sheet. Evenly divide the olive oil, rose harissa, smoked paprika, cumin, and salt over both baking sheets and toss until evenly coated. Place the zucchini mixture on the lower rack and the chickpea mixture on the upper rack. Roast until the vegetables are fork-tender and the halloumi is golden brown, 25 to 35 minutes.

3. **Meanwhile, make the Yogurt Dip:** In a small bowl, stir together the yogurt and salt. Garnish with a drizzle of olive oil and za'atar, if using.

4. **Make the Couscous:** Place the couscous in a medium heatproof bowl. Pour the boiling water over the couscous and cover with a plate to trap the steam. Let the couscous sit, covered, until all the water is absorbed, about 5 minutes. Fluff the couscous with a fork. Stir in the lemon juice, olive oil, salt, and parsley.

5. **Serve:** Drizzle the roasted vegetables with pomegranate molasses (if using) and sprinkle with more parsley. Serve with the herbed couscous, yogurt dip, and pitas, if using.

VEGAN: Omit the halloumi cheese and double up on chickpeas. Use hummus instead of the Greek yogurt. (You can still garnish the hummus with olive oil and za'atar, but you'll likely want to omit the ¼ teaspoon of salt since hummus is usually salted.)

GLUTEN-FREE: Replace the couscous with a cooked gluten-free grain, such as millet or quinoa (you'll need about 3 cups). Use gluten-free pitas or omit.

---

❶ Rose harissa contains some dried rose petals for extra flavour. You can use regular harissa instead. Harissa can be quite spicy—and spice levels vary by brand—so start small and add more to taste.

❷ Pomegranate molasses is a syrup made from pomegranate juice. It has a sweet-and-sour flavour that really perks up dishes. You can often find pomegranate molasses in well-stocked grocery stores or in Middle Eastern grocery stores.

ACTIVE TIME: 20 MINUTES • **TOTAL TIME:** 35 MINUTES • **SERVES** 4 TO 6

PESTO AND GREENS FRITTATA

FRITTATA

8 large **eggs**

¼ cup **whipping (35%) cream** or whole milk

½ teaspoon freshly ground **black pepper**

¼ teaspoon + a pinch of **fine sea salt**, divided

¾ cup shredded **aged cheddar cheese**, divided

2 tablespoons **butter** or extra-virgin olive oil

3 **garlic cloves**, minced

4 cups lightly packed **baby spinach** (4 oz / 113g)

3 **scallions**, thinly sliced

¼ cup **Fresh Basil Pesto** (page 290), Vegan Pesto (page 290), or store-bought, divided

¼ cup drained and minced **sun-dried tomatoes**

Microgreens, for garnish (optional)

RICOTTA CREAM (OPTIONAL)

¼ cup **ricotta cheese**

1 tablespoon **whipping (35%) cream** or whole milk

I have a thing for frittatas. You can fill them with whatever you want, eat them at any time of day, and they taste good warm or cold. Talk about versatility! This version is swirled with pesto and filled with sun-dried tomatoes, spinach, and cheddar cheese. There's also an optional silky ricotta cream for spooning on top. This recipe is intended for a 10-inch cast-iron skillet, but it's easy to modify for a 12-inch skillet instead. ❶

---

1. **Preheat the oven:** Place an oven rack in the upper third of the oven and preheat to 400°F (200°C).

2. **Start the Frittata—whisk the egg mixture:** In a medium bowl, whisk together the eggs, cream, pepper, and ¼ teaspoon of the salt until smooth. Stir in ½ cup of the cheddar.

3. **Cook the vegetables:** In a 10-inch (25 cm) cast-iron or oven-safe skillet ❷, melt the butter over medium heat. Swirl the skillet so the melted butter coats the bottom and up the sides. Add the garlic and cook, stirring constantly, until fragrant, 1 to 2 minutes. Stir in the spinach, scallions, and a pinch of salt and cook, stirring frequently, until the spinach is wilted, about 2 minutes.

4. **Add the egg mixture to the skillet:** Reduce the heat to low. Pour half of the egg mixture into the skillet. Spoon in half of the pesto and scatter with the sun-dried tomatoes. Pour in the remainder of the egg mixture and spoon in the remainder of the pesto. Scatter the remaining ¼ cup cheddar on top.

5. **Bake:** Transfer the skillet to the oven and bake until the eggs are just barely set in the middle, 15 to 18 minutes. Remove from the oven. The eggs will continue to cook in the skillet, so let cool for 10 minutes before slicing.

6. **Meanwhile, make the Ricotta Cream, if using:** In a small bowl, stir together the ricotta and cream until smooth.

7. **Assemble and serve:** Spoon the ricotta cream (if using) over the frittata and sprinkle with microgreens, if using. Cut the frittata into wedges. Serve warm or at room temperature.

---

❶ For a 12-inch (30 cm) skillet, scale up the recipe (to serve 6 to 8): 12 eggs, 6 tablespoons cream, ¾ teaspoon pepper, ¼ to ½ teaspoon salt, 1 cup cheddar cheese, 4 garlic cloves, 6 cups spinach, 4 scallions, 6 tablespoons pesto, ⅓ cup sun-dried tomatoes. Bake for 18 to 20 minutes.

❷ For best results, use a seasoned uncoated cast-iron skillet. An enamelled cast-iron or stainless steel skillet will require extra butter to prevent sticking.

ACTIVE TIME: 30 MINUTES • **TOTAL TIME:** 1 HOUR • **SERVES** 4

BRAISED VEGETABLES WITH PARMESAN CROUTONS

4 tablespoons **extra-virgin olive oil**, divided

2 **carrots**, peeled and cut into ½-inch (1 cm) rounds

1 lb (454g) **leeks** (white and light green parts), cut into ½-inch (1 cm) half-moons ❶

2 **celery ribs**, cut into 1-inch (2.5 cm) lengths

2 cups roughly chopped **green cabbage**

2 large **shallots**, thinly sliced (1 cup)

3 **garlic cloves**, thinly sliced

¾ teaspoon **fine sea salt**

½ teaspoon freshly ground **black pepper**

2 cans (14 fl oz / 398 ml each) **cannellini beans**, drained and rinsed

¾ cup **vegetable stock**

1 teaspoon **grainy Dijon mustard**

2 sprigs **fresh rosemary**

1 pint (300g) **grape** or **cherry tomatoes**

4 cups torn **baguette** or sourdough bread

2 oz (57g) finely grated **Parmesan cheese** (½ cup)

GARNISHES

1 teaspoon **lemon zest**

¼ cup chopped **fresh flat-leaf parsley leaves**

This humble dish is perfect for when you're craving a cozy meal that doesn't leave you feeling heavy. It's easy to make, packed with nourishing vegetables, and topped with *just* enough crisp bread to not feel *too healthy*. The vegetables are braised in a herb-studded broth until tender. A quick trip to the oven crisps the top of the cheesy bread. When it all comes together, this no-fuss, simple meal tastes great and hits the spot.

---

1. Cook the vegetables: In a large Dutch oven or pot, heat 2 tablespoons of the olive oil over medium heat. Scatter in the carrots and cook, undisturbed, until golden brown on the bottom, 3 to 4 minutes. Add the leeks and continue to cook, stirring occasionally, until the carrots are mostly golden brown and the leeks are soft, about 4 minutes. Add 1 tablespoon of the olive oil, celery, cabbage, shallots, garlic, salt, and pepper and cook, stirring frequently, until the garlic is fragrant, 1 to 2 minutes.

2. Add the beans, braising liquid, and tomatoes: Stir in the cannellini beans, vegetable stock, Dijon mustard, and rosemary. Scatter the tomatoes overtop. Cover with a lid and bring to a boil over medium-high heat. Once boiling, reduce the heat to medium-low and simmer until the vegetables are fork-tender and the tomatoes have burst, about 20 minutes. Uncover and let simmer for 10 minutes to allow the broth to reduce.

3. Heat the broiler ❷: Position the rack so the top of the Dutch oven is about 4 inches (10 cm) under the broiler. Set the oven to broil.

4. Meanwhile, prep the bread topping: In a medium bowl, toss the torn baguette with the remaining 1 tablespoon olive oil.

5. Broil and serve: Scatter the bread over the vegetables and sprinkle with the Parmesan. Broil until the bread is toasted and the cheese is melted, 1 to 5 minutes. (Watch carefully, as broil times vary.) Garnish with lemon zest and chopped parsley.

VEGAN: Use grated vegan Parmesan cheese or omit. **GLUTEN-FREE:** Use gluten-free baguette or sourdough.

---

❶ Leeks often have dirt hiding under the first couple of layers, so take the time to rinse thoroughly.

❷ If you do not have a broiler-safe pot, you can instead preheat the oven to 450°F (230°C). If needed, transfer the bean mixture to a 13 x 19-inch (3.5 L) casserole dish (or use an oven-safe pot). Top with the bread and cheese, and bake until the bread is golden brown and the cheese is melted, 10 to 15 minutes.

NOODLES

ACTIVE TIME: 25 MINUTES • TOTAL TIME: 25 MINUTES • SERVES 4

PESTO PANTRY PASTA

12 oz (340g) dried **farfalle** (bow ties; 5 cups)

2 tablespoons **extra-virgin olive oil**

2 **garlic cloves**, minced

½ teaspoon **red pepper flakes**

1 bunch **lacinato kale** (10 oz / 283g), stemmed and thinly sliced ❶

1 can (14 oz / 398 ml) **chickpeas**, drained and rinsed

⅔ cup **roasted red peppers** from a jar, diced

¼ cup drained and minced **sun-dried tomatoes**

¼ teaspoon **fine sea salt**

½ cup **Fresh Basil Pesto** (page 290), Vegan Pesto (page 290), or store-bought

1.3 oz (37g) finely grated **Parmesan cheese** (⅓ cup), more for garnish

⅓ cup **Quick Pickled Red Onions** (page 289) ❷

When your fridge is sparse, this easy one-pot pasta pulls through. Pantry staples—like roasted red peppers, sun-dried tomatoes, and pesto sauce—can jazz up many meals, and this pasta is no exception. This dish comes together quickly while the pasta cooks—all you need to do is chop vegetables and open jars. Leftovers can be eaten warm or as a cold pasta salad. I enjoy it both ways.

---

1. **Cook the pasta:** Bring a large pot of salted water to a boil over high heat. Add the pasta and cook until al dente according to the package directions. Scoop out and reserve 1 cup of pasta water. Drain the pasta.

2. **Cook the other ingredients:** Return the pot to the stovetop and heat the olive oil over low heat. Scatter in the garlic and red pepper flakes and cook until the garlic is fragrant, 1 to 2 minutes. Add the kale, chickpeas, roasted red peppers, sun-dried tomatoes, and salt. Cook until the chickpeas are warm and the kale has softened, 2 to 3 minutes.

3. **Combine and serve:** Return the pasta to the pot along with ¼ cup of the reserved pasta water, pesto, Parmesan, and pickled red onions. Toss, adding more pasta water if needed, a little at a time, until the pasta is coated in silky sauce. Season with more salt, if needed. Divide the pasta among plates or bowls and top with more Parmesan.

VEGAN: Use grated vegan Parmesan cheese or omit. **GLUTEN-FREE:** Use gluten-free pasta (farfalle or penne).

---

❶ Lacinato kale can be replaced with 1 bunch of curly kale (8 oz / 227g) or 3 cups packed chopped spinach.

❷ If you don't have Quick Pickled Red Onions on hand, make them first so they have time to marinate.

ACTIVE TIME: 45 MINUTES • TOTAL TIME: 45 MINUTES • SERVES 4 TO 5

MUSHROOM STROGANOFF

3 tablespoons **grapeseed oil,** divided

1½ lb (680g) **cremini mushrooms**, sliced ❶

2 **yellow onions**, finely chopped (4 cups)

4 **garlic cloves**, minced

1 tablespoon **fresh thyme leaves**

3 tablespoons **all-purpose flour**

3 cups **vegetable stock**

1 tablespoon **tamari**

½ teaspoon **fine sea salt**

12 oz (340g) dried **broad egg noodles** (½-inch / 1 cm wide)

1 oz (28g) finely grated **Parmesan cheese** (¼ cup), more for garnish

⅓ cup **sour cream** ❷

Freshly ground **black pepper**

Chopped **fresh flat-leaf parsley leaves**, for garnish

Mushroom Stroganoff is one of the most popular recipes on the *Evergreen Kitchen* blog. Over the years, readers have written in raving that even kids and veggie-avoiding adults enjoy it. So it felt only right to include a version of the recipe here so that it might win you (and your taste buds) over, too. It'll look like a lot of mushrooms at the beginning, but they shrink down significantly. Cooking them in batches helps the mushrooms brown rather than steam.

---

1. **Sauté the mushrooms and onion:** In a 12-inch (30 cm) skillet, heat 1 tablespoon of the grapeseed oil over medium-high heat. Once the oil is hot, scatter half of the mushrooms into the skillet and sear, undisturbed, until golden brown on the bottom, 3 to 4 minutes. Sauté the mushrooms, stirring frequently, until they are golden brown all over, 4 to 5 minutes. Transfer the mushrooms to a medium bowl and set aside. Add 1 tablespoon of the grapeseed oil to the pan, scatter in the remaining mushrooms and sear, undisturbed, until golden brown on the bottom, 3 to 4 minutes. Add the remaining 1 tablespoon grapeseed oil and the onions. Continue sautéing, stirring occasionally, until the onions are soft and golden brown around the edges, 8 to 10 minutes.

2. **Finish the sauce:** Reduce the heat to medium. Add the reserved cooked mushrooms along with the garlic and thyme. Cook, stirring constantly, until the garlic is fragrant, 1 to 2 minutes. Sprinkle in the flour and toss to coat. Add the vegetable stock, tamari, and salt, stirring to scrape up the brown bits from the bottom of the pan. Bring the sauce to a simmer and cook until it has thickened to the consistency of loose gravy, 5 to 10 minutes.

3. **Meanwhile, cook the noodles:** Bring a large pot of salted water to a boil over high heat. Add the noodles and cook until al dente, according to the package directions. Drain.

4. **Combine the sauce and noodles:** Add the noodles to the sauce, reduce the heat to medium-low, and gently stir to combine. Let the noodles finish cooking in the sauce, stirring occasionally, about 1 minute. Stir in the Parmesan and sour cream. Season with pepper and more salt, if needed. Divide the noodles among bowls. Garnish with more Parmesan and parsley.

VEGAN: Use eggless broad noodles or fusilli pasta. Use vegan sour cream or substitute ¼ cup plain unsweetened barista-style dairy-free milk or creamer. Use grated vegan Parmesan cheese or omit.

GLUTEN-FREE: Replace the flour with white rice flour. Use gluten-free egg noodles or fusilli.

---

❶ For even more mushroom flavour, use 1 lb (454g) cremini mushrooms and ½ lb (227g) shiitake mushrooms.

❷ If you don't have sour cream, you could replace it with full-fat plain Greek yogurt.

SPINACH, PEA, AND PESTO PASTA

12 oz (340g) dried **gemelli** or rotini (4 cups)

10 oz (283g) **frozen peas**

8 oz (227g) **baby spinach**

½ cup **Fresh Basil Pesto** (page 290), Vegan Pesto (page 290), or store-bought

¼ teaspoon **red pepper flakes**

1 oz (28g) finely grated **Parmesan cheese** (¼ cup), more for garnish

Fine sea salt

Freshly ground **black pepper**

This is my go-to meal when I *should* have eaten dinner an hour ago. This pasta tastes fresh and bright, which is impressive since you don't need to chop a single fresh vegetable. If you don't have pesto squirrelled away, I encourage you to make some while the pasta cooks. Store-bought pesto works in a pinch, but since this dish only has a handful of ingredients, you really want each at its best.

1. **Cook the pasta and blanch the peas:** Bring a large pot of salted water to a boil over high heat. Add the pasta and cook 1 minute less than al dente according to the package directions. Scoop out and reserve 1 cup of pasta water. Pour the peas into the pot with the pasta and boil until the peas are bright green and no longer frozen, 30 to 60 seconds. Drain the peas and the pasta together in a colander, then shake to remove excess water.

2. **Combine and serve:** Return the pot to the stovetop over low heat. Add the spinach, drained pasta and peas, pesto, red pepper flakes, and a splash of the reserved pasta water if needed. Toss to combine. Sprinkle in the Parmesan. Toss, adding more pasta water if needed, a little at a time, until the pasta is coated in silky sauce. Season with salt and black pepper to taste. Divide the pasta among bowls and garnish with more Parmesan.

VEGAN: Use grated vegan Parmesan cheese. **GLUTEN-FREE:** Use gluten-free pasta (gemelli, rotini, or penne).

ACTIVE TIME: 25 MINUTES • **TOTAL TIME:** 25 MINUTES • **SERVES** 4

SPICY SESAME ALMOND NOODLES

SPICY ALMOND SAUCE

¼ cup smooth roasted unsalted **almond butter**

2 tablespoons **tamari**

2 tablespoons **grapeseed oil**

1 tablespoon **toasted sesame oil**

1 tablespoon **rice vinegar**

1 **garlic clove**, finely grated

1 teaspoon finely grated **fresh ginger**

2 tablespoons **hot water**

2 to 3 teaspoons **sambal oelek**, divided

NOODLES AND VEGGIES

2 **scallions** (dark part only)

1 cup **snap peas**, trimmed ❶

1 bunch **spinach** (12 oz / 340g)

1 teaspoon **toasted sesame oil**

2 teaspoons **toasted sesame seeds**

Fine sea salt

12 oz (340g) **ramen noodles**

8 oz (227g) **smoked tofu**, cut into bite-size pieces (optional) ❷

In this dish ramen noodles are coated in a silky almond sauce that's flavoured with ginger and sesame oil. It's easy to make and the outcome is delicious. Snap peas and spinach cook in mere minutes, and you can adjust the spice level by adding as little or as much sambal oelek as you'd like. Feel free to substitute whatever veggies you have on hand—just aim for at least one crisp vegetable for texture and variety. If splitting this across meals, store extra sauce in the fridge and cook the noodles fresh when you need them.

---

1. **Make the Spicy Almond Sauce:** In a small bowl, whisk together the almond butter, tamari, grapeseed oil, sesame oil, rice vinegar, garlic, ginger, hot water, and 2 teaspoons of the sambal oelek. Taste and add the remaining 1 teaspoon sambal oelek, if desired.

2. **Start the Noodles and Veggies—make the scallion curls:** Fill a small bowl with ice water. Slice the scallions into 3-inch (8 cm) lengths. Slice each length into razor-thin strips, then submerge them in the ice bath. The scallions will curl as they soak in the water.

3. **Blanch the snap peas:** Bring a large pot of water to a boil over high heat. (Make sure to fill the pot with enough water to cook the ramen after.) Submerge the snap peas in the boiling water and cook until tender and bright green, 1 to 2 minutes. Using a sieve or slotted spoon, scoop out the snap peas and transfer them to a cutting board. Slice the snap peas in half diagonally. Keep the pot of water at a boil.

4. **Blanch the spinach:** Submerge the spinach in the boiling water and cook until softened and dark green, about 30 seconds. Using a sieve or slotted spoon, scoop out the spinach and drain thoroughly. (Keep the pot of water at a boil.) Transfer the spinach to a medium bowl. Drizzle with the sesame oil, sesame seeds, and salt. Toss to coat.

5. **Cook the noodles:** Add the noodles to the boiling water and cook according to the package directions. Drain the noodles.

6. **Assemble:** Divide the noodles among bowls. Drizzle with about half of the sauce. Top with the drained scallion curls, snap peas, spinach, smoked tofu (if using), and the remaining sauce. Stir everything together before digging in.

GLUTEN-FREE: Use gluten-free ramen noodles or rice noodles. Rice noodles tend to stick together when cooked, so toss them with 1 tablespoon of grapeseed oil after cooking.

---

❶ To trim the snap peas, remove the tips and the tough string that runs down the length of the pod.

❷ If tofu isn't your thing, you could replace it with a soft-boiled egg (page 21).

ACTIVE TIME: 35 MINUTES • **TOTAL TIME:** 40 MINUTES • **SERVES** 4

SEARED MUSHROOM AND CREAMY GARLIC PASTA

½ cup raw **cashews** ❶

1½ cups **vegetable stock**

4 tablespoons **extra-virgin olive oil**, divided

1 **yellow onion**, finely chopped (2 cups)

8 **garlic cloves**, minced

2 tablespoons **fresh thyme leaves**, divided

¾ teaspoon **fine sea salt**

¼ teaspoon **red pepper flakes**

8.8 oz (250g) dried **tagliatelle**

12 oz (340g) **mixed mushrooms** (shiitake, cremini, oyster), sliced

1 tablespoon **tamari**

1 oz (28g) finely grated **Parmesan cheese** (¼ cup), more for garnish

Freshly ground **black pepper**

This pasta combines four incredibly delicious ingredients that work so well together: garlic, mushrooms, pasta, and fresh thyme. In fact, I love this combo so much that we served it at our wedding. By "served," I really mean "cooked"—Anguel in his suit and me in my wedding dress. Are we nuts?! Likely. But the meal was so worth it. The only dairy is added at the end, so if you're serving a mixed crowd, it's easy to keep some of the pasta vegan and the rest not.

---

1. **Make the cashew cream:** In a high-speed blender, combine the cashews and vegetable stock. Blend until completely smooth, about 2 minutes, scraping down the sides as needed.

2. **Make the sauce:** In a large Dutch oven or pot, heat 3 tablespoons of the olive oil over medium heat. Add the onion and cook, stirring occasionally, until golden brown around the edges, 8 to 10 minutes. Reduce the heat to low. Add the garlic, 1 tablespoon of the thyme, salt, and red pepper flakes. Cook, stirring frequently, until the garlic is fragrant, 1 to 2 minutes. Pour in the cashew cream and stir to mix. Bring the sauce to a simmer, then cover with a lid. Keep hot over low heat.

3. **Cook the pasta:** Bring a large pot of salted water to a boil over high heat. Add the pasta and cook until al dente according to the package directions. Scoop out and reserve 1 cup of pasta water. Drain the pasta.

4. **Meanwhile, sear the mushrooms:** In a large skillet, heat the remaining 1 tablespoon olive oil over medium-high heat. Once the oil is hot, scatter in the mushrooms and sear, undisturbed, until lightly browned on the bottom, 3 to 4 minutes. Stir, and cook the mushrooms until lightly browned all over, another 5 to 6 minutes. Remove from the heat. Sprinkle with the remaining 1 tablespoon thyme and pour in the tamari. Stir, letting the residual heat continue to cook the mushrooms until the tamari is absorbed, about 1 minute.

5. **Combine:** Add the pasta to the sauce, sprinkle in the Parmesan, and toss to coat. Add a bit of the reserved pasta water, a little at a time, if the sauce is too thick, tossing until the pasta is coated in silky sauce. Add the seared mushrooms, and season with black pepper and more salt, if needed. Gently toss to mix. Divide the pasta among plates. Garnish with more Parmesan.

VEGAN: Use grated vegan Parmesan cheese, or omit and add an extra pinch of salt. Some tagliatelle is made with eggs, so check the package.

GLUTEN-FREE: Use gluten-free pasta (tagliatelle or spaghetti).

---

❶ A high-speed blender can usually blend cashews completely smooth without presoaking. If you don't have a high-speed blender, put the cashews in a medium heatproof bowl, cover with boiling water, and let sit for at least 30 minutes to soften. Drain, then use as directed. If you notice any small pieces of cashews after blending, strain the mixture through a cheesecloth before proceeding.

ACTIVE TIME: 30 MINUTES • **TOTAL TIME:** 30 MINUTES • **SERVES** 6

CREAMY ROASTED RED PEPPER PASTA

1 cup **roasted red peppers** from a jar

⅓ cup **sun-dried tomatoes**, drained

1 lb (454g) dried **rigatoni**

4 tablespoons **extra-virgin olive oil**, divided

1 **yellow onion**, thinly sliced (2 cups)

¼ cup **tomato paste**

5 **garlic cloves**, minced

½ teaspoon **fine sea salt**

½ teaspoon **red pepper flakes**

½ cup **whipping (35%) cream**

2 oz (57g) finely grated **Parmesan cheese** (½ cup), more for serving

Store-bought roasted red peppers and sun-dried tomatoes are a shortcut to big flavour in this recipe. A splash of cream makes it extra luscious. Adding hot pasta water to the cream is a step called tempering, which gently warms the cream before it's added to the hot sauce, preventing it from splitting. Use your knife skills here: aim to slice the onion as thinly as possible so it melds into the sauce.

---

1. **Blend the red peppers and sun-dried tomatoes:** In a blender or food processor, purée the roasted red peppers and sun-dried tomatoes until smooth.

2. **Cook the pasta:** Bring a large pot of salted water to a boil over high heat. Add the pasta and cook until al dente according to the package directions. Scoop out and reserve 1½ cups of pasta water. Drain the pasta.

3. **Meanwhile, make the sauce:** In a large Dutch oven or pot, heat 3 tablespoons of the olive oil over medium heat. Add the onion and cook, stirring occasionally, until soft and golden brown around the edges, 8 to 10 minutes. Add the tomato paste and the remaining 1 tablespoon olive oil and cook, stirring frequently, until the paste darkens slightly, 2 to 3 minutes. Add the garlic, salt, and red pepper flakes and cook until the garlic is fragrant, 1 to 2 minutes. Pour in the roasted red pepper and sun-dried tomato mixture and stir to mix. Cover with a lid and reduce the heat to low to keep the sauce hot.

4. **Temper the cream:** Pour the cream into a heatproof glass measuring cup or small bowl. Pour ¼ cup of the reserved pasta water into the cream and stir to mix.

5. **Combine and serve:** Pour the tempered cream into the sauce and stir to mix. Add the pasta to the sauce. Toss, adding more reserved pasta water if needed, a little at a time, until the pasta is coated in silky sauce. Sprinkle in the Parmesan and toss to combine. Add another splash of pasta water, if needed. Season with more salt, if needed. Divide the pasta among bowls and garnish with more Parmesan.

VEGAN: Replace the whipping cream with plain unsweetened barista-style dairy-free milk or creamer, or leave out the cream and add extra pasta water instead. Use grated vegan Parmesan cheese or omit.

GLUTEN-FREE: Use gluten-free pasta (rigatoni or penne).

ACTIVE TIME: 25 MINUTES • TOTAL TIME: 25 MINUTES • SERVES 4

LEMON AND DILL ORZO SALAD

PASTA SALAD

8.8 oz (250g) dried **orzo** (1⅓ cups)

1 **red bell pepper**, diced

½ **English cucumber**, diced

2 cups finely chopped **spinach**

½ cup crumbled **feta cheese**

3 tablespoons minced **fresh dill**

2 tablespoons pitted and minced **Kalamata olives** ❶

2 tablespoons drained and minced **sun-dried tomatoes**

1 tablespoon drained and minced **capers**

LEMON VINAIGRETTE

⅓ cup **extra-virgin olive oil**

1 teaspoon **lemon zest**

2 to 3 tablespoons **fresh lemon juice**, divided

1 teaspoon **Dijon mustard**

1 teaspoon **honey**

¾ teaspoon **fine sea salt**

½ teaspoon freshly ground **black pepper**

This easy-breezy pasta salad is perfect for outdoor meals. It's bursting with fresh flavours from the lemon, dill, feta, and crisp veggies. You can make this dish in advance. ❶ If you're feeding a crowd, a double batch is easily made, since orzo is commonly sold in 17.6 oz (500g) bags. The most important step is cooking the orzo *just* right. You'll likely want to cook it ever so slightly past al dente, because it won't be added to a warm sauce to finish cooking.

---

1. **Start the Pasta Salad—cook the pasta:** Bring a large pot of salted water to a boil over high heat. Add the pasta and cook until slightly more than al dente according to the package directions. Drain the pasta, rinse under cold running water for 15 seconds to cool it down, then shake to remove excess water.

2. **Meanwhile, make the Lemon Vinaigrette:** In a large bowl, whisk together the olive oil, lemon zest, 2 tablespoons of the lemon juice, Dijon mustard, honey, salt, and pepper until emulsified.

3. **Combine and serve:** Add the pasta to the bowl of vinaigrette, then gently stir until evenly coated. Add the bell pepper, cucumber, spinach, feta, dill, olives, sun-dried tomatoes, and capers, then stir to mix. Taste and adjust seasoning. Add the remaining 1 tablespoon lemon juice and more salt, if needed. Divide the pasta among bowls. ❷

VEGAN: Use vegan feta cheese or omit. Use maple syrup instead of honey. **GLUTEN-FREE:** Use gluten-free orzo.

---

❶ For the best flavour and texture, buy unpitted olives and pit them yourself. To pit, place the flat side of your knife over the olive. Use the palm of your hand to press down on the olive with the flat side of your knife, then discard the pit.

❷ If making the pasta salad in advance, refrigerate in a covered container for up to 2 days. This salad can be eaten at room temperature or cold.

ACTIVE TIME: 30 MINUTES • **TOTAL TIME:** 30 MINUTES • **SERVES** 4 TO 5

SPINACH AND ARTICHOKE PASTA

12 oz (340g) dried **penne** (4 cups)

1 bunch **spinach** (12 oz / 340g), chopped

3 tablespoons **butter**

1½ cups finely chopped **leeks** (white and light green parts)

5 **garlic cloves**, minced

½ teaspoon **red pepper flakes**

2 tablespoons **all-purpose flour**

2 cups **whole** or **2% milk**

¾ teaspoon **fine sea salt**

2 oz (57g) finely grated **Parmesan cheese** (½ cup), more for garnish

¾ cup drained and chopped **marinated artichokes**

¼ cup plain **Greek yogurt** ❶

Freshly ground **black pepper**

If you're looking for a delicious way to eat a whole bunch of spinach, look no further. This easygoing pasta is made with fresh spinach, leeks, and jarred artichokes tossed in a creamy garlic sauce. The sauce is lighter than you'd expect: it's made with milk and Greek yogurt instead of cream, but it doesn't taste like a compromise! The quick-cooking sauce comes together while the pasta boils, so have everything prepped before you start. That way, dinner will be ready in a flash.

---

1. **Cook the pasta:** Bring a large pot of salted water to a boil over high heat. Add the pasta and cook until al dente according to the package directions. About 30 seconds before the pasta is done, submerge the spinach into the water to soften it. Drain the pasta and spinach together in a colander and shake to remove excess water.

2. **Meanwhile, make the sauce:** Melt the butter in a large Dutch oven or 12-inch (30 cm) skillet over medium heat. Add the leeks, garlic, and red pepper flakes and cook, stirring frequently, until the leeks are soft and bright green, 3 to 5 minutes. Reduce the heat, if needed, to prevent the garlic from burning. Sprinkle in the flour and stir to coat. Pour in the milk and stir to mix. Cook, stirring frequently, until the sauce begins to bubble. Let the sauce cook, stirring occasionally, until it thickens and coats the back of a spoon, 1 to 3 minutes. Reduce the heat to low. Stir in the salt, Parmesan, and artichokes.

3. **Combine and serve:** Add the pasta and spinach to the sauce and stir. Let the pasta finish cooking in the sauce, about 1 minute. Stir in the yogurt. Season with black pepper and more salt, if needed. Divide the pasta among bowls and garnish with more Parmesan.

GLUTEN-FREE: Use gluten-free pasta (penne or rotini). Replace the flour with white rice flour.

---

❶ Use full-fat Greek yogurt for the best flavour, but low-fat works as well. In place of Greek yogurt, you could use crème fraîche for even more decadent results.

ACTIVE TIME: 25 MINUTES • **TOTAL TIME:** 25 MINUTES • **SERVES** 2 TO 3

VEGGIE PAD THAI

PAD THAI

4.4 oz (125g) dried medium **rice noodles** ❷

2 tablespoons **grapeseed oil**

8 oz (227g) **firm tofu**, cut into ½-inch (1 cm) cubes

1 **red bell pepper**, thinly sliced

1 large **shallot**, thinly sliced (½ cup)

2 large **eggs**

3 **garlic cloves**, minced

3 **scallions**, cut into 1½-inch (4 cm) lengths

1½ cups **bean sprouts**

1 tablespoon **fresh lime juice**

¼ cup **roasted peanuts**, chopped

¼ cup chopped **fresh cilantro leaves** (optional)

Lime wedges

SAUCE

3 tablespoons **tamari**

3 tablespoons **tamarind concentrate** ❸

2 tablespoons packed **brown sugar**

2 to 3 teaspoons **Sriracha sauce** or sambal oelek

The legit street food vendors in Bangkok probably wouldn't call this pad thai, but it certainly hits the spot for me at home. This version skips the shrimp and fish sauce—two traditional ingredients—to keep things vegetarian. Tamarind provides the tangy flavour that pad thai is known for; it is available at well-stocked grocery stores, Asian grocery stores, and online. This dish cooks quickly, so make sure you have all your veggies prepped before you begin. If you want to scale up the recipe, cook it in batches so you don't overwhelm the pan. If you have a metal spatula, use it for stir-frying—I find it more effective than a stirring spoon. ❶

1. **Soak the noodles:** Bring a large pot of water to a boil over high heat. Once boiling, remove the pot from the heat and submerge the noodles in the water. Let the noodles soak until flexible but still very al dente, 4 to 5 minutes. Drain the noodles in a colander and rinse under cold running water until cool to the touch, 15 to 30 seconds. Drain the noodles thoroughly.

2. **Meanwhile, make the Sauce:** In a small bowl, whisk together the tamari, tamarind concentrate, brown sugar, and Sriracha until smooth.

3. **Start the Pad Thai—sauté the tofu, vegetables, and eggs:** In a large cast-iron skillet or a wok, heat the grapeseed oil over medium-high heat. Once the oil is hot, add the tofu and sauté, stirring frequently, until the tofu is golden brown all over, 3 to 4 minutes. Add the bell pepper and shallot and sauté, stirring frequently, until tender, about 2 minutes. Push the mixture to one side of the skillet. Crack the eggs into the empty side and immediately scramble. Sauté the mixture, stirring constantly, until the eggs begin to set, 30 to 60 seconds. Add the garlic and scallions and sauté, stirring constantly, until the scallions have softened, 1 to 2 minutes.

4. **Add the noodles and sauce:** Scatter the noodles and bean sprouts into the skillet. Pour the sauce overtop. Toss until the noodles are well coated and warmed through, about 1 minute. Drizzle the lime juice over the mixture and toss to coat.

5. **Serve:** Divide the pad thai among plates. Sprinkle with the peanuts and cilantro (if using), and serve with lime wedges.

VEGAN: Omit the eggs.

❶ If you are using a coated nonstick wok, use non-scratching cookware.

❷ Use medium-width rice noodles, about ¼ inch (5 mm) wide.

❸ Tamarind concentrate is a thick, pourable blend of tamarind and water. You can substitute with tamarind paste. To make tamarind paste, in a small bowl, combine ⅓ cup boiling water and ⅓ cup tamarind pulp (from a block of tamarind). Let sit for 10 to 15 minutes to soften, then stir vigorously with a fork to mix. Push the mixture through a sieve to separate the fibres and seeds from the smooth paste. Measure 3 tablespoons of the smooth paste and use as directed.

ACTIVE TIME: 45 MINUTES • **TOTAL TIME:** 45 MINUTES • **SERVES** 4

ROASTED CAULIFLOWER, SMASHED OLIVE, AND LEMON PASTA

1½-lb (680g) head **cauliflower**, cut into florets

⅓ cup + 1 tablespoon **extra-virgin olive oil**, divided

1 teaspoon **fine sea salt**, divided

10 oz (283g) dried **tagliatelle** or linguine

1 **yellow onion**, finely chopped (2 cups)

5 **garlic cloves**, minced

¼ teaspoon **red pepper flakes**

½ cup pitted and chopped **green olives** ❶

1 bunch **lacinato kale** (10 oz / 283g), stemmed and thinly sliced

1 tablespoon drained **capers**

½ teaspoon **lemon zest**

2 tablespoons **fresh lemon juice**

2 oz (57g) finely grated **Parmesan cheese** (½ cup), more for garnish

⅓ cup chopped **fresh dill**, more for garnish

Freshly ground **black pepper**

This pasta gets its magic from caramelized cauliflower, fresh lemon, garlicky olive oil, capers, and olives. Use your favourite firm, green olives—Castelvetrano, Cerignola, and Calabrese are all delicious choices for this dish. Dill adds a nice pop of freshness at the end, especially paired with the lemon. But if dill isn't your thing, you could use chives or parsley instead.

---

1. **Roast the cauliflower:** Place an oven rack in the upper third of the oven and preheat to 450°F (230°C). Line a large baking sheet with parchment paper. Scatter the cauliflower florets on the prepared baking sheet. Drizzle with 1 tablespoon of the olive oil and toss to coat. Sprinkle with ¼ teaspoon of the salt. Roast until the cauliflower is brown around the edges and fork-tender, 20 to 25 minutes, flipping halfway through.

2. **Meanwhile, cook the pasta:** Bring a large pot of salted water to a boil over high heat. Add the pasta and cook until al dente according to the package directions. Scoop out and reserve 1 cup of the pasta water. Drain the pasta.

3. **While the pasta water is coming to a boil, start the sauce:** In a large Dutch oven or 12-inch (30 cm) skillet, heat the remaining ⅓ cup olive oil over medium heat. Add the onion and cook, stirring occasionally, until golden brown around the edges, 8 to 10 minutes. Add the garlic and red pepper flakes and cook, stirring constantly, until the garlic is fragrant, 1 to 2 minutes. Add the olives, kale, capers, remaining ¾ teaspoon salt, and ¼ cup of the reserved pasta water. Cook until the kale starts to wilt, 1 to 2 minutes.

4. **Combine and serve:** Add the pasta to the sauce along with the lemon zest and juice. Sprinkle in the Parmesan. Toss, adding more reserved pasta water if needed, a little at a time, until the pasta is coated in silky sauce. Sprinkle in the dill and season with black pepper and more salt, if needed. Divide the pasta among plates and top with the roasted cauliflower, more Parmesan, and more dill.

VEGAN: Use grated vegan Parmesan cheese or omit. **GLUTEN-FREE:** Use gluten-free pasta (tagliatelle or linguine).

---

❶ For the best flavour and texture, buy unpitted olives and pit them yourself. To pit, place the flat side of your knife over the olive. Use the palm of your hand to press down on the olive with the flat side of your knife, then discard the pit.

ACTIVE TIME: 20 MINUTES • **TOTAL TIME:** 20 MINUTES • **SERVES** 4

MISO BROWN BUTTER PASTA

12 oz (340g) dried **orecchiette** (3½ cups) ❶

⅓ cup **butter**

4 **garlic cloves**, thinly sliced

3 tablespoons **white miso**

1 tablespoon **sambal oelek**

1 teaspoon **rice vinegar**

2 oz (57g) finely grated **Parmesan cheese** (½ cup), more for garnish

Fine sea salt

Minced **fresh chives**, for garnish (about ⅓ cup)

The first pasta I ever cooked for myself was a bowl of noodles tossed in butter and sprinkled with cheese on top. I was so proud. This recipe channels that need-no-veggies attitude with a short list of savvy ingredients. Here, garlic-steeped butter is browned until it smells nutty. Then umami-rich miso, spicy sambal oelek, and salty Parmesan come together in a silky sauce. This pasta also plays nice as a side dish. But there's no shame in tucking straight into a bowl of this comforting pasta—as I often do!

1. **Cook the pasta:** Bring a large pot of salted water to a boil over high heat. Add the pasta and cook until al dente according to the package directions. Scoop out and reserve 1 cup of pasta water. Drain the pasta. Set aside the pot.

2. **Meanwhile, make the brown butter:** Melt the butter in a small saucepan over medium heat. Using a silicone spatula, stir frequently to scrape up the brown bits from the bottom of the pan. Once the butter begins to foam, 3 to 5 minutes in, scatter the garlic into the pot and cook, stirring constantly, until the butter and garlic are golden brown, 2 to 5 minutes. Immediately remove the pot from the heat.

3. **Combine and serve:** To the pasta pot, add the miso, sambal oelek, rice vinegar, and ½ cup of the reserved pasta water and whisk vigorously until the miso is fully dissolved. Add the drained pasta and brown butter and toss to coat. Sprinkle in the Parmesan. Toss, adding more pasta water if needed, a little at a time, until the pasta is coated in silky sauce. Taste and season with salt, if needed. Divide the pasta among bowls and top with more Parmesan and chives.

VEGAN: Use vegan butter and Parmesan. Depending on the brand of vegan butter, it may not brown, but it will still taste delicious. I've had luck getting Miyoko's brand to brown.

GLUTEN-FREE: Use gluten-free pasta (orecchiette, shells, or elbow).

❶ Orecchiette can be replaced with other small noodles, such as small shells or elbow macaroni.

ACTIVE TIME: 25 MINUTES • **TOTAL TIME:** 25 MINUTES • **SERVES** 5

GINGER SOY SOBA SALAD WITH SPICY PEANUT SAUCE

SOBA SALAD

8 oz (227g) **soba noodles** ❶

8 oz (227g) **smoked tofu,** cut into ½-inch (1 cm) cubes (optional)

1 **red bell pepper**, thinly sliced

1 **celery rib**, thinly sliced

1 cup shredded **red cabbage**

3 **scallions**, thinly sliced

½ cup chopped **fresh cilantro leaves**

2 tablespoons **toasted sesame seeds**

PEANUT SAUCE (OPTIONAL)

3 tablespoons smooth unsalted **peanut butter** ❷

2 to 3 teaspoons **sambal oelek**

2 to 3 tablespoons **hot water**

DRESSING

3 tablespoons **fresh lime juice**

3 tablespoons **tamari**

2 tablespoons **toasted sesame oil**

2 tablespoons **grapeseed oil**

1½ teaspoons finely grated **fresh ginger**

This noodle salad is brimming with crisp vegetables and a refreshing ginger-lime-soy sauce. It's make-ahead friendly—and sturdy enough to pack for picnics, potlucks, and camping weekends. I like to serve a spicy peanut sauce on the side. Creamy sauces tend to make noodles gummy over time, so drizzling it on right before eating keeps them nice and slick. If someone's sensitive to nuts or spice, they can skip the sauce; the noodles will still taste delicious without it.

---

1. **Start the Soba Salad—cook the soba:** Bring a large pot of unsalted water to a boil over high heat. Add the soba and cook according to the package directions. (Be careful not to overcook the noodles.) Drain the noodles in a colander and rinse under cold running water, until cool to the touch, 30 to 60 seconds, then shake to remove excess water.

2. **Meanwhile, make the Peanut Sauce, if using:** In a small bowl, whisk together the peanut butter, 2 teaspoons of the sambal oelek, and 2 tablespoons of the hot water. Add as much of the remaining 1 tablespoon hot water, if needed, to make the sauce smooth and pourable. Taste and add the remaining 1 teaspoon sambal oelek, if desired.

3. **Make the Dressing:** In a large bowl, whisk together the lime juice, tamari, sesame oil, grapeseed oil, and ginger.

4. **Assemble:** Add the soba noodles to the dressing and toss to coat. Add the smoked tofu, bell pepper, celery, cabbage, scallions, cilantro, and sesame seeds. Toss to mix. Serve room temperature or cold, with the peanut sauce (if using) on the side for drizzling.

GLUTEN-FREE: Use 100% buckwheat soba noodles.

---

❶ Soba are Japanese noodles primarily made from buckwheat and often wheat flour. If you're looking for a gluten-free option, check the labels for 100% buckwheat.

❷ Can be replaced with smooth roasted unsalted almond butter.

ACTIVE TIME: 35 MINUTES • **TOTAL TIME:** 45 MINUTES • **SERVES** 6

ROASTED BUTTERNUT SQUASH PASTA WITH TOASTED HAZELNUTS

4 cups peeled **butternut squash** cut into ½-inch (1 cm) cubes ❶

¼ cup + 1 tablespoon **extra-virgin olive oil**, divided

2 tablespoons **fresh thyme leaves**, divided

1¼ teaspoons **fine sea salt**, divided

½ cup raw **hazelnuts**

1 **yellow onion**, finely chopped (2 cups)

4 **garlic cloves**, minced

¼ teaspoon **red pepper flakes**

1 lb (454g) dried **penne** (5⅓ cups)

⅓ cup raw **cashews** ❷

2½ cups **vegetable stock**

2 teaspoons **white wine vinegar**

Pinch of **ground nutmeg** (optional)

Freshly ground **black pepper**

This pasta is *saucy*, and the way it's cooked is all about building flavour. The silky butternut squash sauce is infused with fresh thyme, garlic, and hazelnuts—yum! The olive oil does double duty, toasting the hazelnuts and then flavouring the sauce with the nutty oil. You'll roast the butternut squash to bring out its flavours. Cutting the squash into small cubes maximizes its surface area so it quickly browns in the oven.

---

1. **Roast the butternut squash:** Place an oven rack in the upper third of the oven and preheat to 450°F (230°C). Scatter the butternut squash on a large baking sheet. Drizzle with 1 tablespoon of the olive oil, toss to coat, then sprinkle with 1 tablespoon of the thyme and ¼ teaspoon of the salt. Roast until the squash is fork-tender and brown around the edges, 25 to 30 minutes.

2. **Meanwhile, toast the hazelnuts:** In a large Dutch oven or pot, heat the remaining ¼ cup olive oil over medium heat. Add the hazelnuts and cook, stirring frequently, until fragrant and golden brown, 4 to 6 minutes. Scoop out the nuts, leaving the oil in the pot. Transfer the nuts to a cutting board, let cool slightly, and then roughly chop.

3. **Start cooking the sauce:** Return the pot, with the oil, to medium heat. Carefully scatter in the onion and cook, stirring frequently, until golden brown around the edges, 5 to 7 minutes. Reduce the heat to low. Add the garlic and red pepper flakes and cook, stirring constantly, until the garlic is fragrant, about 1 minute. Transfer the mixture to a high-speed blender. Set aside the pot.

4. **Meanwhile, cook the pasta:** Bring a separate large pot of salted water to a boil over high heat. Add the pasta and cook until al dente according to the package directions. Drain the pasta.

5. **Blend and heat the sauce:** To the blender with the onion mixture, add the roasted butternut squash, cashews, vegetable stock, white wine vinegar, nutmeg (if using), and the remaining 1 teaspoon salt. Blend until completely smooth, 1 to 2 minutes. Pour the sauce back into the pot, then stir in the remaining 1 tablespoon thyme. Cover with a lid and reduce the heat to medium-low to keep the sauce hot.

6. **Combine and serve** ❸**:** Add the pasta to the hot sauce and toss to combine. Let the pasta finish cooking in the sauce, stirring frequently, about 1 minute. Divide the pasta among bowls. Garnish with the hazelnuts and black pepper to taste. Serve immediately while the pasta sauce is hot and silky.

GLUTEN-FREE: Use gluten-free pasta (penne or rotini).

---

❶ You'll need about a 1½-lb (680g) squash before trimming and peeling.

❷ If you don't have a high-speed blender, presoak the cashews: Place them in a medium heatproof bowl, cover with boiling water, and let soak until soft, about 30 minutes. Drain, then add to the blender along with the rest of the sauce.

❸ If you're planning for leftovers, I recommend refrigerating extra sauce separately (for up to 3 days), then cooking the pasta fresh. Warm the sauce over medium-low heat, and add a splash of water to thin, if needed.

ACTIVE TIME: 25 MINUTES • **TOTAL TIME:** 30 MINUTES • **SERVES** 4

COCONUT GREEN CURRY PASTA

8.8 oz (250g) dried **spaghetti** or linguine

3 tablespoons **grapeseed oil**, divided

1 large **shallot**, thinly sliced (½ cup)

1 **carrot**, peeled and cut into matchsticks

1 cup trimmed **asparagus** cut into 2-inch (5 cm) lengths

3 **garlic cloves**, minced

1 **red bell pepper**, thinly sliced into 2-inch (5 cm) lengths

8 oz (227g) **Brussels sprouts**, trimmed and thinly sliced

½ teaspoon **fine sea salt**, divided

4 to 5 tablespoons **green curry paste** ❶

1 can (14 fl oz / 398 ml) **full-fat coconut milk**

Freshly ground **black pepper**

¼ cup chopped **fresh cilantro leaves**

Lime wedges

Green curry paste is a quick way to jazz up all kinds of meals. Here, it mixes with creamy coconut milk to make a velvety sauce for spaghetti noodles. It might sound like an odd combination, but give this one a shot—it really works! Adding curry paste to hot oil is called "blooming," and it helps amplify the spices' flavour. And don't forget that squeeze of fresh lime at the end—the acid really brightens the flavour.

1. **Cook the pasta:** Bring a large pot of salted water to a boil over high heat. Add the pasta and cook until al dente according to the package directions. Drain the pasta.

2. **Meanwhile, sauté the vegetables:** In a 12-inch (30 cm) skillet or a large Dutch oven, heat 1 tablespoon of the grapeseed oil over medium heat. Add the shallot and cook, stirring frequently, until golden brown around the edges, 2 to 3 minutes. Add the carrots and asparagus and cook, stirring frequently, until tender, 2 to 3 minutes. Add the garlic, bell pepper, Brussels sprouts, and ¼ teaspoon of the salt and cook, stirring frequently, until the Brussels sprouts are bright green, about 2 minutes. Transfer the vegetables to a medium bowl.

3. **Make the curry sauce:** In the same skillet over low heat, add the remaining 2 tablespoons grapeseed oil and the green curry paste (careful, it's going to sizzle!). Stir to mix with the oil, and cook until fragrant, about 1 minute. Pour in the coconut milk and the remaining ¼ teaspoon salt, then stir to mix. Keep warm, over low heat, until the pasta is ready.

4. **Combine:** Add the pasta to the skillet and toss to coat. Add the vegetables and toss to mix. Season with black pepper and more salt, if needed. Toss to combine. Divide the noodles among bowls. Top with chopped cilantro and serve with lime wedges.

GLUTEN-FREE: Use gluten-free pasta (spaghetti or linguine).

❶ The intensity of curry pastes varies significantly by brand. If you are using a milder brand (like Thai Kitchen), use 5 tablespoons of green curry paste. If in doubt, start with 4 tablespoons and add more to taste. Curry pastes can contain shrimp, so check the label to confirm if it is vegan.

CLASSIC-ISH COMFORT FOOD

ACTIVE TIME: 40 MINUTES • TOTAL TIME: 1 HOUR • SERVES 4

MEATLESS MEATBALLS WITH GARLIC BREAD

MEATLESS MEATBALLS

1 lb (454g) **cremini mushrooms**, roughly chopped

8 oz (227g) **globe eggplant**, peeled and diced (2½ cups)

1 cup finely chopped **yellow onion**

5 **unpeeled garlic cloves**

4 tablespoons **extra-virgin olive oil**, divided

½ teaspoon **fine sea salt**

½ cup **quick rolled oats**

¼ cup chopped **fresh flat-leaf parsley leaves**, more for garnish

2 tablespoons **nutritional yeast**

2 tablespoons **tamari**

1 tablespoon **dried oregano**

½ teaspoon freshly ground **black pepper**

1 cup **panko breadcrumbs**

2 cups **marinara sauce**

Finely grated **Parmesan cheese**, for garnish

GARLIC BREAD

1 **demi-baguette** (or ½ regular baguette)

3 **garlic cloves**

¼ teaspoon **fine sea salt**

2 tablespoons **extra-virgin olive oil**

Spaghetti and meatballs is a bona fide classic. But can I let you in on a secret? I'm there for the meatballs. These veggie "meatballs" are so good, they can stand on their own. Broiling the eggplant and mushrooms quickly adds flavour and draws out excess moisture. Serve these with freshly made garlic bread and the best marinara you can get your hands on. These meatballs freeze well for make-ahead meals. ❶ And heck, if you still want spaghetti, these would taste great with it too.

1. **Set the oven to broil:** Place the oven racks in the upper and lower thirds of the oven and set to broil. Set aside 2 large baking sheets; line 1 with parchment paper.

2. **Start the Meatless Meatballs—broil the vegetables:** Scatter the mushrooms, eggplant, and onion on the unlined baking sheet. Place the unpeeled garlic cloves on a small piece of foil and set it on the baking sheet. Drizzle 2 tablespoons of the olive oil over the vegetables and a little bit over the garlic. Wrap the foil tightly around the garlic. Toss to coat the vegetables, then sprinkle with the salt. Broil on the upper rack until the vegetables are browned around the edges, 8 to 12 minutes, stirring halfway through. (Watch carefully, as broil times vary.) Remove from the oven and open the foil so the garlic cloves can cool slightly. Set the oven to 425°F (220°C). (You'll want the oven at the correct temperature to bake the meatballs, step 4.)

3. **Combine in a food processor:** Scrape the broiled mushrooms, eggplant, and onion into a food processor. Add the oats, parsley, nutritional yeast, tamari, oregano, and pepper. Peel the garlic cloves, and using a fork, mash them on a cutting board, then add to the food processor. Pulse until the mixture is almost fully pulverized but is not yet a paste (flecks of parsley should be visible), scraping down the sides as needed. Scatter in the panko and pulse just until mixed.

4. **Bake the meatballs:** Scoop 3-tablespoon portions of the eggplant mixture (about the size of a golf ball) onto the lined baking sheet. (You should have about 20 balls.) Using dampened hands, roll each portion into a smooth ball. Generously brush the meatballs all over with the remaining 2 tablespoons olive oil. Bake on the upper rack until the meatballs are firm and golden, 25 to 30 minutes, shaking the pan halfway through for even browning.

CONTINUED ON NEXT PAGE

VEGAN: Use vegan Parmesan cheese or omit. **GLUTEN-FREE:** Use gluten-free panko breadcrumbs and baguette.

❶ To freeze the baked meatballs, let them cool completely, then freeze on the baking sheet until they are firm to the touch. Transfer the meatballs to freezer bags or airtight containers and store in the freezer for up to 3 months. To reheat, place the frozen meatballs on a parchment-lined baking sheet and bake in a 250°F (120°C) oven until warmed through, about 20 minutes.

CONTINUED FROM PREVIOUS PAGE

5. **Meanwhile, make the Garlic Bread:** Cut the baguette in half crosswise, then slice each piece horizontally in half, so you end up with 4 pieces of bread. Place the garlic cloves on the cutting board, then sprinkle with the salt. Using a fork, mash the garlic into a paste. Transfer the paste to a small bowl, add the olive oil, and stir to mix. Arrange the bread cut side up on the unlined baking sheet and brush with the garlicky oil. Bake on the lower rack until golden brown around the edges, 5 to 7 minutes.

6. **Heat the marinara sauce and serve:** In a small saucepan, heat the marinara sauce, stirring occasionally, over medium heat. Cover with a lid so the sauce doesn't splatter. Divide the marinara among bowls. Top with the meatballs, Parmesan, and parsley. Serve with the garlic bread.

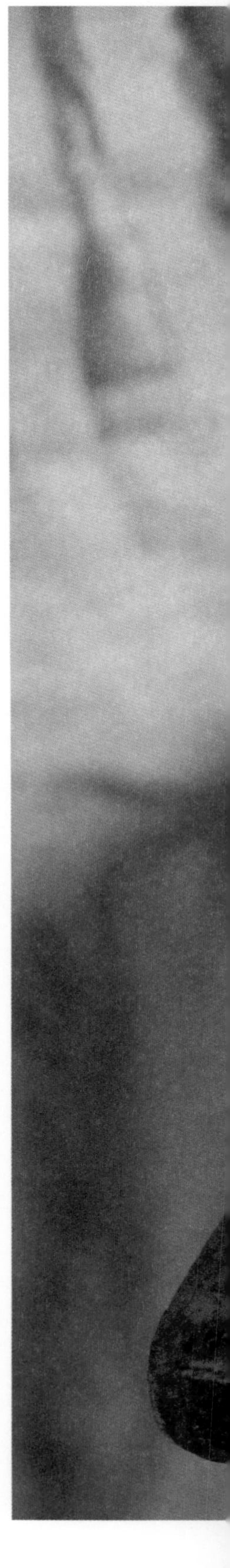

VEGGIE SKILLET POT PIE

2 tablespoons **grapeseed oil**, divided

1 **yellow onion**, finely chopped (2 cups)

1½ cups peeled and diced **carrots**

8 oz (227g) **cremini mushrooms**, quartered

4 **garlic cloves**, minced

¼ cup **all-purpose flour**

3½ cups **vegetable stock**

3 cups **russet potatoes** cut into ½-inch cubes (10.6 oz / 300g)

1 tablespoon **fresh thyme leaves**

1¼ teaspoons **fine sea salt**

½ teaspoon freshly ground **black pepper**

1 can (14 oz / 398 ml) **navy beans**, drained and rinsed

1 cup **frozen green peas**

¼ cup chopped **fresh chives**

1 lb (454g) **frozen puff pastry** (2 sheets), defrosted in fridge overnight ❶

This dish is the ultimate comfort food. It's a stick-to-your-ribs meal that won't leave you needing to take a nap afterwards. The base is made with potatoes, carrots, mushrooms, and green peas coated in a delicious gravy. We even sneak some beans in for extra protein. Everything gets topped with a shatteringly crisp golden-brown pastry. Store-bought puff pastry saves the work of fussing around with a traditional crust. Better yet, this entire dish comes together in a single pan, which can also be brought directly to the table.

---

1. **Preheat the oven:** Place an oven rack in the centre position and preheat to 400°F (200°C). Line a large baking sheet with parchment paper.

2. **Sauté the vegetables:** In a 12-inch (30 cm) oven-safe skillet, heat 1 tablespoon of the grapeseed oil over medium-high heat. Add the onion and sauté, stirring frequently, until golden brown around the edges, 3 to 5 minutes. Add the carrots and mushrooms and sauté, stirring occasionally, until the mushrooms are lightly browned, 3 to 4 minutes. Add the garlic and sauté, stirring constantly, until fragrant, 1 to 2 minutes.

3. **Simmer the filling:** To the skillet, add the remaining 1 tablespoon grapeseed oil and the flour, and toss to coat. Add the vegetable stock, stirring to incorporate the flour until no clumps remain. Add the potatoes, thyme, salt, and pepper. Bring to a boil, then reduce the heat to medium and simmer, stirring frequently, until the potatoes are fork-tender, about 15 minutes. Stir in the navy beans, peas, and chives. Remove from the heat.

4. **Meanwhile, prep the puff pastry:** Unroll a pastry sheet onto a lightly floured work surface. Using a rolling pin, gently smooth out any creases. Cut the pastry into nine 3-inch (8 cm) squares. Repeat with the other pastry sheet. Transfer the pastry squares to the prepared baking sheet and freeze for 10 minutes. ❷

5. **Assemble and bake:** Layer the chilled pastry squares, slightly overlapping, over the filling in the skillet (you may have some squares left over ❸). Transfer the skillet to the oven and bake until the puff pastry is golden brown, about 30 minutes.

VEGAN: Use a vegan puff pastry. Many of the inexpensive big brands are vegan-friendly because they use vegetable oils instead of butter. Just be sure to read the ingredient label.

---

❶ You can also use a block of puff pastry (rather than sheets), but you'll need to roll it out until it is ¼ inch (5 mm) thick. Transfer to a parchment-lined baking sheet and chill in the fridge for at least 15 minutes before cutting as directed.

❷ Chilling the puff pastry and letting it rest will help minimize shrinkage in the oven.

❸ There are many ways to use extra puff pastry. Make a cobbler by layering squares over a fruit filling. Or brush them with melted butter, sprinkle with cinnamon sugar, and bake. Or take them on a savoury route: brush with melted butter and sprinkle with grated cheese and black pepper before baking.

ACTIVE TIME: 40 MINUTES • TOTAL TIME: 40 MINUTES • SERVES 4

BARBECUE PULLED MUSHROOM SANDWICHES

DATE BARBECUE SAUCE

⅔ cup **water**

¼ cup firmly packed pitted **Medjool dates**

2 tablespoons **tomato paste**

2 tablespoons **tamari**

2 tablespoons **apple cider vinegar**

1 teaspoon **grapeseed oil**

½ teaspoon freshly ground **black pepper**

¼ teaspoon **garlic powder**

¼ teaspoon **smoked sweet paprika**

3 tablespoons **fresh lemon juice**

SLAW

1½ cups shredded **green cabbage**

2 tablespoons **mayonnaise**, more for serving

1 tablespoon **apple cider vinegar**

2 teaspoons **grainy Dijon mustard**

2 **scallions**, thinly sliced

Fine sea salt

Freshly ground **black pepper**

SEARED MUSHROOMS

1 lb (454g) **trumpet (king oyster) mushrooms**

2 tablespoons **grapeseed oil**

4 **brioche buns** or other soft buns, sliced in half horizontally and lightly buttered

Grab the napkins! These saucy sandwiches are filled with pulled mushrooms coated in a sweet and smoky barbecue sauce and topped with a zippy cabbage slaw. Many store-bought barbecue sauces are loaded with sugar, but my version uses dates for natural sweetness. The sauce conveniently simmers while you shred the mushrooms (see page 17 for a how-to). It will look like a lot of mushrooms at the start, but they'll shrink as they cook. Use the biggest skillet you have—12-inch (30 cm) if you have one, but 10-inch (25 cm) will work fine too.

---

1. **Make the Date Barbecue Sauce:** In a small saucepan, combine the water, dates, tomato paste, tamari, apple cider vinegar, grapeseed oil, pepper, garlic powder, and smoked paprika. Cover with a lid and simmer over medium heat for 15 to 20 minutes for the flavours to meld. Transfer the mixture to a high-speed blender and add the lemon juice. Blend until smooth, scraping down the sides as needed.

2. **Meanwhile, make the Slaw:** In a medium bowl, combine the cabbage, mayonnaise, apple cider vinegar, and grainy Dijon mustard. Toss until the cabbage is evenly coated. Stir in the scallions. Season with salt and pepper to taste.

3. **Start the Seared Mushrooms—prep the mushrooms:** Cut the caps off the mushrooms and slice them as thinly as possible. Rake a fork down the mushroom stems to shred them (see page 17).

4. **Cook the mushrooms:** In your largest skillet, heat the grapeseed oil over medium-high heat. Once the oil is hot, scatter the prepared mushrooms into the skillet and sear, undisturbed, until golden brown on the bottom, 3 to 4 minutes. Sauté, stirring occasionally, until the mushrooms are golden brown all over, 3 to 4 minutes. Reduce the heat to low. Let the skillet cool down slightly (about 1 minute), then pour the barbecue sauce over the mushrooms. Toss to coat, then cook for 1 to 2 minutes to let the mushrooms absorb some of the sauce.

5. **Warm the buns:** Place an oven rack in the centre position and preheat to 300°F (150°C). Place the buns on a baking sheet and bake until warm but still soft, 3 to 5 minutes.

6. **Assemble:** Spread the mayonnaise on the top and bottom halves of the buns. Divide the mushrooms and slaw evenly among the bottom halves, then finish the sandwiches with the tops. Serve hot with plenty of napkins.

VEGAN: Use vegan buns and brush them with vegan butter or olive oil. Use vegan mayonnaise. **GLUTEN-FREE:** Use gluten-free buns.

ACTIVE TIME: 30 MINUTES • **TOTAL TIME:** 45 MINUTES • **SERVES** 6

HEALTHIER MACARONI AND CHEESE

4 tablespoons **butter**, divided

4 cups minced **cauliflower florets** (1 lb / 454g)

½ cup chopped **yellow onion**

3 **garlic cloves**, minced

3½ cups **whole** or **2% milk**

1½ teaspoons **Dijon mustard**

¾ teaspoon **fine sea salt**

¼ teaspoon **cayenne pepper** (optional)

12 oz (340g) dried **elbow macaroni** (3 cups)

4 cups shredded **sharp cheddar cheese** (1 lb / 454g), divided ❶

2 oz (57g) finely grated **Parmesan cheese** (½ cup)

½ cup **panko breadcrumbs**

Freshly ground **black pepper**

Let's face it, any *good* mac and cheese probably won't be your healthiest meal of the week. But sneaking in a whole pound of cauliflower certainly can't hurt. Rather than using a traditional béchamel sauce, this recipe blends cauliflower, garlic, and onion until silky smooth. It's going to look like a lot of sauce, but that's what you want! Baked mac and cheese benefits from extra sauce so it doesn't dry out in the oven.

1. **Preheat the oven:** Place an oven rack in the upper third of the oven and preheat to 425°F (220°C).

2. **Make the sauce:** In a medium saucepan, melt 2 tablespoons of the butter over medium heat. Add the cauliflower, onion, and garlic, cover with a lid, and cook, stirring occasionally, until the cauliflower is soft, 10 to 12 minutes. (Reduce the heat to medium-low if the vegetables start to brown.) Transfer the mixture to a high-speed blender. Add the milk, Dijon mustard, salt, and cayenne, if using. Blend until silky smooth.

3. **Meanwhile, cook the noodles:** Bring a large pot of salted water to a boil over high heat. Add the noodles and cook until al dente according to the package directions. Drain the noodles and return to the pot, off the heat. Stir in 1 tablespoon of the butter until melted and the noodles are coated.

4. **Combine:** Pour the sauce over the noodles and toss to coat. Stir in 3½ cups of the cheddar and the Parmesan. The cheese probably won't melt completely at this point—this is fine. Transfer the mixture to a 13 x 9-inch (3.5 L) casserole dish. Evenly sprinkle with the remaining ½ cup cheddar.

5. **Top with panko and bake:** In a small heatproof bowl, melt the remaining 1 tablespoon butter in the microwave in 15-second intervals. Add the panko, stir to mix, then sprinkle evenly over the cheese. Transfer to the oven and bake until the cheese is melted and the panko is golden brown, 12 to 18 minutes. Garnish with pepper to taste.

GLUTEN-FREE: Use gluten-free pasta (macaroni noodles or small shells) and gluten-free panko breadcrumbs.

❶ Shred your own cheese—it will melt smoother and taste better. Pre-shredded cheese might be convenient, but it usually has additives to prevent the shreds from clumping.

ACTIVE TIME: 25 MINUTES • TOTAL TIME: 35 MINUTES • SERVES 6

VEGETABLE RAGU

1 **yellow onion**, roughly chopped (2 cups)

1 **carrot**, peeled and roughly chopped

1 **celery rib**, roughly chopped

4 tablespoons **extra-virgin olive oil**, divided

8 oz (227g) **shiitake mushrooms**, stems trimmed

6 **garlic cloves**, minced

¼ cup **tomato paste**

½ cup **dry red wine** ❶

1 can (28 fl oz / 796 ml) **crushed fire-roasted tomatoes** ❷

2 tablespoons **tamari**

2 teaspoons **dried oregano**

½ teaspoon **fine sea salt**

½ teaspoon freshly ground **black pepper**

17.6 oz (500g) dried **pappardelle**

1.3 oz (37g) finely grated **Parmesan cheese** (⅓ cup), more for garnish

A deeply flavoured *vegetarian* ragu might sound like a paradox, but this one is delicious nonetheless. Caramelized tomato paste, fire-roasted tomatoes, and tamari all bring umami magic to this dish. Meaty shiitake mushrooms add subtle texture—without making things too mushroom-forward. The food processor makes quick work of mincing, but chop the vegetables into roughly similar sizes first. This way, the food processor will mince the vegetables more evenly so they easily meld into the luscious sauce.

1. **Mince the vegetables and cook:** In a food processor, combine the onion, carrot, and celery and pulse until minced. ❸ In a large Dutch oven or pot, heat 3 tablespoons of the olive oil over medium heat. Transfer the minced vegetables to the pot. Add the mushrooms to the food processor, pulse until minced, then add them to the pot. Cook, stirring occasionally, until the vegetables are very soft, 8 to 10 minutes.

2. **Build the rest of the sauce:** Add the remaining 1 tablespoon olive oil, garlic, and tomato paste to the pot and cook, stirring continuously, until the tomato paste darkens slightly, 2 to 3 minutes. (Reduce the heat, if needed, to prevent the garlic from burning.) Pour in the red wine and let boil for 1 minute, stirring to scrape up the brown bits from the bottom of the pot. Add the tomatoes, tamari, oregano, salt, and pepper. Stir to mix. Reduce the heat to low, cover with a lid, and simmer for at least 15 minutes for the flavours to meld.

3. **Meanwhile, cook the pasta:** Bring a large pot of salted water to a boil over high heat. Add the pasta and cook until al dente according to the package directions. Scoop out and reserve 1 cup of pasta water. Drain the pasta.

4. **Combine:** Add the pasta to the sauce and toss to coat. Sprinkle in the Parmesan. Toss, adding more reserved pasta water if needed, a little at a time, until the noodles are coated in a silky sauce. Divide the pasta among bowls and garnish with more Parmesan.

VEGAN: Use vegan Parmesan cheese or omit. Some pappardelle is made with eggs, so check the label.

GLUTEN-FREE: Use gluten-free pasta (pappardelle or tagliatelle).

❶ Use a dry red wine, such as a Merlot or Pinot Noir. Alternatively, you can replace the wine with vegetable stock.

❷ Instead of crushed tomatoes, you can use a 28 fl oz (796 ml) can of diced fire-roasted tomatoes. Pulse the tomatoes in a blender until smooth, then use as directed.

❸ If you don't have a food processor, mince the onion, carrot, celery, and mushrooms by hand as finely as you can so they meld into the sauce.

ACTIVE TIME: 20 MINUTES • **TOTAL TIME:** 40 MINUTES • **MAKES** TWO 8-INCH (20 CM) PIZZAS

MEDITERRANEAN PESTO PIZZA

PIZZA

1 batch **Quick Pizza Dough** (page 297) or 1 lb (454g) store-bought, room temperature ❶

1 to 2 tablespoons **extra-virgin olive oil**

½ cup **pizza sauce** ❷

½ teaspoon **dried oregano**

2 cups shredded **low-moisture mozzarella** (8 oz / 227g)

1 medium **shallot**, minced (¼ cup)

1 small **red bell pepper**, diced

¼ cup pitted and sliced **Kalamata olives**

3 tablespoons drained and minced **sun-dried tomatoes**

2 tablespoons drained **capers**

½ cup crumbled **feta cheese**

Freshly ground **black pepper**

FOR GARNISH

2 cups lightly packed **arugula**

Fresh Basil Pesto (page 290), Vegan Pesto (page 290), or store-bought

Parmesan cheese

Red pepper flakes (optional)

Pizza is one of those no-recipe recipes. Add a hefty amount of cheese and more than likely, it's going to be a winner. But if you're looking for some pizza topping inspiration, here you go: sun-dried tomatoes, capers, shallots, red peppers, and crumbled feta. The toppings are mostly pantry ingredients, so it can be thrown together at a moment's notice. Even better, the toppings don't require any precooking. There are two types of sauce here (because why choose if you don't need to?). Save the pesto for drizzling at the end, so its delicate flavours stay fresh and vibrant.

1. **Preheat the oven:** Place an oven rack in the lower third of the oven and preheat to 475°F (240°C). Set aside 2 large baking sheets.

2. **Start the Pizza—roll out the dough:** Cut the pizza dough into 2 equal portions. Loosely cover 1 portion of dough with plastic wrap or a clean kitchen towel to prevent it from drying out. On a lightly floured work surface, using your hands or a rolling pin, stretch or roll 1 portion of dough into an 8-inch (20 cm) circle. Transfer it to one of the baking sheets. Repeat with the remaining piece of dough and transfer it to the second baking sheet.

3. **Add the toppings:** Lightly brush the olive oil over the stretched dough. Evenly divide and spread the pizza sauce over each pizza, leaving a 1-inch (2.5 cm) border around the edge, then sprinkle with the oregano. Over each pizza, sprinkle ½ cup of the mozzarella over the pizza sauce. Sprinkle each pizza evenly with the shallot, bell pepper, olives, sun-dried tomatoes, and capers. Sprinkle each pizza with ½ cup of the remaining mozzarella. Divide the feta between the pizzas and season generously with black pepper.

4. **Bake:** Bake the pizzas, one at a time, until the crust is golden brown on the bottom and the cheese is melted, 10 to 14 minutes. Top with the arugula, drizzle with pesto, and sprinkle with Parmesan and red pepper flakes, if using.

VEGAN: Use your favourite meltable vegan mozzarella cheese, vegan feta, and vegan Parmesan.

GLUTEN-FREE: Use your favourite gluten-free pizza dough.

❶ If the pizza dough is refrigerated, let it sit on the counter to come up to room temperature before rolling.

❷ Pizza sauce is typically made with uncooked tomatoes, so it has a brighter tomato flavour compared with pasta sauces, which have been cooked down. Passata can be substituted for pizza sauce, if needed.

ACTIVE TIME: 55 MINUTES • **TOTAL TIME:** 1 HOUR 15 MINUTES • **SERVES** 6 TO 8

SHEPHERD'S PIE

1 cup raw **walnuts**

3 tablespoons **extra-virgin olive oil**

1 can (5.5 fl oz / 156 ml) **tomato paste**

1 **yellow onion**, diced (2 cups)

2 **carrots**, peeled and diced

2 **celery ribs**, finely diced

4 **garlic cloves**, minced

1 tablespoon **fresh thyme leaves**, more for garnish

2 teaspoons minced **fresh rosemary leaves**

¾ teaspoon **fine sea salt**

3 tablespoons **all-purpose flour**

2 cups **vegetable stock**

2 cans (14 fl oz / 398 ml each) **lentils**, drained and rinsed

2 tablespoons **tamari**

Freshly ground **black pepper**

2 cups **frozen peas**

1 batch **Garlic Mashed Potatoes** (page 301) ❷

1 to 2 tablespoons **butter**, melted (optional)

When you're looking for a dish that shows someone you care, shepherd's pie is a solid option. Fluffy homemade mashed potatoes spooned over a cozy filling is kind of like a hug in a bowl. To help with timing, you can prep this dish the night before and bake it the next day. ❶ Or recruit a helper to oversee the mashed potatoes. Regardless how you go about it, everyone at the table will love you for making it.

1. **Crumble the walnuts:** In a food processor, pulse the walnuts until they are crumbled into pieces about the size of coarsely ground coffee.

2. **Cook the tomato paste and aromatics:** In a large braiser or pot, heat the olive oil over medium heat. Add the tomato paste, onion, carrots, celery, and crumbled walnuts and cook, stirring occasionally, until the vegetables are fork-tender, 12 to 14 minutes. Add the garlic, thyme, rosemary, and salt and cook, stirring continuously, until fragrant, 1 to 2 minutes.

3. **Simmer the filling:** Scatter in the flour and toss to coat evenly. Pour in the vegetable stock and stir to scrape up the brown bits from the bottom of the pot. Pour in the lentils and tamari and stir to mix. Simmer the mixture until the vegetables are soft, about 10 minutes. Season with pepper and more salt, if needed. Stir in the frozen peas.

4. **Preheat the oven:** Place an oven rack in the upper third of the oven and preheat to 450°F (230°C).

5. **Assemble and bake:** Keep the filling in the braiser (if oven-safe) or transfer it to a 13 x 9-inch (3.5 L) casserole dish. Spoon the mashed potatoes over the filling, using the back of the spoon to create a swooping texture on top to encourage the high spots to brown. ❷ Place the braiser on a baking sheet to catch any drips. Bake until the potatoes are golden brown, about 20 minutes. Drizzle the melted butter (if using) over the potatoes and garnish with thyme.

VEGAN: Use melted vegan butter or olive oil over the potatoes or omit. Make the Garlic Mashed Potatoes with vegan substitutes (page 301).

GLUTEN-FREE: Replace the flour with white rice flour.

❶ You can assemble this dish the day before and bake it the next day. Cover and refrigerate overnight. Let the dish come to room temperature (about 30 minutes) before baking as directed.

❷ It is easier to get smooth, fluffy swoops when you're working with hot mashed potatoes. I usually make the Garlic Mashed Potatoes at the same time as the filling, but you could also make it before. Just keep it in a pot, covered with a lid, over low heat. Thin with a splash of milk, if needed, before spooning it over the filling.

STAUB
STAUB

ACTUALLY GOOD FRIED RICE

2 cups **cooked** and **cooled jasmine rice** (page 302) or other medium-grain white rice (page 303) ❶

3 tablespoons **grapeseed oil**, divided

3 large **eggs**

1 **carrot**, peeled and diced

1 **celery rib**, diced

1 large **shallot**, minced (½ cup)

3 **garlic cloves**, minced

2 teaspoons minced **fresh ginger**

1 tablespoon **tamari**

⅔ cup **frozen peas**

1½ teaspoons **toasted sesame oil**

¼ teaspoon **fine sea salt**

2 **scallions**, thinly sliced

Sambal oelek or Sriracha sauce, for serving (optional)

"Just tell them this is *actually* good"—that was my mom's advice for naming this recipe. She's adamant that you should never trust a fried rice recipe that doesn't call for day-old rice. Come to think of it, I'm not sure she's *ever* used a recipe for fried rice. But here's one anyway. The trick to avoiding clumpy fried rice is to let the rice grains dry out. Day-old rice accomplishes this, but if you didn't plan ahead, see the tip below. Turn on your hood fan and open your windows: fried rice needs to be cooked at ripping hot heat, very quickly. If you're looking to scale up the recipe, cook extra batches separately rather than crowding the pan.

1. **Get the rice and other ingredients ready:** Use your hands to break up any clumps of rice. Arrange all your prepped ingredients next to the stove. (This dish cooks quickly, so you'll want everything prepped before you begin.)

2. **Cook the eggs, then the vegetables:** In a large wok ❷ or cast-iron skillet, heat 1 tablespoon of the grapeseed oil over high heat. Once the oil is hot, crack the eggs into the pan and scramble them until mostly set but still slightly runny, 30 to 45 seconds. Transfer the scrambled eggs to a medium bowl. Add 1 tablespoon of the grapeseed oil to the pan. Add the carrot and sauté until tender but still crisp, about 1 minute. Add the celery and sauté until tender but still crisp, about 1 minute. Transfer the vegetables to the bowl with the eggs.

3. **Cook the aromatics and rice:** Add the remaining 1 tablespoon grapeseed oil to the pan. Scatter in the shallot, garlic, and ginger and sauté, stirring continuously, until fragrant, about 15 seconds. Add the cooked rice and sauté, tossing continuously, until the rice is crispy and heated through, about 3 minutes. Pour in the tamari and toss to coat.

4. **Combine:** Return the scrambled eggs and sautéed vegetables to the pan along with the frozen peas. Sauté, tossing continuously, until the peas are defrosted, 1 to 2 minutes. Add the sesame oil and salt. Taste and season with more salt, if needed. Spoon the rice into bowls, then top with scallions and sambal oelek, if using.

VEGAN: Skip the eggs. If desired, you can add cubed smoked tofu (about 1 cup). Smoked tofu is already cooked, so just toss it in the wok before the vegetables to warm it up.

❶ Day-old rice is recommended. Otherwise, spread freshly cooked rice out on a baking sheet and let it cool on the counter for 15 minutes to let the steam escape. Transfer the rice to the fridge and let it cool on the baking sheet for 45 minutes before using.

❷ A wok is great for fast, high-heat cooking because it provides different zones of heat and makes tossing easy. I recommend an uncoated wok because nonstick coatings usually can't handle high heat. An uncoated cast-iron skillet is a good alternative, especially on an induction or electric stovetop. It will take longer to heat up, but once it does, it'll retain the heat as you add cold ingredients to the pan. Use a metal spatula for stir-frying if you're using an uncoated wok, otherwise use non-scratching cookware.

ACTIVE TIME: 30 MINUTES • **TOTAL TIME:** 1 HOUR • **SERVES** 6

VEGETABLE BOURGUIGNON

4 tablespoons **extra-virgin olive oil**, divided

2 lb (907g) **carrots**, peeled and cut into ½-inch (1 cm) rounds

1 lb (454g) **cremini mushrooms**, halved

1 lb (454g) thawed **frozen peeled pearl onions** [1]

3 **celery ribs**, diced

5 **garlic cloves**, minced

2 tablespoons **tamari**

3 tablespoons **all-purpose flour**

1 cup **dry red wine** [2]

3 cups **vegetable stock**

2 tablespoons **white miso**

½ teaspoon **fine sea salt**

4 sprigs **fresh thyme**

1 **dried bay leaf**

Freshly ground **black pepper**

1 batch **Garlic Mashed Potatoes** (page 301) [3]

Chopped **fresh flat-leaf parsley leaves**, for garnish

Living in the Pacific Northwest means ~~always talking about~~ putting up with the rain. When the chilly weather starts to set in, I look forward to making bourguignon. This version doesn't have beef—instead, the veggies are the main feature. Miso paste gives extra depth of flavour. This recipe is less wine-forward than some traditional bourguignons, but you can always pour more wine into the pot if you'd like. Or pour the extra wine into a glass and enjoy it while cooking. The bourguignon is delicious spooned over garlic mashed potatoes, but you could keep it simple with crusty bread served on the side instead.

1. **Brown the carrots:** In a large Dutch oven or pot, heat 1 tablespoon of the olive oil over medium heat. Add the carrots and cook, stirring occasionally, until the carrots are golden brown, about 10 minutes. Transfer the carrots to a medium bowl.

2. **Brown the mushrooms:** Drizzle 2 tablespoons of the olive oil into the pot. Add the mushrooms and cook, stirring occasionally, until the mushrooms are browned, about 8 minutes. Transfer the mushrooms to the bowl with the carrots.

3. **Brown the pearl onions and celery:** Drizzle the remaining 1 tablespoon olive oil into the pot. Add the pearl onions and celery and cook, stirring occasionally, until the onions are golden brown, 6 to 8 minutes.

4. **Combine and simmer:** Return the carrots and mushrooms to the pot. Add the garlic and tamari and cook, stirring frequently, until the garlic is fragrant, 1 to 2 minutes. Sprinkle in the flour and toss to coat. Pour in the red wine and let boil for 1 minute, stirring to scrape up the brown bits from the bottom of the pot. Add the vegetable stock, miso, salt, thyme, and bay leaf. Stir to mix. Cover with the lid slightly ajar and bring the mixture to a boil over medium-high heat. Once boiling, reduce the heat to low and simmer until the carrots and onion are fork-tender, about 30 minutes. Uncover and simmer for another 5 minutes to let the mixture reduce slightly.

5. **Serve:** Discard the thyme sprigs and bay leaf. Season with pepper, and more salt, if needed. Divide the garlic mashed potatoes among bowls, then ladle the vegetable bourguignon overtop. Garnish with the parsley.

VEGAN: Make the Garlic Mashed Potatoes with vegan substitutes (page 301).

GLUTEN-FREE: Instead of using all-purpose flour, in a small bowl, whisk together 2 tablespoons cornstarch and 3 tablespoons water. Wait to add the cornstarch slurry until the end, after the soup has simmered for 30 minutes. Then pour in the cornstarch slurry and stir to mix. Increase the heat to medium-high and bring the mixture to a boil. Let boil until slightly thickened, about 1 minute. Reduce the heat and simmer for 5 minutes, then continue with step 5.

[1] If you can't find frozen pearl onions, use 1 lb (454g) chopped yellow onions instead. Or use fresh pearl onions, but budget extra time because you'll need to blanch and peel them before using.

[2] Use a dry red wine such as a Pinot Noir or Cabernet Sauvignon. Don't use cooking wine.

[3] I usually make the Garlic Mashed Potatoes at the same time as the bourguignon, but you could also make it before. Just keep it in a pot, covered with a lid, over low heat. Thin with a splash of milk, if needed, before serving.

ACTIVE TIME: 30 MINUTES • **TOTAL TIME:** 50 MINUTES • **SERVES** 4

PEA FRITTERS AND FRIES WITH TARTAR SAUCE

FRIES

1½ lb (680g) **russet potatoes** ❶

2 tablespoons **extra-virgin olive oil**

¼ teaspoon **fine sea salt**

FRITTERS

¾ cup **frozen peas**

2 cups **cooked** and **cooled quinoa** ❷

1¾ cups shredded **low-moisture mozzarella** (7 oz / 200g)

1 cup loosely packed minced **baby spinach**

2 **scallions**, thinly sliced

½ teaspoon freshly ground **black pepper**

½ teaspoon **fine sea salt**

4 large **eggs**, whisked

⅔ cup dry **breadcrumbs**

TARTAR SAUCE

1 cup plain **Greek yogurt**

¼ cup minced **dill pickle**

¼ cup minced **fresh dill**

2 tablespoons drained **capers**, minced

1 tablespoon **fresh lemon juice**

½ teaspoon freshly ground **black pepper**

¼ teaspoon **fine sea salt**

Growing up in Vancouver, my family ate a lot of fish. In the summer, I loved our family trips to Granville Island, where we'd get to order fish and chips from the "blue shack" on the pier. The chips were my favourite part: I *loved* dipping my fries in the tartar sauce. This recipe makes a yummy tartar sauce from Greek yogurt instead of mayonnaise. The fritters are packed with peas, spinach, scallions, and cheese. They're a great way to use up extra quinoa, but since quinoa cooks up so quickly, you can also just make it fresh. This recipe requires 2 large baking sheets (18 x 13 inches / 46 x 33 cm), so if yours are smaller, make a half batch.

1. **Preheat the oven:** Place the oven racks in the upper and lower thirds of the oven and preheat to 425°F (220°C). Line 2 large baking sheets with parchment paper.

2. **Make the Fries:** Cut the potatoes lengthwise into quarters, then slice each quarter in half to make 8 equal-sized wedges. Transfer the potatoes to one of the prepared baking sheets. Drizzle the potatoes with the olive oil and toss to coat, then spread out in an even layer and sprinkle with the salt. Bake on the lower rack until the fries are golden brown and crispy, 40 to 45 minutes, flipping halfway through. Season with more salt, if needed.

3. **Meanwhile, start the Fritters—mix the batter:** Rinse the frozen peas in a colander under warm running water until defrosted, about 30 seconds, then let sit in the sink to drain. In a large bowl, combine the cooked quinoa, mozzarella, spinach, scallions, pepper, and salt. Using your fingertips, lightly squish the peas as you add them to the bowl. Pour in the eggs and stir until well mixed. Sprinkle in the breadcrumbs and stir to mix.

4. **While the fries are baking, shape and bake the fritters:** Pack the mixture into a ¼-cup measuring cup. Turn the measuring cup over on the other prepared baking sheet and shake it to release the mixture. ❸ Repeat with the remaining mixture, spacing the fritters evenly on the baking sheet. (You should have 15 to 18 fritters.) Using damp fingertips, smooth out the shape of the fritters and tuck in any loose spinach. Bake on the upper rack until golden brown and firm to the touch, about 30 minutes.

5. **Meanwhile, make the Tartar Sauce:** In a small bowl, stir together the yogurt, pickle, dill, capers, lemon juice, pepper, and salt. Taste and adjust seasonings, if needed.

6. **Serve:** Divide the hot fries and pea fritters among plates and serve with a generous scoop or two of tartar sauce.

GLUTEN-FREE: Use gluten-free breadcrumbs.

❶ If you can, choose small russet potatoes for bite-size wedges that cook quicker. Potato skins have a lot of flavour, so skip peeling them for this recipe.

❷ Usually, ⅔ cup dried quinoa will yield about 2 cups cooked quinoa, but measure after cooking to be sure.

❸ If you're having trouble getting the mixture to release from the measuring cup, you can instead use damp hands to form the fritters by hand.

SMOKY GOUDA MUSHROOM MELTS

ROASTED MUSHROOMS

3 tablespoons **water**

2 tablespoons **tamari**

1 tablespoon **grapeseed oil**

1 tablespoon **Dijon mustard**

1 teaspoon **garlic powder**

1 teaspoon coarsely ground **black pepper** ❶

¾ teaspoon **smoked sweet paprika**

4 **portobello mushroom caps**, sliced into ½-inch (1 cm) thick strips

CARAMELIZED ONIONS

1 tablespoon **grapeseed oil**

1 **yellow onion**, thinly sliced (2 cups)

¼ teaspoon **fine sea salt**

Pinch of **baking soda** (optional) ❷

GARLIC MAYO

¼ cup **mayonnaise**

1 or 2 **garlic cloves**, finely grated

FOR SERVING

1 **baguette**

Softened **butter**

Sliced **smoked Gouda** or cheddar cheese ❸

If you (or anyone else) doubts that a vegetarian sandwich can be delicious, make this one! The combination of smoky roasted mushrooms, creamy garlic mayo, and caramelized onions is impossible to resist—especially once you add melted smoked Gouda cheese. Roasting the mushrooms is as simple as tossing everything together in a baking dish—then letting the oven do the heavy lifting. When caramelizing onions, I like to add a pinch of baking soda to speed up the browning process.

1. **Preheat the oven:** Place an oven rack in the centre position and preheat to 450°F (230°C).

2. **Make the Roasted Mushrooms:** In a 13 x 9-inch (3.5 L) casserole dish, whisk together the water, tamari, grapeseed oil, Dijon mustard, garlic powder, pepper, and smoked paprika. Add the mushrooms, toss to coat, and bake until the marinade has been absorbed and the mushrooms are tender, 20 to 25 minutes, stirring halfway through.

3. **Meanwhile, make the Caramelized Onions:** In a large skillet, heat the grapeseed oil over medium heat. Scatter in the onion and sprinkle with the salt and baking soda, if using. Cook, stirring frequently, until the onions are golden brown, 15 to 20 minutes. If the onions start to stick, deglaze the skillet with splashes of water as needed.

4. **Make the Garlic Mayo:** In a small bowl, whisk together the mayonnaise and garlic.

5. **Assemble and bake:** Cut the baguette into quarters, then slice each piece horizontally in half, so you end up with 8 pieces of bread. Place the baguette halves cut side up on a baking sheet and lightly butter them. Evenly divide the mushrooms, caramelized onions, and Gouda among the bottom halves. Bake until the bread is toasted and the cheese is melted, 3 to 5 minutes. Spread the garlic mayo on the top halves and close the sandwiches.

VEGAN: Use vegan mayonnaise and butter. Use your favourite meltable smoked vegan cheese.

GLUTEN-FREE: Use gluten-free bread (baguette or ciabatta).

❶ Use a pepper grinder on the coarse setting or a small spice grinder. Alternatively, place the peppercorns in a freezer bag and set the bag on a sturdy cutting board. Place a heavy skillet on top, then push down on the skillet to crush the peppercorns.

❷ The baking soda helps the onions caramelize faster. You don't need much, just a small pinch will do. You can leave it out, but if you do, budget more time for caramelizing the onions, about 10 more minutes.

❸ If you can't find smoked Gouda or smoked cheddar cheese, use regular Gouda or aged cheddar (the flavour will be milder).

ACTIVE TIME: 1 HOUR 15 MINUTES • **TOTAL TIME:** 1 HOUR 15 MINUTES • **SERVES** 4 TO 6

CRISPY VEGGIE POTSTICKERS

POTSTICKERS

3 tablespoons **grapeseed oil**, divided, more for cooking

8 oz (227g) **cremini mushrooms**, minced

½ cup peeled and minced **carrot**

3 cups shredded **green cabbage**

3 **garlic cloves**, minced

1 tablespoon minced **fresh ginger**

1 tablespoon **toasted sesame oil**

1 tablespoon **tamari**

2 teaspoons **rice vinegar**

½ teaspoon **sambal oelek**

½ teaspoon **fine sea salt**

2 **scallions**, thinly sliced

16 oz (454g) round **potsticker wrappers**, room temperature [1]

DIPPING SAUCE

2 tablespoons **tamari**

4 teaspoons **rice vinegar**

1 teaspoon **sambal oelek**

½ teaspoon **toasted sesame oil**

VEGAN: Use vegan wrappers.

[1] One package typically contains about 40 to 55 wrappers. Potsticker wrappers can be found in the refrigerated section of well-stocked grocery stores and Asian grocery stores. Let the wrappers come to room temperature before using, so they are more pliable.

[2] Uncooked potstickers can be frozen for up to 3 months. Cover the baking sheet of potstickers with plastic wrap and transfer to the freezer. Once the potstickers are firm, transfer to freezer bags or airtight containers. (This method ensures they don't stick together.) Cook from frozen as directed.

Having a stash of homemade frozen potstickers means you're always 15 minutes away from a delicious meal. Potstickers are a type of Chinese dumpling that are usually pan-fried until crispy on the bottom. These ones are filled with mushrooms, carrots, and cabbage seasoned with ginger, garlic, and toasted sesame oil. Wrapping them takes a bit of time (and practice), but it's definitely time well spent. I'm a novice when it comes to wrapping potstickers, but see page 130 for one way to do it (or check out some of the amazing tutorials available online). Use a nonstick pan for cooking the potstickers—it makes all the difference.

1. Start the Potstickers—sauté the vegetables: In a large nonstick skillet, heat 2 tablespoons of the grapeseed oil over medium heat. Add the mushrooms and carrots and sauté, stirring occasionally, until the carrots are soft, 8 to 10 minutes. Add the remaining 1 tablespoon grapeseed oil, cabbage, garlic, and ginger and cook, stirring frequently, until the cabbage has softened but is still bright green, about 2 minutes. Remove from the heat.

2. Mix the filling: In a large bowl, stir together the sesame oil, tamari, rice vinegar, sambal oelek, and salt. Add the sautéed vegetables (set aside the skillet) and stir well to coat. Stir in the scallions. Let the mixture cool until no longer steaming, 5 to 10 minutes.

3. Wrap the potstickers (page 130): Fill a small bowl with cold water (for dipping your fingers). Line a large baking sheet with parchment paper. On a dry work surface, lay out 1 potsticker wrapper, keeping the remaining wrappers in the package, covered with a slightly dampened paper towel so they don't dry out. Dip your finger in the water and run it along the edge of the wrapper. Scoop 1 tablespoon of the filling into the centre of the wrapper. Fold the wrapper in half to create a semicircle. Either press the wrapper together to seal it or go one step further by pleating (see page 130). Place the potsticker on the baking sheet. Continue with the remaining potstickers and filling. [2]

4. Cook the potstickers: Set aside the skillet's lid or a baking sheet large enough to cover the skillet. Lightly coat the bottom of the skillet with grapeseed oil and heat over medium heat. Working in batches, place a single layer of potstickers in the skillet and cook until golden brown on the bottom, 1 to 2 minutes. Carefully pour about ½ cup water into the skillet and immediately cover with the lid. Cook until almost all the water has evaporated and the tops of the potstickers look steamed, about 5 minutes. Remove the lid and cook, uncovered, until all the water is evaporated. Transfer the cooked potstickers to a plate. Repeat with the remaining potstickers, adding more oil to the pan, as needed (or freeze the rest).

5. Meanwhile, make the Dipping Sauce: Whisk together the tamari, rice vinegar, sambal oelek, and sesame oil.

6. Serve: Divide the potstickers among plates and serve with small bowls of dipping sauce on the side.

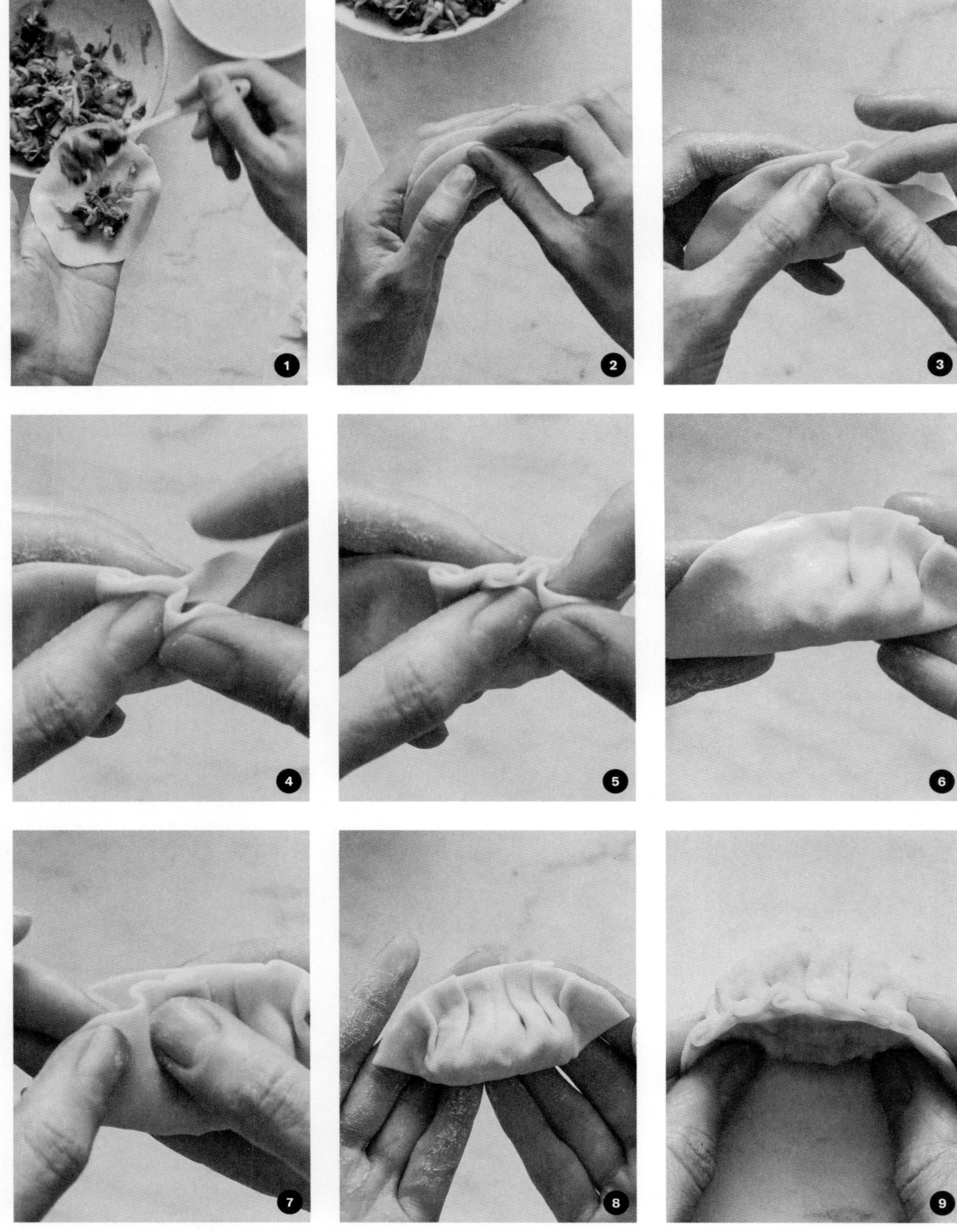
1
2
3
4
5
6
7
8
9

ACTIVE TIME: 30 MINUTES • **TOTAL TIME:** 30 MINUTES • **SERVES** 2

BUFFALO-SAUCED CAULIFLOWER WITH RANCH CELERY SALAD

CRISPY CAULIFLOWER

1½-lb (680g) head **cauliflower**

2 tablespoons + 1 teaspoon **grapeseed oil**, divided

¼ cup **panko breadcrumbs**

Fine sea salt

Freshly ground **black pepper**

CREAMY WHITE BEANS

1 can (14 fl oz / 398 ml) **cannellini beans**, drained and rinsed

1 **garlic clove**

2 tablespoons **fresh lemon juice**

2 to 4 tablespoons **water**

A pinch of **fine sea salt**

CELERY SALAD

¼ cup plain **Greek yogurt**

1 tablespoon minced **fresh chives**

1 tablespoon minced **fresh dill**

1 tablespoon minced **fresh flat-leaf parsley leaves**

1 tablespoon **fresh lemon juice**

¼ teaspoon **garlic powder**

Fine sea salt

8 **celery ribs**, thinly sliced

BUFFALO SAUCE

3 tablespoons **hot sauce** (such as Frank's Red Hot sauce)

1 tablespoon **butter**, melted

1 teaspoon **fresh lemon juice**

¼ teaspoon **garlic powder**

This recipe is loosely inspired by Buffalo cauliflower wings—but with dinner vibes. Juicy cauliflower is seared in a screaming hot skillet until brown. Then it's drizzled with Buffalo sauce and sprinkled with crispy panko (I like to add the panko last so it doesn't get soggy). The creamy white beans underneath it all are there to catch any extra sauce, and provide protein to keep you full. A crisp ranch celery salad rounds it all out. If your celery has the leaves attached, keep them, because they're tasty and cute in this salad.

1. **Preheat the oven:** Place an oven rack in the centre position and preheat to 425°F (220°C).

2. **Start the Crispy Cauliflower—cut the "steaks":** Remove the tough outer leaves from the cauliflower (leave the tender inner leaves attached). Trim the stem to create a flat base. Resting the cauliflower on its stem, use a large knife to cut the cauliflower in half from top to bottom. Cut a 1¼-inch (3 cm) slice from the cut side of each half. You should end up with 2 "steaks" with the stem attached (this holds the cauliflower together). Reserve the remaining loose florets for another use. ❶

3. **Toast the panko:** In a large oven-safe skillet ❷, heat 1 teaspoon of the grapeseed oil over medium heat. Scatter in the panko, toss to coat, and cook, stirring frequently, until golden brown, 3 to 5 minutes. Transfer the panko to a small bowl. Season with salt and pepper to taste. Wipe the skillet clean.

4. **Meanwhile, make the Creamy White Beans:** In a blender, combine the beans, garlic, lemon juice, 2 tablespoons of the water, and salt. Process until smooth and creamy, scraping down the sides as needed, and adding more water, a little at a time, if needed. Taste and season with a bit more salt, if needed. (Go light on the seasoning, though, because the Buffalo sauce is quite salty.)

5. **Continue the Crispy Cauliflower—cook the "steaks":** In the same skillet, heat 1 tablespoon of the grapeseed oil over medium-high heat. Once the oil is hot, lay the cauliflower steaks in the skillet and cook until brown on the bottom, 3 to 5 minutes. Carefully turn the steaks over. Add the remaining 1 tablespoon grapeseed oil to the skillet, and using a flexible spatula, lift up the steaks so the oil can slide underneath. Cook until the other side is seared, 3 to 5 minutes. Season with salt and pepper. Transfer the skillet to the oven and roast until the cauliflower stem is fork-tender, 6 to 10 minutes.

CONTINUED ON NEXT PAGE

VEGAN: For the Celery Salad, replace the Greek yogurt with 3 tablespoons vegan mayo + 2 extra teaspoons fresh lemon juice. (You'll need a total of 1 tablespoon + 2 teaspoons lemon juice for the salad.)

GLUTEN-FREE: Use gluten-free panko breadcrumbs.

❶ I usually use the cauliflower florets for the Healthier Macaroni and Cheese (page 113).

❷ Use a 12-inch (30 cm) skillet if you have one because it'll make it easier to sear both the cauliflower steaks at once.

CONTINUED FROM PREVIOUS PAGE

6. **Meanwhile, make the Celery Salad:** In a medium bowl, whisk together the yogurt, chives, dill, parsley, lemon juice, and garlic powder. Season with salt to taste. Add the celery and toss to coat.

7. **Make the Buffalo Sauce:** In a small bowl, whisk together the hot sauce, melted butter, lemon juice, and garlic powder.

8. **Assemble:** Divide the creamy white beans between plates. Nestle the cauliflower steaks on top. Drizzle the Buffalo sauce over the cauliflower and beans, then scatter the toasted panko on top. Serve with the ranch celery salad on the side.

ACTIVE TIME: 45 MINUTES • **TOTAL TIME:** 1 HOUR 5 MINUTES • **MAKES** 9 HAND PIES

SAVOURY CHEDDAR APPLE HAND PIES

1 cup diced **Yukon Gold potato** (5.3 oz / 150g)

2 tablespoons **grapeseed oil**, divided

1 tablespoon **Dijon mustard**

¾ teaspoon **fine sea salt**, divided

1 cup thinly sliced **yellow onion** (1 small onion)

3 **garlic cloves**, minced

2 tablespoons **fresh thyme leaves** [2]

½ teaspoon freshly ground **black pepper**, more for garnish

2 tablespoons **all-purpose flour**

1½ cups **whole milk**

1 cup diced **Gala apple** (1 small apple) [3]

½ cup **frozen peas**

1½ cups shredded **aged cheddar cheese** (6 oz / 170g), divided

1 lb (454g) **frozen puff pastry** (2 sheets), defrosted in fridge overnight

1 large **egg**, whisked

I didn't know that sliced apple with cheddar cheese was a match made in heaven, until my friend Andrea showed me the light. That was all the way back in grade school, and now, decades later, I still love this combination. These savoury hand pies are stuffed with oven-roasted potatoes, sautéed onions, melted cheddar cheese, and crisp apple. Try to squeeze in as much filling as you can—the more the merrier. You can enjoy the hand pies on their own, or pair them with soup like the Roasted Tomato Soup (page 201). Leftovers make for a yummy breakfast on the go, lunch, or snack the next day. [1]

---

1. **Preheat the oven:** Place an oven rack in the centre position and preheat to 425°F (220°C). Line 2 large baking sheets with parchment paper.

2. **Roast the potatoes:** Pile the potatoes onto one of the prepared baking sheets. Drizzle with 1 tablespoon of the grapeseed oil and Dijon mustard, then toss to coat. Evenly spread the potatoes on the baking sheet and sprinkle with ¼ teaspoon of the salt. Roast until the potatoes are golden brown and fork-tender, 15 to 20 minutes. Remove from the oven. Reduce the oven temperature to 400°F (200°C). (You'll want the oven at the correct temperature to bake the hand pies, step 6.)

3. **Meanwhile, start the filling:** In a large nonstick skillet, heat the remaining 1 tablespoon grapeseed oil over medium heat. Add the onion and cook, stirring occasionally, until golden brown around the edges, 8 to 10 minutes. Add the garlic, thyme, pepper, and the remaining ½ teaspoon salt and cook, stirring constantly, until fragrant, 1 to 2 minutes.

4. **Simmer the filling:** Sprinkle in the flour and stir to coat. Pour in the milk and stir to mix. Bring to a simmer over medium heat and cook, stirring frequently, until the mixture has thickened to the consistency of gravy, 2 to 3 minutes. Remove the skillet from the heat. Stir in the roasted potatoes, apple, peas, and 1 cup of the cheddar. Set aside to cool.

5. **Prepare the puff pastry:** Unroll the puff pastry onto a lightly floured work surface. Using a rolling pin, gently smooth out any creases. Cut each sheet of pastry into nine 3½-inch (9 cm) squares, for a total of 18 squares.

CONTINUED ON NEXT PAGE

---

[1] Puff pastry is best baked fresh. You can freeze unbaked hand pies. Brush the frozen pies with egg wash and sprinkle with cheese and pepper, then bake. Frozen hand pies may take an extra 5 minutes in the oven. Leftover baked hand pies will keep, refrigerated in an airtight container, for up to 2 days. Reheat in a 250°F (120°C) oven until warmed through, 10 to 12 minutes.

[2] Fresh thyme leaves are best for this recipe. In a pinch, substitute with 2 teaspoons of dried thyme.

[3] You can use another sweet apple, such as Pink Lady, Fuji, or Honeycrisp. Peeling is not necessary, but you can if you want. Finely dice the apples (not a rough chop) so they mix evenly in the filling.

CONTINUED FROM PREVIOUS PAGE

6. Assemble and bake: Arrange 9 pastry squares on the second baking sheet. ❹ Pile the filling into the middle of each square, leaving a ⅓-inch (8 mm) border around the outer edges. Brush the edges with the egg. Top the filling with one of the remaining pastry squares. Crimp the edges with a fork to seal, then brush the tops with the egg. Sprinkle the remaining ½ cup cheddar on top and garnish generously with pepper. Bake until the pastry is golden brown and the cheese is melted, 20 to 25 minutes, rotating the sheet front to back halfway through.

❹ All the hand pies should *just* fit on a half sheet pan (18 x 13 inches / 46 x 33 cm). If you're using a smaller baking sheet, divide the hand pies between 2 sheets; position the oven racks in the upper and lower thirds of the oven and bake as instructed, swapping top and bottom positions and rotating the sheets front to back halfway through.

BOWL FOOD

ACTIVE TIME: 15 MINUTES • **TOTAL TIME:** 25 MINUTES • **SERVES** 2

PESTO GRAIN BOWLS WITH JAMMY EGGS

1 cup **pearled farro** ❶

2 large **eggs**

⅓ cup **Fresh Basil Pesto** (page 290), Vegan Pesto (page 290), or store-bought

1 tablespoon **fresh lemon juice**

Fine sea salt

Freshly ground **black pepper**

2 cups lightly packed **baby spinach**

¼ cup crumbled **feta cheese**

2 tablespoons chopped **almonds**

1 tablespoon drained and minced **sun-dried tomatoes**

1½ teaspoons drained **capers**, minced

Red pepper flakes

Quick Pickled Red Onions (page 289) ❷

This dish celebrates one of my favourite grains—farro. It's especially delicious tossed with fresh pesto and lemon. I like to top this bowl with pickled red onions, salty feta cheese, and an egg with a jammy yolk. The toppings are flexible, but if you do make substitutions, try to cover a variety of flavours and textures. Farro cook times vary significantly: it's not often clear what kind of farro you're buying, so check the recommended cook time on the package—and if there isn't one, just keep checking for doneness at regular intervals.

1. **Cook the farro:** Rinse the farro in a sieve under cold running water for 30 seconds. Transfer the farro to a medium saucepan. Cover with 3 inches (8 cm) of water and bring to a boil over medium-high heat. Once boiling, reduce the heat to medium-low, cover with the lid, and simmer until the farro is tender but still slightly chewy, 15 to 20 minutes. Drain the farro and return to the pot, off the heat.

2. **Meanwhile, boil the eggs:** Bring a small saucepan of water to a boil over medium-high heat. Gently lower the eggs into the water. Adjust the heat, if needed, to maintain a gentle boil and cook the eggs for 6½ minutes (adjust timing based on your desired doneness; see page 21). Fill a medium bowl with ice water and gently lower the cooked eggs into the bowl to cool.

3. **Assemble:** Add the pesto and lemon juice to the pot of farro and stir to mix. Season the farro with salt and black pepper to taste, then divide it between two bowls. Peel the eggs and cut in half lengthwise. (If you are not serving this right away, hold off on cutting the eggs until just before assembling.) Top with the eggs, spinach, feta, almonds, sun-dried tomatoes, capers, red pepper flakes, and pickled red onions.

GLUTEN-FREE: Replace the farro with about 3 cups cooked short-grain brown rice (page 303).

❶ Farro is sold as pearled, semi-pearled, or whole. You can substitute semi-pearled or whole farro, but they will need to cook for 35 to 40 minutes.

❷ If you don't have Quick Pickled Red Onions on hand, make them first so they have time to marinate.

ACTIVE TIME: 35 MINUTES • **TOTAL TIME:** 45 MINUTES • **SERVES** 4

BIBIMBAP WITH CRISPY RICE

BIBIMBAP

1 tablespoon **toasted sesame oil**

1 bunch **spinach** (12 oz / 340g), chopped

1 tablespoon **toasted sesame seeds**

4 tablespoons **grapeseed oil**, divided

8 oz (227g) **shiitake mushrooms**, sliced

2 **garlic cloves**, minced

1 teaspoon minced **fresh ginger**

2 teaspoons **tamari**

4 cups **cooked medium-grain white rice** (page 303)

¼ teaspoon **fine sea salt**

4 **large eggs**

2 **carrots**, peeled and cut into matchsticks

½ **English cucumber**, thinly sliced

SAUCE

3 tablespoons **gochujang** [1]

4 teaspoons **honey**

1 tablespoon **toasted sesame oil**

1 tablespoon **rice vinegar**

1 tablespoon **water**

When bibimbap is served in a hot stone pot (dolsot), the bottom layer of rice audibly sizzles to a crisp. At home, I use a humble skillet to create a crispy layer of rice. Once the rice gets a golden-brown crust, it's scooped into bowls and topped with a rainbow of veggies, a fried egg, and a drizzle of gochujang sauce. Use a spoon to mix everything together before eating, so the delicious sauce and runny egg yolk get a chance to mingle with the rice.

---

1. **Start the Bibimbap—cook the spinach:** In a large nonstick skillet, heat the sesame oil over medium heat. Scatter in the spinach and cook, stirring frequently, until it's wilted, 2 to 4 minutes. Transfer the spinach to a small bowl. Stir in the sesame seeds.

2. **Cook the mushrooms:** In the same skillet, heat 1 tablespoon of the grapeseed oil over medium heat. Scatter in the mushrooms and cook, stirring occasionally, until the mushrooms begin to brown, 6 to 8 minutes. Add the garlic, ginger, and tamari and cook, stirring frequently, until the garlic is fragrant and the tamari has been absorbed, about 2 minutes. Transfer the mushroom mixture to another small bowl.

3. **Crisp the rice:** In the same skillet, heat 2 tablespoons of the grapeseed oil over medium heat. Scatter in the rice, sprinkle with the salt, and cook, undisturbed, until golden brown on the bottom, 10 to 12 minutes. Using a flexible spatula, flip the rice in sections, and cook for 3 to 4 minutes, until pale golden on the bottom and warmed through. Divide the rice among bowls. Set aside the skillet.

4. **Meanwhile, make the Sauce:** In a small bowl, whisk together the gochujang, honey, sesame oil, rice vinegar, and water until smooth.

5. **Continue the Bibimbap—fry the eggs:** Return the skillet to the stovetop and heat the remaining 1 tablespoon grapeseed oil over medium-low heat. Crack the eggs, one at a time, into the skillet. Cover with a lid and cook the eggs until the whites are set but the yolk is still runny, 2 to 3 minutes.

6. **Assemble:** Top each bowl of rice with the spinach, mushrooms, carrots, cucumber, fried egg, and a drizzle of sauce. Serve the remaining sauce on the side. Mix everything together before digging in.

VEGAN: Omit the egg. Replace the honey with maple syrup or granulated sugar. (If you use sugar, you may need a bit of extra water to thin.)

---

[1] Gochujang is a spicy Korean red chili paste with rice and fermented soybeans. It is often packaged in a small red rectangular tub and can be found at Korean grocery stores, well-stocked grocery stores, or online. Gochujang is often vegan and gluten-free, but check the label to confirm.

ACTIVE TIME: 20 MINUTES • **TOTAL TIME:** 45 MINUTES • **SERVES** 4

POLENTA WITH ROASTED TOMATOES AND BASIL OIL

POLENTA

3 cups **vegetable stock**

2 cups **water**

½ teaspoon **fine sea salt**

1 cup **fine cornmeal** ❶

1.3 oz (37g) finely grated **Parmesan cheese** (⅓ cup), more for garnish

1 tablespoon **butter**

BAKED TOMATOES AND BEANS

1 lb (454g) **cherry** or **grape tomatoes** ❷

1 can (14 fl oz / 398 ml) **navy** or **cannellini beans**, drained and rinsed

1 tablespoon **extra-virgin olive oil**

¼ teaspoon **fine sea salt**

BASIL OIL

½ cup packed **fresh basil leaves** (0.75 oz / 21g)

¼ cup **extra-virgin olive oil**

2 tablespoons **water**

½ teaspoon **white wine vinegar**

¼ teaspoon **fine sea salt**

This dish makes the most of summer's sweet tomatoes and fragrant basil. The soft polenta acts as the perfect pillow for nestling roasted tomatoes and beans into—and it becomes especially delicious when drizzled with basil oil. Some people say polenta is high maintenance, but I don't think you need to be scared! I usually keep the lid on, to prevent sputtering as it simmers, then just do an occasional check-in and stir as it cooks. There's a point at about the 15-minute mark where the polenta might look ready. But keep cooking it in line with the recipe timing, so that it fully hydrates and becomes its best self.

---

1. **Preheat the oven:** Place an oven rack in the centre position and preheat to 425°F (220°C).

2. **Make the Polenta:** Combine the vegetable stock, water, and salt in a large pot. Cover with the lid slightly ajar and bring to a boil over medium-high heat. Once boiling, stream the polenta into the pot while whisking vigorously so it doesn't clump. Continue stirring as the mixture thickens, 1 to 3 minutes. Reduce the heat to low, cover with the lid, and continue to cook, stirring vigorously every 10 minutes, until the polenta is smooth and creamy, 30 to 35 minutes total. Stir in the Parmesan and butter. Season with more salt, if needed.

3. **Meanwhile, make the Baked Tomatoes and Beans:** Scatter the tomatoes and beans in a 13 x 9-inch (3.5 L) casserole dish. Add the olive oil and salt and toss to coat. Bake until the tomatoes are lightly browned and bursting, about 30 minutes, stirring halfway through.

4. **Make the Basil Oil:** In a food processor or blender, combine the basil, olive oil, water, white wine vinegar, and salt. Pulse until the basil is minced and the oil is green, scraping down the sides as needed.

5. **Assemble:** Drizzle 2 tablespoons of the basil oil over the tomatoes and beans, then stir gently to coat. Spoon the polenta into bowls. Top with the tomatoes and beans, drizzle with the basil oil, and garnish with more Parmesan.

VEGAN: Use vegan butter or substitute olive oil. Use grated vegan Parmesan cheese or omit.

---

❶ The cornmeal doesn't necessarily need to be labelled "for polenta." Just look for a fine or medium grind, if you prefer.

❷ Multicoloured tomatoes look extra pretty for this dish.

ACTIVE TIME: 15 MINUTES • **TOTAL TIME:** 45 MINUTES • **SERVES** 4

CHARRED SWEET POTATOES WITH TOMATO CHILI JAM

This recipe brings together sweet, spicy, soft, and crispy. Charred sweet potatoes get piled high with a tomato chili jam, roasted chickpeas, tangy feta cheese, and a shower of fresh cilantro. There's very little active cooking required: the oven does the roasting while the tomato chili jam simmers on the stovetop (mostly unattended). At the end, you get to swoop in, assemble these pretty bowls, and dig in. If you're feeling sassy, spike the tomato chili jam with a splash of bourbon.

TOMATO CHILI JAM

1 can (28 fl oz / 796 ml) **whole peeled tomatoes**

4 **garlic cloves**, finely grated

¼ cup firmly packed **dark brown sugar**

¼ cup **bourbon** or whiskey (optional)

1 tablespoon **tamari**

½ to ¾ teaspoon **red pepper flakes** ❶

SWEET POTATOES AND CHICKPEAS

4 small **sweet potatoes** (2 lb / 907g total), sliced in half lengthwise ❷

2 tablespoons **grapeseed oil**, divided

½ teaspoon **fine sea salt**, divided

1 can (14 fl oz / 398 ml) **chickpeas**, drained, rinsed, and patted dry

FOR SERVING

Cooked short-grain brown rice (page 303)

½ cup crumbled **feta cheese**

Fresh cilantro leaves ❸

1. **Preheat the oven:** Place the oven racks in the upper and lower thirds of the oven and preheat to 450°F (230°C). Set aside 2 large baking sheets.

2. **Make the Tomato Chili Jam:** Pour the tomatoes and their juices into a medium saucepan. Use your hands to crush the tomatoes. Stir in the garlic, brown sugar, bourbon (if using), tamari, and red pepper flakes and bring to a gentle boil over medium heat. Continue to cook, stirring occasionally, until the mixture reduces to a thick sauce, 35 to 40 minutes.

3. **Meanwhile, char the Sweet Potatoes:** Place the sweet potatoes on one of the baking sheets. Brush them with 1 tablespoon of the grapeseed oil, ensuring the cut sides are generously oiled (to prevent sticking and encourage browning). Sprinkle the cut sides with ¼ teaspoon of the salt. Arrange the sweet potatoes cut side down on the baking sheet and roast on the lower rack until the flesh is deeply browned around the edges and fork-tender in the middle, 20 to 30 minutes.

4. **At the same time, roast the Chickpeas:** Scatter the chickpeas on the second baking sheet. Drizzle with the remaining 1 tablespoon grapeseed oil and toss to coat. Sprinkle with the remaining ¼ teaspoon salt. Roast the chickpeas on the upper rack until crisp and golden brown, 20 to 30 minutes.

5. **Assemble:** Divide the rice among bowls. Top with the sweet potatoes, chickpeas, tomato chili jam, feta, and cilantro.

VEGAN: Use vegan feta cheese or omit.

❶ This isn't intended to be knock-your-head-off spicy. At ½ teaspoon, the spice is present but barely noticeable when eaten alongside all the other ingredients. For slightly more heat, go with ¾ teaspoon.

❷ Grocery store labelling sometimes mixes up sweet potatoes and yams. Look for thin reddish-brown skin and an orange interior.

❸ Don't like cilantro? Use thinly sliced scallions instead.

ACTIVE TIME: 20 MINUTES • **TOTAL TIME:** 30 MINUTES • **SERVES** 3

SHORTCUT BROTHY BEANS

¼ cup **extra-virgin olive oil**, more for garnish

1 tablespoon **tomato paste**

2 large **shallots**, thinly sliced (1 cup)

5 **garlic cloves**, minced

1 tablespoon **fresh thyme leaves**

2 cups **vegetable stock**

½ teaspoon freshly ground **black pepper**

¼ teaspoon **fine sea salt**

2 cans (14 fl oz / 398 ml each) **butter** or **cannellini beans**, drained and rinsed ❷

1 tablespoon **white miso**

3 cups packed chopped **Swiss chard**, spinach, or lacinato kale

Lemon wedges

Grilled **crusty bread** or focaccia, for serving (optional)

It's hard to beat home-cooked beans, but sometimes you don't have hours to spend cooking. This dish instead infuses canned beans with heaps of flavour, in a fraction of the time. In addition to the usual suspects—shallots, garlic, and herbs—tomato paste and miso add an extra depth of flavour. It's an impressive level-up for canned beans! You can easily double the recipe if you want extra beans on hand for other meals throughout the week. ❶

1. **Cook the tomato paste, shallots, and herbs:** In a large Dutch oven or pot, heat the olive oil over medium heat. Add the tomato paste and shallots and cook, stirring frequently, until the shallots are soft and the tomato paste has darkened, about 5 minutes. Add the garlic and thyme and cook, stirring continuously, until fragrant, about 1 minute.

2. **Add the stock and simmer:** Add the vegetable stock, pepper, and salt. Cover with a lid and bring to a boil. Once boiling, reduce the heat to medium-low and simmer for 5 minutes to let the flavours meld.

3. **Add the beans, seasonings, and greens:** Pour the beans into the pot and gently stir to mix. Cover with a lid and cook over medium-low heat until the beans are warmed through, about 10 minutes. Stir in the miso until fully dissolved. (It's okay if some beans get squished while doing this—it'll thicken the broth.) Stir in the Swiss chard. Taste and season with more salt, if needed.

4. **Serve:** Serve the beans hot with lemon on the side and bread for dipping, if using.

GLUTEN-FREE: Use gluten-free bread or omit.

❶ For an even heartier meal, you could top with a soft-boiled egg (page 21), crumbled feta, and fresh herbs. Or spoon the beans over rice. They can also be added as a protein-boost in soups, pastas, bowls, etc.

❷ I recommend using "no salt added" beans, so you have control over seasoning at the end.

ACTIVE TIME: 30 MINUTES • **TOTAL TIME:** 45 MINUTES • **SERVES** 4 TO 5

FALAFEL BOWLS

These falafel bowls are as delicious as they are satisfying. This recipe calls for soaking dried chickpeas overnight, so make sure you plan ahead. As much as I love to encourage substitutions, in this recipe using dried chickpeas is a MUST. Canned chickpeas will introduce too much moisture and make the falafel mushy. As you pulse the mixture, it might be tempting to throw in extra binders, but trust me, it doesn't need it. Use a light hand when shaping and don't compact the falafel too much—you don't want them to be dense. These homemade falafel balls are baked rather than deep-fried. If you have an air-fryer, use it for an even crispier exterior. ❶

FALAFEL

1 cup dried **chickpeas**, soaked for 18 to 24 hours ❷

1½ cups lightly packed chopped **fresh flat-leaf parsley leaves**

⅔ cup finely chopped **yellow onion**

4 **garlic cloves**, minced

2 **scallions**, roughly chopped

1 tablespoon **fresh lemon juice**

2 teaspoons **ground cumin**

1 teaspoon **ground coriander**

1¼ teaspoons **fine sea salt**

4 tablespoons **extra-virgin olive oil**, divided

QUICK PICKLED RED CABBAGE

2 cups shredded **red cabbage**

½ teaspoon **fine sea salt**

2 tablespoons **granulated sugar**

½ teaspoon freshly ground **black pepper**

1 cup **boiling water**

½ cup **white wine vinegar**

FOR SERVING

Tzatziki (page 293), Vegan Tzatziki (page 293), or store-bought

Chopped **English cucumber**

Pitas, warmed

1. **Preheat the oven:** Place an oven rack in the upper third of the oven and preheat to 425°F (220°C). Line a large baking sheet with parchment paper.

2. **Start the Falafel—mix:** Drain the soaked chickpeas and transfer them to a food processor. Add the parsley, onion, garlic, scallions, lemon juice, cumin, coriander, salt, and 1 tablespoon of the olive oil. Pulse, scraping down the sides as needed, until the chickpeas form finely ground crumbs but are not yet completely puréed.

3. **Form and bake the falafel ❶:** Scoop 2-tablespoon portions of the chickpea mixture (about the size of a ping-pong ball) and arrange them on the prepared baking sheet. (You should have about 20 balls.) Using your fingertips, gently flatten the balls into thick patties. Generously brush both sides of the patties with the remaining 3 tablespoons olive oil. (It might seem like a lot of oil, but it ensures the falafel get golden brown and don't dry out.) Bake for 15 minutes, until golden brown on the bottom. Flip and bake until golden brown on the other side, another 10 to 15 minutes.

4. **Meanwhile, make the Quick Pickled Red Cabbage:** In a medium heatproof bowl, combine the cabbage and salt. Using your hands, rub the salt into the cabbage. ❸ Add the sugar, pepper, boiling water, and white wine vinegar. Stir well to combine. Cover the bowl and let sit for at least 20 minutes to soften.

5. **Assemble and serve:** Arrange the falafel, tzatziki, cucumber, and pickled red cabbage ❹ in shallow bowls. Serve with pitas on the side.

GLUTEN-FREE: Use gluten-free pitas or omit.

❶ If using an air-fryer, you can keep the falafel scoops rounded (rather than flattening) and there's no need to flip them halfway through. Set the air-fryer to 400°F (200°C) and bake for 12 to 15 minutes.

❷ To soak the chickpeas, place the dried chickpeas in a large bowl and fill the bowl with plenty of cold water. Make sure they're well covered because the chickpeas will at least double in size. Cover and let sit for 18 to 24 hours.

❸ If your hands get stained from the red cabbage, simply rub baking soda and a little water on your hands, then rinse under a running tap. Repeat if needed.

❹ Refrigerate extra pickled red cabbage, in a jar with a tight-fitting lid, for up to 2 weeks.

ACTIVE TIME: 35 MINUTES • TOTAL TIME: 40 MINUTES • SERVES 4

PEANUT-GLAZED TOFU RICE BOWLS

BAKED TOFU

16 oz (454g) **extra-firm tofu,** patted dry and cut into ½-inch (1 cm) cubes

1 tablespoon **tamari**

1 tablespoon **grapeseed oil**

4 teaspoons **cornstarch**

PEANUT BUTTER SAUCE

⅓ cup smooth unsalted **peanut butter** ❶

2 tablespoons **tamari**

2 to 3 teaspoons **sambal oelek** or Sriracha sauce

½ teaspoon **garlic powder**

3 tablespoons **hot water**

1 tablespoon **brown sugar** ❷

2 tablespoons **fresh lime juice**

EDAMAME

1½ cups **frozen shelled edamame**

1 tablespoon **toasted sesame seeds**

2 teaspoons **toasted sesame oil**

Fine sea salt

FOR SERVING

Cooked jasmine rice (page 302)

2 **carrots**, peeled and cut into matchsticks

1 **English cucumber**, chopped

1 or 2 **ripe mangoes**, peeled and cubed ❸

¼ cup **roasted peanuts,** chopped

2 **scallions**, thinly sliced

Lime wedges

These fresh and colourful rice bowls are topped with peanut-glazed tofu, sesame-kissed edamame, sweet mango, and a rainbow of fresh veggies. They're great for dinner and packing up for lunch the next day. The tofu, edamame, and peanuts all provide protein to keep you feeling full. You can substitute different veggies based on what you have on hand—just aim for colour and crunch.

---

1. **Preheat the oven:** Place an oven rack in the centre position and preheat to 425°F (220°C). Line a large baking sheet with parchment paper.

2. **Make the Baked Tofu:** Place the tofu on the prepared baking sheet. Drizzle the tamari over the tofu, and using your fingers, toss until most of the tamari is absorbed. Drizzle the grapeseed oil over the tofu and toss to coat. Sprinkle the cornstarch over the tofu and toss to coat. Spread the tofu in an even layer, then bake until golden brown, 25 to 30 minutes.

3. **Meanwhile, make the Peanut Butter Sauce:** In a small bowl, combine the peanut butter, tamari, sambal oelek, and garlic powder. Stir with a fork until a thick paste forms. Add the water and brown sugar. Stir vigorously until the mixture is completely smooth. Stir in the lime juice.

4. **Make the Edamame:** Bring a medium saucepan of water to a boil. Once boiling, add the edamame and cook until bright green and fork-tender, about 4 minutes. Drain, then return the edamame to the pot, off the heat. Add the sesame seeds, sesame oil, and salt to taste. Toss to coat.

5. **Assemble:** Drizzle 3 tablespoons of the peanut butter sauce over the hot tofu on the baking sheet and toss to coat. Divide the rice among bowls. Top with the tofu, edamame, carrots, cucumber, and mango. Garnish with the remaining peanut butter sauce, peanuts, and scallions. Serve with lime wedges.

---

❶ Can be replaced with smooth roasted unsalted almond butter.

❷ You can use light or dark brown sugar. In a pinch, you could also use granulated or coconut sugar.

❸ I usually use two Ataulfo mangoes. Ataulfo mangoes tend to be on the smaller side, so if you opt for a larger variety, one mango should be sufficient.

ACTIVE TIME: 20 MINUTES • **TOTAL TIME:** 1 HOUR • **SERVES** 4

SMASHED POTATOES AND ROASTED CAULIFLOWER BOWLS

POTATOES AND CAULIFLOWER

1 lb (454g) **baby potatoes**

2-lb (907g) head **cauliflower**, cut into florets

2 tablespoons **extra-virgin olive oil**

1 tablespoon **za'atar**

½ teaspoon **fine sea salt**

HERB SAUCE

1 cup loosely packed **fresh cilantro leaves**

1 cup loosely packed **fresh flat-leaf parsley leaves**

⅓ cup crumbled **feta cheese**, more for serving

3 tablespoons **fresh lemon juice**

2 tablespoons **extra-virgin olive oil**

1 **garlic clove**

¼ teaspoon **fine sea salt**

Cold water (about 2 tablespoons)

FOR SERVING

4 cups **mixed greens**

1 cup **hummus**

Quick Pickled Red Onions (page 289) ❶

Chopped **pistachios**

Potatoes with craggy, crispy edges and oven-roasted cauliflower make for a dish that's as much about texture as it is about taste. The green herb sauce is made from fresh herbs (of course), as well as feta cheese and lemon. The result is a bright-tasting sauce that's delicious drizzled over, well, everything. Serve with mixed greens, creamy hummus, pickled onions, and chopped nuts. What a feast!

---

1. **Preheat the oven:** Place the oven racks in the upper and lower thirds of the oven and preheat to 425°F (220°C). Line 2 large baking sheets with parchment paper.

2. **Start the Potatoes and Cauliflower—boil the potatoes:** Add the potatoes to a large pot of salted water. Cover with the lid slightly ajar and bring to a boil. Cook the potatoes until fork-tender, 8 to 12 minutes. Drain the potatoes.

3. **Roast the cauliflower and potatoes:** Mix and evenly scatter the cauliflower and potatoes on the prepared baking sheets. Drizzle with the olive oil and toss to coat. Using the palm of your hand, press down on the potatoes to flatten them to ½ inch (1 cm). Sprinkle the za'atar and salt over the vegetables. Roast until golden brown around the edges, 30 to 35 minutes, flipping the vegetables and swapping top and bottom positions halfway through.

4. **Meanwhile, make the Herb Sauce:** In a food processor, combine the cilantro, parsley, feta, lemon juice, olive oil, garlic, and salt. Pulse until finely minced. With the food processor running, slowly pour in the water, 1 tablespoon at a time, until a smooth, slightly runny sauce forms, scraping down the sides as needed.

5. **Assemble:** In a medium bowl, toss the mixed greens with just enough herb sauce to lightly coat (about ⅓ cup). Divide the dressed greens, cauliflower and potatoes, herb sauce, and hummus among shallow bowls. Garnish with the pickled red onions, pistachios, and more feta.

VEGAN: For the Herb Sauce, replace the feta cheese with 2 tablespoons pine nuts, ½ teaspoon lemon zest, and an extra pinch of salt. Use vegan feta for garnish or omit.

---

❶ If you don't have Quick Pickled Red Onions on hand, make them first so they have time to marinate.

BURRITO BOWLS WITH SMOKY SOFRITAS

BURRITO BOWLS

2 tablespoons **grapeseed oil**, divided

1 **white onion**, diced (2 cups)

12 oz (340g) **extra-firm tofu**

¼ cup **tomato paste**

2 tablespoons **tamari**

2 **garlic cloves**, minced

1 tablespoon **ground cumin**

1 teaspoon **dried oregano**

1 canned **chipotle pepper** in adobo, minced + 1 tablespoon **adobo sauce** ❶

1 can (14 fl oz / 398 ml) **diced fire-roasted tomatoes**

1 can (14 fl oz / 398 ml) **pinto beans**, drained and rinsed

1 cup **vegetable stock**

2 teaspoons **red wine vinegar**

Fine sea salt

Cooked rice (page 302), for serving

Lime wedges

SUGGESTED TOPPINGS (OPTIONAL)

Pitted, peeled, and chopped **avocado**

Quick Pickled Red Onions (page 289) ❷

Chopped **romaine lettuce**

Shredded **cheddar cheese**

Chopped **fresh cilantro leaves**

Hot sauce

I'll admit, this recipe is shamelessly inspired by the sofritas made popular by Chipotle restaurants. While there are many ways to over-complicate tofu prep, this version keeps things simple. The onion and crumbled tofu are cooked in a nonstick skillet, which lets the tofu cook long enough to get golden brown without tons of oil. Once the tofu has crisped up, it's ready to absorb the flavours of the sauce—which gets done directly in the same pan. You certainly don't need to use all the toppings listed below, but if you're feeling inspired, load it up!

---

1. **Start the Burrito Bowls—cook the tofu and onion:** In a large nonstick skillet, heat 1 tablespoon of the grapeseed oil over medium heat. Add the onion and, using your hands, crumble the tofu into the skillet. Cook, stirring occasionally, until the onion is soft and the tofu is golden brown, 12 to 15 minutes.

2. **Add the seasonings:** Add the remaining 1 tablespoon grapeseed oil and tomato paste to the skillet. Stir well to mix, then cook, stirring frequently, until the tomato paste darkens slightly, 2 to 3 minutes. Pour in the tamari and stir with a flexible spatula to scrape up the brown bits from the bottom of the skillet. Add the garlic, cumin, and oregano and cook, stirring constantly, until the garlic is fragrant, 1 to 2 minutes.

3. **Simmer the sauce:** Add the chipotle pepper and adobo sauce, tomatoes, pinto beans, and vegetable stock. Stir to mix. Bring to a simmer over medium heat and cook for 10 to 12 minutes, to let the flavours meld and allow the sauce to thicken. Stir in the red wine vinegar. Season with salt to taste.

4. **Assemble and serve:** Divide the rice among bowls. Spoon the tofu and pinto bean mixture over the rice. Garnish with toppings of your choice and serve with lime wedges.

VEGAN: Use vegan shredded cheese or omit.

---

❶ If you're sensitive to spice, choose a small pepper.

❷ If you don't have Quick Pickled Red Onions on hand, make them first so they have time to marinate.

ACTIVE TIME: 30 MINUTES • **TOTAL TIME:** 45 MINUTES • **SERVES** 4

ORANGE GINGER AND SESAME MEATBALLS

MEATBALLS

12 oz (340g) **extra-firm tofu,** patted dry

3 **garlic cloves**, minced

2 teaspoons minced **fresh ginger**

2 tablespoons **tamari**

1 tablespoon **toasted sesame oil**

3 **scallions**, thinly sliced, more for garnish

½ cup + ⅓ cup **panko breadcrumbs**, divided

SAUCE

½ teaspoon **orange zest** (optional)

1 cup **fresh orange juice**

3 tablespoons **honey**

1 teaspoon **tamari**

2 **garlic cloves**, minced

1 teaspoon minced **fresh ginger**

4 teaspoons **cornstarch**

2 tablespoons **cold water**

1 tablespoon **rice vinegar**

¼ to ½ teaspoon **red pepper flakes**

FOR SERVING

Cooked jasmine rice (page 302)

Toasted sesame seeds, for garnish

These tasty protein-packed "meatballs" are made with tofu and flavoured with scallions and toasted sesame oil. They come together quickly in a food processor and are baked in the oven. Then all you need to do is make the orange and ginger sauce. The sauce is sweet, salty, and bright. Go for a generous drizzle all over the meatballs and rice. I usually cook up jasmine rice for serving, but feel free to pick your favourite rice for this.

1. **Preheat the oven:** Place an oven rack in the centre position and preheat to 375°F (190°C). Line a large baking sheet with parchment paper.

2. **Start the Meatballs—mix:** Crumble the tofu into a food processor. Add the garlic, ginger, tamari, and sesame oil and process until smooth. Add the scallions and ½ cup of the panko. Pulse just until the panko is evenly distributed.

3. **Form the meatballs:** Scoop 2-tablespoon portions of the tofu mixture (about the size of a ping-pong ball) and roll between your palms to form smooth balls. Arrange them on the prepared baking sheet. (You should have about 16 balls.) Place the remaining ⅓ cup panko in a small bowl. Roll the meatballs, one at a time, in the panko to coat. Bake until the meatballs are firm and golden brown, 30 to 35 minutes.

4. **Meanwhile, start the Sauce—combine and simmer:** In a small saucepan, combine the orange zest (if using), orange juice, honey, tamari, garlic, and ginger and bring to a boil over medium-high heat. Once boiling, reduce the heat to medium and simmer, stirring occasionally, for 5 minutes to let the flavours infuse.

5. **Thicken the sauce:** In a small bowl, whisk together the cornstarch and cold water until smooth. Pour the cornstarch mixture into the sauce and whisk to combine. Bring to a boil, then reduce the heat to medium-low and cook, stirring occasionally, until it thickens slightly, 2 to 3 minutes. Whisk in the rice vinegar and red pepper flakes. Keep the sauce warm over low heat, stirring occasionally, until the meatballs are ready.

6. **Assemble and serve:** Scoop the rice into bowls, top with the meatballs, and generously drizzle with the sauce. Garnish with scallions and sesame seeds.

VEGAN: Replace the honey with maple syrup. (The sauce will be slightly darker, but still tasty.)

GLUTEN-FREE: Use gluten-free panko breadcrumbs.

HANDHELDS

ACTIVE TIME: 30 MINUTES • **TOTAL TIME:** 30 MINUTES • **SERVES** 4

SHAWARMA-SPICED MUSHROOM PITA

4 (8 inch / 20 cm) **pitas**

SHAWARMA MUSHROOMS

1¼ teaspoons **smoked sweet paprika**

1 teaspoon **ground cumin**

¾ teaspoon **ground coriander**

½ teaspoon **garlic powder**

½ teaspoon **onion powder**

½ teaspoon **fine sea salt**

¼ teaspoon freshly ground **black pepper**

¼ teaspoon **ground turmeric**

3 tablespoons **grapeseed oil**, divided

12 oz (340g) **oyster mushrooms**, torn into bite-size pieces

GARLIC YOGURT

1 cup plain **Greek yogurt**

2 **garlic cloves**, finely grated

Pinch of **fine sea salt**

FOR SERVING

1 cup sliced **English cucumber**

1 cup **cherry tomatoes**, halved

1 cup sliced **romaine lettuce**

Quick Pickled Red Onions (page 289) or thinly sliced red onion ❶

These yummy pitas might leave you wondering why all meals aren't handhelds. Shawarma is a Middle Eastern dish made from seasoned rotisserie-cooked meat. But here, seared mushrooms are the juicy, meatless canvas for absorbing the flavourful and smoky spice blend. Wrap them up in a soft pita along with creamy garlic yogurt, crisp fresh veggies, and tangy pickled onions—then dig in.

---

1. **Warm the pita:** Place an oven rack in the centre position and preheat to 300°F (150°C). Stack the pitas and wrap them tightly in foil. Bake until warmed through, 15 to 20 minutes. Remove from the oven but leave the pitas wrapped in foil to keep warm until serving.

2. **Meanwhile, start making the Shawarma Mushrooms—mix the spices:** In a small bowl, whisk together the smoked paprika, cumin, coriander, garlic powder, onion powder, salt, pepper, and turmeric.

3. **Sear the mushrooms:** In a large skillet, heat 2 tablespoons of the grapeseed oil over medium-high heat. Once the oil is hot, scatter the mushrooms into the skillet and sear, undisturbed, until golden brown on the bottom, 3 to 4 minutes. Sauté the mushrooms, stirring frequently, until they are golden brown all over, 4 to 5 minutes. Reduce the heat to medium. Add the remaining 1 tablespoon grapeseed oil and the spice mixture. Toss to coat the mushrooms, and cook, stirring frequently, until the spices are fragrant, 1 to 2 minutes. Taste and season with more salt, if needed.

4. **Meanwhile, make the Garlic Yogurt:** In a small bowl, whisk together the yogurt, garlic, and salt.

5. **Assemble:** Spread the garlic yogurt over the warm pitas. Divide the mushrooms over each pita, then top with the cucumber, tomatoes, lettuce, and pickled red onions. Roll up the pita and enjoy.

VEGAN: Omit the Garlic Yogurt and spread a couple tablespoons of toum (Lebanese garlic sauce) or vegan mayonnaise on each pita instead.

GLUTEN-FREE: Use gluten-free pitas.

---

❶ If you don't have Quick Pickled Red Onions on hand, make them first so they have time to marinate.

GRILLED HALLOUMI SKEWERS WITH THAI BASIL AND LIME VINAIGRETTE

SKEWERS

8.8 oz (250g) **halloumi cheese**

2 **bell peppers** (red, orange, or yellow), cut into 1½-inch (4 cm) pieces

1 **zucchini** (12 oz / 340g), cut into ½-inch (1 cm) rounds

8 oz (227g) **cremini mushrooms** ❷

1 small **red onion**, cut into 1-inch (2.5 cm) pieces

2 tablespoons **grapeseed oil**, more for grilling

½ teaspoon **fine sea salt**

¼ teaspoon freshly ground **black pepper**

VINAIGRETTE

⅓ cup finely chopped **fresh Thai basil leaves** ❸

¼ cup **grapeseed oil**

½ teaspoon **lime zest**

2 tablespoons **fresh lime juice**

¾ teaspoon finely grated **fresh ginger**

½ teaspoon **fine sea salt**

FOR SERVING

Cooked jasmine rice (page 302; optional)

Chopped **pistachios** or roasted peanuts

1 **lime**, cut into wedges

Sure, barbecued veggies are a crowd-pleaser. But want to know what's even more popular? Grilled cubes of cheese. Halloumi is a firm cheese that gets crispy and golden brown on the grill without melting. To prevent halloumi from splitting when you skewer it, cut the cheese into big cubes and slowly slide them onto the thinnest skewers you can find. ❶ Or skip the skewers to save time and cook everything in a grill basket or in a stovetop grill pan brushed generously with oil. Serve these skewers over a bed of rice, drizzle the fresh thai basil and lime vinaigrette on top, and watch it all disappear.

1. **Start the Skewers—assemble:** Cut the halloumi into 1-inch (2.5 cm) cubes. (If the block of halloumi has a seam, cut along the seam to prevent splitting.) In a large bowl, combine the halloumi, bell peppers, zucchini, mushrooms, and onion. Toss with the grapeseed oil, salt, and pepper. Carefully thread alternating vegetables and halloumi onto skewers. (You should get about twelve [10-inch / 25 cm] skewers.)

2. **Preheat the grill:** Prepare the grill for direct cooking over medium-high heat.

3. **Meanwhile, make the Vinaigrette:** In a small bowl, whisk together the Thai basil, grapeseed oil, lime zest, lime juice, ginger, and salt.

4. **Continue with the Skewers—grill:** Generously brush the grill with grapeseed oil to prevent sticking. Place the skewers on the grill and cook until the mushrooms and zucchini are tender and the cheese is golden brown, 3 to 4 minutes per side.

5. **Assemble and serve:** Scoop the rice (if using) onto a serving platter. Lay the grilled skewers on top. Drizzle with the vinaigrette and sprinkle with pistachios. Serve with lime wedges.

VEGAN: Use extra-firm tofu instead of halloumi cheese. Since halloumi is salty, season the tofu generously with salt and freshly ground black pepper before combining it with the vegetables in step 1.

❶ If using bamboo skewers, soak them in room-temperature water for at least 30 minutes before using to prevent burning.

❷ Mushrooms with caps larger than 1½ inches (4 cm) can be sliced in half, top to bottom.

❸ Thai basil has a thicker purple stem and heartier leaves than Italian basil. It can be found fresh in well-stocked grocery stores (often packaged with the other fresh herbs) or head to your nearest Asian grocery store.

ACTIVE TIME: 45 MINUTES • **TOTAL TIME:** 45 MINUTES • **SERVES** 4

CRISPY TOFU BANH MI

CRISPY TOFU

12 oz (340g) **extra-firm tofu**

2 tablespoons **grapeseed oil**, divided

¾ cup **panko breadcrumbs**

2 teaspoons **cornstarch**

QUICK PICKLED CARROTS ❶

⅔ cup **boiling water**

1 tablespoon **granulated sugar**

½ teaspoon **fine sea salt**

⅔ cup **rice vinegar**

1 large **carrot**, peeled and cut into matchsticks

SRIRACHA LIME SAUCE

2 tablespoons **tamari**

2 tablespoons **Sriracha sauce**

Zest and juice of 1 **lime**

1 teaspoon **garlic powder**

FOR SERVING

1 **baguette**

Mayonnaise

½ **English cucumber**, thinly sliced

2 **radishes**, thinly sliced (optional)

Fresh cilantro leaves

In my early twenties, I used to eat at the same banh mi shop each week. It was around the corner from my Toronto apartment, and they made a killer crispy tofu, which inspired this recipe. Instead of deep-frying, I use pan-toasted panko breadcrumbs. There are a few components to this sandwich, but don't let that deter you. One bite and it'll all be worth it.

1. **Start the Crispy Tofu—slice and dry the tofu:** Line a large baking sheet with a clean kitchen towel or paper towel. Cut the tofu crosswise into ⅓-inch (8 mm) slices (you should get 8 to 12 slices). Place the tofu in a single layer on the lined baking sheet. Cover the tofu with the kitchen towel or paper towel and let dry for at least 10 minutes.

2. **Meanwhile, make the Quick Pickled Carrots:** Combine the boiling water, sugar, and salt in a small heatproof jar or container. Stir until the sugar and salt are dissolved. Stir in the rice vinegar and carrots and let sit for at least 15 minutes to marinate.

3. **Make the Sriracha Lime Sauce:** In a small bowl, whisk together the tamari, Sriracha, lime zest and juice, and garlic powder.

4. **Continue the Crispy Tofu—toast the panko:** In a large nonstick skillet, heat 1 tablespoon of the grapeseed oil over medium heat. Scatter in the panko, toss to coat, and cook, stirring frequently, until golden brown, 3 to 5 minutes. Transfer the panko to a plate to cool. Set aside the skillet.

5. **Dust the tofu with cornstarch:** Uncover the tofu and sprinkle 1 teaspoon of the cornstarch on top of the tofu. Using your fingers, rub the cornstarch into the tofu until it's no longer visible. Flip and repeat on the other side of the tofu with the remaining 1 teaspoon cornstarch.

6. **Pan-fry the tofu:** In the skillet, heat the remaining 1 tablespoon grapeseed oil over medium heat. Place the dusted tofu in the skillet and fry until golden brown, 2 to 4 minutes per side. Drizzle 4 tablespoons of the Sriracha lime sauce over the tofu (keep the small amount of extra sauce). Flip the tofu to coat both sides and cook until the sauce is mostly absorbed but the outside of the tofu is still moist, about 1 minute. ❷ Remove the skillet from the heat.

CONTINUED ON NEXT PAGE

VEGAN: Use vegan mayonnaise. **GLUTEN-FREE:** Use gluten-free panko breadcrumbs and baguette.

❶ You can make a larger batch of Quick Pickled Carrots by adding more carrots to the jar, so long as they are submerged under the pickling liquid. Store covered in the fridge for up to 2 weeks.

❷ The moisture from the sauce will help the panko stick to the tofu. If you cooked the tofu a bit longer and it is dry on the outside, you can correct this by lightly brushing the extra Sriracha Lime Sauce on the tofu at the end of step 6 before coating with the toasted panko.

CONTINUED FROM PREVIOUS PAGE

7. **Coat the tofu:** Working with 1 slice at a time, dip the tofu in the panko and using your fingers, press the panko onto both sides. Transfer the coated tofu to a large plate. Repeat to coat the remaining tofu.

8. **Assemble:** Cut the baguette into quarters, then slice each piece horizontally in half, so you end up with 8 pieces of bread. Generously spread mayonnaise on the baguette halves. Divide the crispy tofu, quick pickled carrots, cucumber, and radishes (if using) evenly among the bottom halves. Drizzle with any remaining Sriracha lime sauce and top with a little cilantro. Finish the sandwiches with the tops.

ACTIVE TIME: 30 MINUTES • **TOTAL TIME:** 30 MINUTES • **SERVES** 4

CHIPOTLE MUSHROOM TACOS WITH PINEAPPLE JALAPEÑO SALSA

12 (6-inch / 15 cm) **corn tortillas**

PINEAPPLE SALSA

1½ cups diced **fresh pineapple** ❶

1 **jalapeño pepper**, ribs and seeds removed, minced

2 tablespoons chopped **fresh cilantro leaves**

1 tablespoon **fresh lime juice**

CHIPOTLE MUSHROOMS

⅓ cup **fresh orange juice**

1 canned **chipotle pepper** in adobo, minced + 2 tablespoons **adobo sauce** ❷

2 tablespoons **tamari**

2 **garlic cloves**, finely grated

2 teaspoons **ground cumin**

2 tablespoons **grapeseed oil**

1 lb (454g) **oyster mushrooms**, torn into thin pieces

FOR SERVING

Quick Pickled Red Onions (page 289) ❸

Everyday Guacamole (page 298) or store-bought

These tacos are downright delicious. Using your hands to tear the oyster mushrooms creates craggy edges that sear up nicely in the skillet. The mushrooms are then coated in a chipotle orange sauce that's spicy, salty, *and* sweet. For toppings, pineapple jalapeño salsa, guacamole, and pickled red onions really round out all the flavours and textures. If you like things extra spicy, serve with extra hot sauce on the side.

1. **Warm the tortillas:** Position a rack in the centre position and preheat to 300°F (150°C). Divide the tortillas into 2 stacks and wrap in foil. Place in the oven until warmed through, about 15 minutes. Remove from the oven but leave the tortillas wrapped in foil to keep warm until serving.

2. **Meanwhile, make the Pineapple Salsa:** In a small bowl, combine the pineapple, jalapeño, cilantro, and lime juice. Toss to coat.

3. **Start the Chipotle Mushrooms—make the sauce:** In a small bowl, whisk together the orange juice, chipotle pepper and adobo sauce, tamari, garlic, and cumin.

4. **Cook the mushrooms:** In a large skillet, heat the grapeseed oil over medium-high heat. Once the oil is hot, add the mushrooms and sear, undisturbed, until golden brown on the bottom, 3 to 4 minutes. Sauté, stirring occasionally, until golden brown all over, 4 to 5 minutes. Reduce the heat to medium-low. Pour in the sauce and toss to coat the mushrooms and cook, stirring constantly, for 2 minutes to let the flavours meld.

5. **Serve:** Scoop the mushrooms into a small serving bowl. Serve with the pineapple salsa, pickled red onions, guacamole, and warmed tortillas. Assemble the tacos at the table.

❶ Use fresh pineapple. Canned or thawed frozen pineapple won't have the same taste and texture.

❷ This makes for a slightly spicy mushroom filling. If you're sensitive to spice, choose a small pepper and add adobo sauce in small increments, to taste.

❸ If you don't have Quick Pickled Red Onions on hand, make them first so they have time to marinate.

ACTIVE TIME: 45 MINUTES • TOTAL TIME: 45 MINUTES • SERVES 6

SWEET POTATO BLACK BEAN BURGERS WITH CHIPOTLE MAYO

My brother, who is very much *not* a vegetarian, is obsessed with these burgers. Smoked paprika, chipotle peppers, and adobo sauce give them a bit of kick. A mixture of sweet potato, black beans, and cooked rice hits that moist-but-not-too-mushy texture that is so important in a veggie burger. Nothing is worse than a dry burger, veggie or otherwise! These burgers freeze well—you can even cook them in the oven from frozen. ❶ The toppings are a choose-your-own-adventure situation, but the chipotle mayo is a must.

CHIPOTLE MAYO

6 tablespoons **mayonnaise**

2 tablespoons **adobo sauce** from canned chipotles in adobo

BURGER PATTIES

3 tablespoons **grapeseed oil**, divided, more for brushing

1 **yellow onion**, finely chopped (2 cups)

2 cups shredded **sweet potato** (1 large potato)

2 **garlic cloves**, minced

¼ cup **tomato paste**

⅓ cup raw **pepitas**

2 canned **chipotle peppers** in adobo + 1 tablespoon **adobo sauce**

2 teaspoons **ground cumin**

1¼ teaspoons **fine sea salt**

½ teaspoon **smoked sweet paprika**

1 can (14 fl oz / 398 ml) **black beans**, drained and rinsed

1½ cups **cooked short-grain brown rice** (page 303) ❷

¾ cup dry **breadcrumbs**

FOR SERVING (OPTIONAL)

6 **burger buns**, toasted

Everyday Guacamole (page 298) or sliced avocado

Lettuce

Sliced **tomatoes**

Quick Pickled Red Onions (page 289)

1. **Make the Chipotle Mayo:** In a small bowl, whisk together the mayonnaise and adobo sauce.

2. **Start the Burger Patties:** In a large nonstick skillet, heat 1 tablespoon of the grapeseed oil over medium heat. Scatter the onion and sweet potato into the skillet and cook, stirring occasionally, until they are golden brown around the edges, 10 to 12 minutes. Add the garlic and tomato paste and cook, stirring frequently, until the garlic is fragrant and softened, 2 to 3 minutes.

3. **Combine in a food processor:** Transfer the onion and sweet potato mixture to a food processor. (Set aside the skillet.) Add the remaining 2 tablespoons grapeseed oil, pepitas, chipotle peppers and adobo sauce, cumin, salt, and smoked paprika. Pulse until smooth, scraping down the sides as needed. Add the black beans, cooked rice, and breadcrumbs. Pulse just until evenly mixed but not puréed.

4. **Shape the patties:** Divide the mixture into 6 portions (about ¾ cup each). Using your hands, shape and flatten into patties ¾ inch (2 cm) thick.

5. **Cook the burgers and assemble:** Give the skillet a quick wipe, then heat it over medium heat (or prepare a grill for direct cooking over medium heat). Generously brush both sides of the burger patties with grapeseed oil. Place the patties in the skillet and cook until browned on the bottom, 3 to 6 minutes. Flip and cook until browned on the other side and the burger is firm to the touch, 3 to 6 minutes. Place on toasted buns and top with chipotle mayo and toppings of your choice.

VEGAN: Use vegan mayonnaise and burger buns. **GLUTEN-FREE:** Use gluten-free breadcrumbs and burger buns.

❶ These burger patties are meal-prep friendly. To refrigerate, store uncooked patties in an airtight container in the fridge for up to 3 days. Cook on the stovetop or barbecue as directed. To freeze, place the uncooked patties on a parchment-lined baking sheet, freeze until firm, then transfer to an airtight container or freezer bag and freeze for up to 3 months. To cook from frozen, brush both sides of the patties generously with grapeseed oil, then bake at 425°F (220°C) on a parchment-lined baking sheet until browned and firm, 30 to 40 minutes, flipping halfway through.

❷ Typically, ½ cup uncooked short-grain brown rice yields 1½ cups cooked rice, but measure after cooking to be sure. See page 303 for cooking instructions. If you must substitute, choose a sticky short-grain white rice, like sushi rice.

ACTIVE TIME: 25 MINUTES • **TOTAL TIME:** 25 MINUTES • **SERVES** 2

CURRY VEGETABLE FRITTERS

1 cup grated **Yukon Gold potato** (4.6 oz / 130g) ❶

1 cup peeled and grated **carrot** (4.1 oz / 115g)

1 cup finely chopped **broccoli florets** (3 oz / 85g)

3 **scallions**, thinly sliced

1½ teaspoons **curry powder**

1 teaspoon **ground cumin**

½ teaspoon **fine sea salt**

⅓ cup **chickpea flour** (or ½ cup all-purpose flour) ❷

2 large **eggs**, whisked

2 tablespoons **grapeseed oil**, more if needed

Flaky sea salt, for garnish

Tzatziki (page 293), Vegan Tzatziki (page 293), or store-bought, for serving

For busy nights when you want a low-effort, light meal, these fritters are a great go-to. You can eat them on their own or serve up some fresh veggies on the side. Go ahead and eat them on the couch while watching your favourite show—that's my preferred fritter-eating position. To make these fritters, all you have to do is grate some veggies, mix them in a bowl, and pan-fry them until golden brown. Chickpea flour is my favourite binder to use here, because it's tasty, gluten-free, and a source of protein, but all-purpose flour works too.

1. **Preheat the oven:** Place an oven rack in the centre position and preheat to 300°F (150°C). Place a cooling rack inside a baking sheet.

2. **Mix the fritter batter:** In a large bowl, stir together the potato, carrot, broccoli, scallions, curry powder, cumin, and sea salt. Sprinkle in the chickpea flour and toss to coat. Pour in the eggs and stir until well mixed.

3. **Pan-fry the fritters:** In a large cast-iron or nonstick skillet, heat the grapeseed oil over medium heat. Working in batches, drop small mounds of batter (about 3 tablespoons each) into the hot oil. (Do not overcrowd the skillet.) Fry the fritters until golden brown on the bottom, 2 to 3 minutes. Flip and cook until the other side is golden brown, 2 to 3 minutes. Add a bit more grapeseed oil to the skillet, if needed, to prevent the fritters from sticking. Transfer the fitters to the prepared baking sheet and keep warm in the oven while you cook the remaining fritters.

4. **Serve:** Transfer the fritters to a serving platter and sprinkle with flaky salt. Serve with tzatziki on the side for dipping.

❶ Replace with other thin-skinned yellow or red potatoes, if desired.

❷ Chickpea flour, also called garbanzo flour and besan, is gluten-free and has a slightly nutty flavour. Chickpea flour is often found in the gluten-free baking aisle or at Indian grocery stores. If substituting all-purpose flour, these fritters won't be gluten-free.

ACTIVE TIME: 25 MINUTES • TOTAL TIME: 25 MINUTES • SERVES 2

MUSHROOM AND GOAT CHEESE TOASTS

1 medium **shallot**, minced (¼ cup)

1 tablespoon **white wine vinegar**

1 tablespoon **grapeseed oil**

6 oz (170g) **mixed mushrooms**, torn into bite-size pieces

1 tablespoon **butter**, more for spreading

1 cup thinly sliced **leeks** (white and light green parts)

2 **garlic cloves**, minced

1 tablespoon **fresh thyme leaves**

Flaky sea salt

Freshly ground **black pepper**

⅓ cup **soft goat cheese** (2.5 oz / 71g)

2 tablespoons **whole milk**

1 **demi-baguette** ❶

Microgreens (optional)

Warm buttered bread, creamy goat cheese, and garlicky seared mushrooms. What's not to love?! A wild mushroom mix works well here, but feel free to use your favourites—I'm pretty sure all mushrooms taste great when cooked with leeks, thyme, and butter. The quick pickled shallots add a pop of acidity to complement the umami-rich mushrooms. Microgreens make for a pretty garnish, but these toasts are still delicious without them.

---

1. **Quick-pickle the shallots:** In a small bowl, toss the shallots with the white wine vinegar. Let sit for at least 10 minutes.

2. **Cook the mushroom mixture:** In a large skillet, heat the grapeseed oil over medium-high heat. Once the oil is hot, scatter in the mushrooms and sauté, stirring occasionally, until golden brown, 6 to 8 minutes. Reduce the heat to medium-low. Add the butter, leeks, garlic, and thyme and cook, stirring frequently, until the leeks are soft, 1 to 2 minutes. Season with flaky salt and pepper to taste. Transfer the mushroom mixture to a medium bowl. Set aside the skillet.

3. **Meanwhile, make the goat cheese spread:** In a small bowl, using a fork, vigorously stir together the goat cheese and milk until it is soft and spreadable.

4. **Toast the bread:** Heat the skillet over medium heat. Cut the baguette into halves, then slice each piece horizontally so you end up with 4 pieces of bread. Lightly butter the baguette halves. Place the baguette halves buttered side down in the skillet and cook until the edges are golden brown, about 2 minutes.

5. **Assemble:** Spread the goat cheese mixture on the buttered side of the baguette halves. Top with the mushroom mixture, some drained pickled shallots, microgreens (if using), and flaky salt and pepper to taste.

GLUTEN-FREE: Use gluten-free baguette.

---

❶ You can replace the demi-baguette with half a full-sized baguette.

ACTIVE TIME: 30 MINUTES • **TOTAL TIME:** 30 MINUTES • **SERVES** 4

CAPRESE PESTO PANINI

1 piece **focaccia** (about 10 inches / 25 cm square) ❶

1 ball (8.8 oz / 250g) **fresh mozzarella cheese**

2 **beefsteak** or **heirloom tomatoes** (1 lb / 454g)

½ cup **Fresh Basil Pesto** (page 290) or store-bought

2 tablespoons drained and minced **sun-dried tomatoes**

2 cups lightly packed **baby spinach**

Extra-virgin olive oil, for brushing

Balsamic glaze, for serving (optional)

You don't need a fancy panini press to be a sandwich superstar. Just cook these sandwiches on a hot grill pan or skillet, with another heavy pan on top for the full panini experience. Made with focaccia and piled high with juicy tomatoes, creamy mozzarella cheese, and pesto, this panini is even better if you drizzle it with balsamic glaze. Try to buy the ripest tomatoes you can get your hands on—it's worth it!

---

1. Prep the ingredients: Using a serrated knife, cut the focaccia into quarters and then cut each quarter in half horizontally. Cut the mozzarella and tomatoes into ¼-inch (5 mm) slices.

2. Assemble the sandwiches: Divide the pesto evenly among the tops and bottoms of the focaccia pieces. Layer the fresh tomatoes, mozzarella, sun-dried tomatoes, and spinach evenly on the bottom halves. Close the sandwiches with the top halves. Brush the tops with the olive oil.

3. Grill the sandwiches: Heat a large grill pan or skillet over medium-low heat. Working in batches of 1 or 2, place the sandwiches oiled side down in the skillet. Use a heavy skillet or pan to press down with moderate pressure on the sandwiches as they cook until golden on the bottom, about 3 minutes. Brush the top of the sandwiches with olive oil, then carefully flip. Grill the other side until golden, about 3 minutes.

4. Serve: Slice the sandwiches in half. Serve hot, with the balsamic glaze for drizzling, if using.

GLUTEN-FREE: Use gluten-free focaccia or ciabatta.

---

❶ Ciabatta bread can be used instead. If your ciabatta bread is very rounded on top, you can trim the top so it sits flatter in the pan. Focaccia is usually saltier than ciabatta, so you may want to sprinkle flaky sea salt over the ciabatta after brushing it with olive oil.

VEGGIE SUSHI WITH SRIRACHA MAYO

1½ cups **sushi rice**

1¾ cups **water**

1 lb (454g) **sweet potatoes**, cut into ⅓-inch (8 mm) thick matchsticks ❶

2 tablespoons + 2 teaspoons **grapeseed oil**, divided

¾ teaspoon **fine sea salt**, divided

⅓ cup **panko breadcrumbs**

⅓ cup **mayonnaise**

3 to 4 teaspoons **Sriracha sauce**

2 tablespoons **rice vinegar**

2 teaspoons **granulated sugar**

4 sheets **sushi nori**

1 **mini cucumber**, cut into matchsticks

½ **avocado**, pitted, peeled, and sliced

FOR SERVING

Soy sauce

Wasabi (optional)

Miso soup, warm (optional)

If you love sushi but don't have great plant-based options nearby, I highly recommend taking matters into your own hands. These rolls have a rainbow of veggies tucked inside and are then topped with Sriracha mayo and crispy panko for crunch. It's not traditional, but it's definitely delicious. If you're new to rolling sushi, follow the step-by-step on page 187. You can usually get a sushi mat from the grocery store, but in a pinch, a doubled-up tea towel works too.

---

1. **Preheat the oven:** Place the oven racks in the upper and lower thirds of the oven and preheat to 425°F (220°C). Line 2 large baking sheets with parchment paper.

2. **Cook the rice:** Rinse the rice in a sieve under cold running water, while swishing the rice with your fingertips, until the water almost runs clear, about 1 minute. Shake the sieve to remove excess water (too much water will throw off your ratios, so drain well). Add the rice and water to a Dutch oven or medium pot with a tight-fitting lid and bring to a boil over high heat. Once the water is boiling, immediately cover with the lid, reduce the heat to medium-low, and cook until the water has been absorbed, 15 to 16 minutes. Don't peek until the end. Remove from the heat and let sit, with the lid on, for 10 minutes to steam.

3. **Meanwhile, bake the sweet potatoes:** Scatter the sweet potatoes on one of the prepared baking sheets. Drizzle with 2 tablespoons of the grapeseed oil and toss to coat. Sprinkle with ¼ teaspoon of the salt. Bake on the upper rack until fork-tender, 20 to 30 minutes. Transfer to a medium plate to cool.

4. **At the same time, toast the panko:** Pile the panko in the middle of the second baking sheet. Drizzle with the remaining 2 teaspoons grapeseed oil and ¼ teaspoon of the salt. Toss to mix, then spread the panko into an even layer. Bake on the lower rack until golden brown, 2 to 4 minutes. Transfer the panko to a small bowl to cool.

5. **Make the Sriracha mayo:** In a small bowl, whisk together the mayonnaise and Sriracha. Transfer half the sauce to a squeeze bottle (or small freezer bag with a corner snipped off) for drizzling.

6. **Make the rice seasoning:** In a small bowl, vigorously whisk together the rice vinegar, sugar, and remaining ¼ teaspoon salt until the sugar and salt are dissolved.

CONTINUED ON NEXT PAGE

VEGAN: Use vegan mayonnaise. **GLUTEN-FREE:** Use gluten-free panko breadcrumbs.

---

❶ About 2 small sweet potatoes. I like to use an orange and a purple potato for extra colour, but that's optional.

CONTINUED FROM PREVIOUS PAGE

7. **Season the rice:** Transfer the cooked rice to a large bowl. Pour the rice seasoning overtop. Using a rice paddle or silicone spatula, gently fold the rice for 1 minute to distribute the rice seasoning and cool the rice. Cover the bowl with a damp kitchen towel to prevent the rice from drying out.

8. **Fill and roll the sushi:** Lay a sushi mat (or a kitchen towel folded in half) on the counter with a short side facing you. Cover the mat with a piece of plastic wrap, then place a sheet of nori on top shiny side down. Using the rice paddle or dampened hands, evenly spread a quarter of the rice over the nori, leaving the top 1-inch (2.5 cm) border bare. Spread some Sriracha mayo in the middle of the rice, then lay the sweet potato, cucumber, and avocado on top. Use the mat to roll the sushi up tightly. Press gently to seal and shape the roll until it is nice and round. Repeat to roll the remaining sushi.

9. **Slice, garnish, and serve:** Wipe a sharp knife with a damp kitchen towel. Slice each sushi roll into 8 to 10 pieces. Drizzle the pieces with the Sriracha mayo and sprinkle with toasted panko. Serve the sushi with small dishes of soy sauce for dipping, along with wasabi and bowls of miso soup, if using.

ACTIVE TIME: 25 MINUTES • **TOTAL TIME:** 25 MINUTES • **SERVES** 4

SEARED HALLOUMI SANDWICHES WITH ROASTED RED PEPPER SPREAD

HERB SAUCE

⅓ cup minced **fresh flat-leaf parsley leaves**

3 tablespoons minced **shallot**

2 tablespoons **extra-virgin olive oil**

2 tablespoons drained **capers**, minced

Zest and juice of 1 **lemon**

¼ teaspoon **red pepper flakes**

RED PEPPER SPREAD

⅓ cup raw **walnuts**

⅔ cup **roasted red peppers** from a jar

¼ teaspoon **smoked sweet paprika**

¼ teaspoon **fine sea salt**

SEARED HALLOUMI

1 tablespoon **extra-virgin olive oil**

8.8 oz (250g) **halloumi cheese**, cut into 12 slices

FOR SERVING

8 slices **whole grain bread**

½ **English cucumber**, thinly sliced

Sometimes the messier the sandwich, the better. These ones are made with a roasted red pepper spread that comes together in minutes. Slices of skillet-seared halloumi cheese are then nestled on top. Halloumi, while delicious, is quite salty, so the herb sauce and sliced cucumbers balance it out with a hint of acidity and freshness. Do grab some extra napkins, because you'll need them.

---

1. **Make the Herb Sauce:** In a small bowl, stir together the parsley, shallot, olive oil, capers, lemon zest and juice, and red pepper flakes.

2. **Make the Red Pepper Spread:** In a large nonstick or cast-iron skillet, toast the walnuts over medium heat, stirring frequently, until fragrant and slightly toasted, about 5 minutes. Transfer the nuts to a food processor, along with the roasted red peppers, smoked paprika, and salt. Pulse until smooth, scraping down the sides as needed. Set aside the skillet.

3. **Make the Seared Halloumi ❶:** In the skillet, heat the olive oil over medium heat. Once the oil is hot, working in batches if needed, place the slices of halloumi in the skillet and sear until golden brown, 1 to 2 minutes per side.

4. **Assemble:** Toast the bread. For each sandwich, spread a generous amount of roasted red pepper spread on both slices of the bread. On the bottom 4 halves of the sandwiches, evenly layer the cucumber and halloumi. Spoon the herb sauce on top and then finish the sandwiches with the remaining 4 slices of bread.

GLUTEN-FREE: Use gluten-free whole grain bread.

---

❶ A nonstick pan or well-seasoned cast-iron pan works best to prevent the cheese from sticking. If you need to use a different type of pan, like stainless steel, use more olive oil for frying. Halloumi cheese develops a delicious crispy crust when seared, so you don't want to lose it to the bottom of the pan!

ACTIVE TIME: 35 MINUTES • **TOTAL TIME:** 1 HOUR • **SERVES** 4

CHEESY MUSHROOM CALZONES

1 tablespoon **extra-virgin olive oil**, more for brushing

8 oz (227g) **cremini mushrooms**, sliced

2 **garlic cloves**, minced

2 cups packed stemmed and thinly sliced **lacinato kale** ❶

½ teaspoon **red pepper flakes**

Pinch of **fine sea salt**

1 cup shredded **low-moisture mozzarella cheese** (4 oz / 113g) ❷

1 cup shredded **aged cheddar cheese** (4 oz / 113g)

2 oz (57g) finely grated **Parmesan cheese** (½ cup)

¼ teaspoon freshly ground **black pepper**

1 batch **Quick Pizza Dough** (page 297) or 1 lb (454g) store-bought, room temperature ❸

1 to 1½ cups **marinara sauce**, for dipping

In a pizza-obsessed world, calzones often don't get the attention they deserve. Essentially a folded pizza, they are quite literally *stuffed full* of delicious toppings (more toppings, in fact, than a pizza could reasonably hold). Plus, the dough gets golden brown on *both* sides. As an added bonus, the filling doesn't cool as rapidly as pizza, so you don't need to stress if dinner is ready but not everyone's at the table yet. Since calzones take up less real estate in the oven, you can bake them all in one go.

---

1. **Preheat the oven:** Place an oven rack in the centre position and preheat to 425°F (220°C). Line a large baking sheet with parchment paper.

2. **Cook the mushroom and kale filling:** In a large skillet, heat the olive oil over medium heat. Scatter in the mushrooms and cook, stirring occasionally, until golden, 6 to 8 minutes. Add the garlic and cook, stirring constantly, until fragrant, 1 to 2 minutes. Add the kale, red pepper flakes, and salt. Cook, stirring frequently, until the kale is wilted, 1 to 2 minutes.

3. **Meanwhile, combine the cheeses:** In a medium bowl, combine the mozzarella, cheddar, Parmesan, and black pepper. Toss to combine.

4. **Assemble the calzones:** Fill a small bowl with room-temperature water. Cut the pizza dough into 4 equal portions. On a lightly floured work surface, using your hands or a rolling pin, stretch or roll 1 piece of dough into a 7-inch (18 cm) circle. Spoon one-quarter of the mushroom filling and cheese mixture over half of the circle, leaving a 1-inch (2.5 cm) border of exposed dough around the outer edge. Dip a finger into the bowl of water and run it around the outer edge of the dough to moisten it. Fold the dough over the filling, then crimp the edges to seal. Transfer the calzone to the prepared baking sheet. Repeat with the remaining dough, mushroom filling, and cheese.

5. **Bake the calzones:** Brush the tops of the calzones generously with olive oil. Bake until golden brown, 20 to 25 minutes.

6. **Heat the marinara sauce and serve:** When the calzones are almost done baking, heat the marinara sauce in a small saucepan over low heat. Serve the calzones hot with a small bowl of warm marinara sauce on the side for dipping.

GLUTEN-FREE: Use your favourite gluten-free pizza dough.

---

❶ Curly kale can be used instead. Kale can be replaced with 3 cups of chopped spinach.

❷ Low-moisture mozzarella, also called pizza mozzarella, comes in a block or ball. It is different from fresh mozzarella packed in water, which is also delicious, but too watery for this recipe.

❸ If the pizza dough is refrigerated, let it sit on the counter to come up to room temperature before rolling. It will be easier to stretch.

ACTIVE TIME: 15 MINUTES • **TOTAL TIME:** 25 MINUTES • **SERVES** 4

BLISTERED TOMATOES AND WHIPPED RICOTTA TOASTS

TOASTS

1 lb (454g) **cherry tomatoes** on the stem or loose

3 tablespoons **extra-virgin olive oil**, divided

1 teaspoon **fine sea salt**, divided

⅓ cup raw **walnuts**

16 oz (454g) **ricotta cheese** (1¾ cups)

2 teaspoons **lemon zest**

¼ cup **fresh lemon juice**

8 thick slices **sourdough bread**

GARNISHES

Fresh basil leaves

Extra-virgin olive oil, for drizzling

Freshly ground **black pepper**

Flaky sea salt

On the days when I really don't feel like cooking, I usually find myself putting *something* on top of toast. That said, this creamy whipped ricotta is so good, it's hard not to eat it straight off the spoon. Once combined with juicy blistered tomatoes, toasted walnuts, and fresh basil, this simple dinner instantly feels fancier than it should. This recipe can be easily halved, if needed.

1. **Preheat the oven:** Place the oven racks in the upper and lower thirds of the oven and preheat to 425°F (220°C). Line 2 large baking sheets with parchment paper.

2. **Bake the tomatoes:** Place the tomatoes on one of the prepared baking sheets and drizzle with 1 tablespoon of the olive oil. Sprinkle with ¼ teaspoon of the salt. Bake on the upper rack until the tomatoes slightly burst, 15 to 20 minutes.

3. **Meanwhile, toast the walnuts:** Scatter the walnuts on the second baking sheet. Bake on the lower rack until slightly toasted and fragrant, 2 to 4 minutes, shaking the pan halfway through. Transfer the walnuts to a cutting board to cool, then roughly chop.

4. **Whip the ricotta:** In a food processor, combine the ricotta, lemon zest, lemon juice, remaining 2 tablespoons olive oil, and remaining ¾ teaspoon salt. Purée until smooth and fluffy, scraping down the sides as needed.

5. **Assemble just before eating:** Toast the bread (either in a toaster or using the residual heat from baking the tomatoes). Spread a generous amount of whipped ricotta on each slice. Top with the cherry tomatoes, walnuts, basil, a drizzle of olive oil, pepper, and flaky salt. ⓘ

GLUTEN-FREE: Use gluten-free sourdough or whole grain bread.

ⓘ Refrigerate extra whipped ricotta in an airtight container for up to 3 days. Cherry tomatoes can be gently reheated in a nonstick skillet on the stove or cooked fresh. Toasted walnuts can be stored in an airtight container at room temperature.

ACTIVE TIME: 30 MINUTES • TOTAL TIME: 30 MINUTES • SERVES 4

FRICO-STYLE QUESADILLAS

QUESADILLAS

1 small **sweet potato** (8 oz / 227g)

1 tablespoon **grapeseed oil**

2 teaspoons **ground cumin**

1½ teaspoons **chili powder**

¼ teaspoon **fine sea salt**

3 cups medium-shredded **aged cheddar cheese** (9 oz / 255g), divided ❶

4 (8 to 10-inch / 20 to 25 cm) **flour tortillas**

1 can (14 fl oz / 398 ml) **pinto** or **black beans**, drained and rinsed

1 cup chopped **spinach**

3 **scallions**, thinly sliced

⅓ cup **Quick Pickled Red Onions** (page 289) or thinly sliced red onion ❷

⅓ cup **roasted red pepper** from a jar, thinly sliced

FOR SERVING (OPTIONAL)

Everyday Guacamole (page 298) or store-bought

Pico de gallo or other salsa

Hot sauce

Just when you thought quesadillas couldn't get better, these cheesy pockets of goodness have an extra layer of melted cheese on the *outside*. The filling is made from cumin-spiced sweet potato, beans, greens, quick pickled red onions, and roasted red pepper. Plus more cheese, of course! If you have a 12-inch (30 cm) skillet, you can speed things up by cooking two quesadillas at once: when it's time for the frico (melted cheese), just lift up the quesadilla with a flexible spatula, scatter some cheese underneath, and lower the quesadilla back on top.

1. **Preheat the oven:** Place an oven rack in the centre position and preheat to 300°F (150°C). Place a cooling rack inside a baking sheet.

2. **Cook the sweet potato filling:** Grate the skin-on sweet potato on the large holes of a box grater. In a large nonstick skillet, heat the grapeseed oil over medium heat. Scatter in the shredded sweet potato, cumin, chili powder, and salt. Cook, stirring occasionally, until the sweet potato is tender and golden brown around the edges, 8 to 10 minutes. Transfer the sweet potato to a medium bowl. Set aside the skillet.

3. **Meanwhile, organize the other fillings:** The quesadillas will be assembled directly in the skillet, so arrange 2 cups of the cheddar, tortillas, beans, spinach, scallions, pickled red onions, and roasted red peppers close by. (I like everything on a baking sheet.) Reserve the remaining 1 cup cheddar for sprinkling in step 5.

4. **Cook the quesadilla:** Place a tortilla in the skillet over medium heat. Scatter one-quarter of the fillings (sweet potatoes, cheddar, beans, spinach, scallions, pickled red onions, and roasted red peppers) over one half of the tortilla, layering the cheese throughout the fillings so that it holds everything together once melted. Fold the other half of the tortilla over the fillings. Cook until the quesadilla is golden brown on the bottom, 2 to 3 minutes. Flip the quesadilla and cook the other side until golden brown, 2 to 3 minutes.

5. **Add the frico cheese to the quesadilla:** Sprinkle ¼ cup of the reserved cheddar onto the empty side of the skillet, then flip the quesadilla onto the cheese. Cook until the cheese is melted and golden brown, about 2 minutes. Use a flexible spatula to lift the quesadilla while keeping the cheese attached. Transfer the quesadilla to the rack, cheese side up. Slide the baking sheet into the oven to keep warm while you make the remaining quesadillas.

6. **Serve:** Slice the quesadillas into wedges. Serve with guacamole, pico de gallo, and hot sauce, if using.

VEGAN: Use your favourite meltable vegan cheddar cheese. **GLUTEN-FREE:** Use gluten-free tortillas (corn, rice, or gluten-free flour blends).

❶ Grating the cheese on the medium holes on a box grater will make lighter cheese shreds, which I find easier to scatter more evenly through the quesadilla. If your box grater doesn't have medium holes, opt for the large ones.

❷ If you don't have Quick Pickled Red Onions on hand, make them first so they have time to marinate.

ACTIVE TIME: 30 MINUTES • **TOTAL TIME:** 40 MINUTES • **SERVES** 4

BALSAMIC VEGETABLE AND GOAT CHEESE SANDWICHES

GOAT CHEESE SPREAD

4 oz (113g) **soft goat cheese**

¼ cup **whole milk**

BALSAMIC MARINADE

2 tablespoons **extra-virgin olive oil**, more for brushing

2 tablespoons **balsamic vinegar**

1 **garlic clove**, finely grated

1 teaspoon **lemon zest**

1 tablespoon **fresh lemon juice**

2 teaspoons **Dijon mustard**

1 teaspoon **dried oregano**

½ teaspoon freshly ground **black pepper**

¼ teaspoon **fine sea salt**

GRILLED VEGETABLES

1 **zucchini** (12 oz / 340g), cut into ½-inch (1 cm) rounds

2 **bell peppers** (red, orange, or yellow), cut into strips 1 inch (2.5 cm) wide

1 **red onion**, cut into ⅓-inch (8 mm) rounds ❷

2 tablespoons **grapeseed oil**

½ teaspoon **fine sea salt**

¼ cup chopped **fresh flat-leaf parsley leaves**

FOR SERVING

4 **ciabatta buns**

1 cup lightly packed **arugula**

These colourful sandwiches are perfect for easy summer dinners. Once you finish grilling the veggies, they get popped into a balsamic marinade until it's time to eat. When serving a crowd, I like to make things easy (. . . on me!) by spreading the pretty veggies on a platter and letting everyone build their own sandwich. These vegetables might be even more delicious the next day, so consider doubling the batch so you can stash away extras for the week. ❶

---

1. **Make the Goat Cheese Spread:** In a small bowl, using a fork, vigorously stir together the goat cheese and milk until it is soft and spreadable.

2. **Make the Balsamic Marinade:** In a large bowl, whisk together the olive oil, balsamic vinegar, garlic, lemon zest, lemon juice, Dijon mustard, oregano, pepper, and salt.

3. **Make the Grilled Vegetables:** Prepare the grill for direct cooking or heat a large stovetop grill pan over medium-high heat. Combine the zucchini, bell peppers, and red onion in a second large bowl. Drizzle with the grapeseed oil and sprinkle with the salt. Toss to coat. Working in batches, place the vegetables on the grill and cook until fork-tender and golden brown, 2 to 4 minutes per side. Transfer the grilled vegetables to the bowl with the balsamic marinade. Toss to coat. Let the grilled vegetables marinate for 5 to 10 minutes. Stir in the parsley.

4. **Toast the buns:** Cut the buns in half horizontally and lightly brush the cut sides with the olive oil. Place them cut-side down on the grill over indirect heat. Alternatively, if using a stovetop grill pan, grill the buns over medium-low heat until warm and lightly toasted, about 2 minutes.

5. **Assemble:** Spread the goat cheese on the bun halves. Divide the grilled vegetables among the bottom halves of the buns. Arrange some arugula on top of the vegetables, then finish the sandwiches with the tops.

VEGAN: Omit the Goat Cheese Spread and use another creamy element—like toum (a Lebanese garlic sauce), vegan mayonnaise, or mashed avocado.

GLUTEN-FREE: Use gluten-free ciabatta buns or similar buns.

---

❶ Refrigerate the marinated veggies in an airtight container for up to 3 days. They can be enjoyed at room temperature, or reheat in a 425°F (220°C) oven until warmed through, 5 to 10 minutes.

❷ A larger red onion will yield larger rings, which are more likely to stay on the grates. Otherwise, if using a barbecue, use a grill basket to prevent smaller pieces of onion from falling through the grates (or use water-soaked bamboo skewers).

SOUPS

ACTIVE TIME: 20 MINUTES • **TOTAL TIME:** 45 MINUTES • **SERVES** 6

ROASTED TOMATO SOUP WITH CHEESY BREAD

SOUP

2 tablespoons **butter**

1 lb (454g) **yellow onions,** chopped (3 cups)

5 **garlic cloves**, minced

2 cans (28 fl oz / 796 ml each) **crushed fire-roasted tomatoes** ❶

2 cups **vegetable stock**

2 teaspoons **celery salt**

½ cup **whipping (35%) cream**

1 tablespoon **granulated sugar**

Fine sea salt

Freshly ground **black pepper**

CHEESY BREAD (OPTIONAL)

6 thick slices **sourdough** or **ciabatta bread**

1 to 2 tablespoons softened **butter**

6 oz (170g) shredded **sharp cheddar cheese** (1½ cups)

Chopped **fresh flat-leaf parsley leaves,** for garnish

I'll let you in on a not-so-secret secret ingredient for amazing tomato soup: celery salt. This unfussy soup comes together quickly, and the fire-roasted tomatoes provide an extra depth of flavour. The Cheesy Bread is optional, but I've yet to meet someone who turns it down. Plus, it's easy to make while the soup is simmering.

1. **Start the Soup—sauté the onions and garlic:** Melt the butter in a large Dutch oven or pot over medium heat. Add the onions and cook, stirring occasionally, until golden brown around the edges, 8 to 10 minutes. Add the garlic and cook, stirring frequently, until fragrant, 1 to 2 minutes.

2. **Add liquids and simmer:** Add the tomatoes, vegetable stock, and celery salt and stir to mix. Cover with the lid slightly ajar and bring the soup to a boil over medium-high heat. Reduce the heat to medium-low and simmer, partially covered, for 15 to 20 minutes for the flavours to meld.

3. **Meanwhile, make the Cheesy Bread, if using:** Place an oven rack in the centre position and preheat to 450°F (230°C). Arrange the bread on a large baking sheet. Lightly butter the tops of the bread and evenly sprinkle with the cheddar. Bake until the cheese is golden brown, 5 to 8 minutes. Sprinkle the bread with the parsley, then slice into 2-inch-wide (5 cm) strips.

4. **Blend and serve:** Stir the cream and sugar into the soup, then transfer to a blender, working in batches if needed. Blend until silky smooth. Season with salt and pepper to taste. Pour the soup into bowls and serve with the cheesy bread, if using.

VEGAN: Use vegan butter or extra-virgin olive oil. Instead of cream, use a plain unsweetened barista-style dairy-free milk or creamer. If making the Cheesy Bread, use your favourite meltable vegan cheddar cheese.

GLUTEN-FREE: If making the Cheesy Bread, use gluten-free bread.

❶ You can use diced fire-roasted tomatoes instead, since it'll all be blended at the end.

ACTIVE TIME: 30 MINUTES • **TOTAL TIME:** 45 MINUTES • **SERVES** 5

SILKY CAULIFLOWER SOUP WITH CHEESE AND PEPPER CRISPS

2-lb (907g) head **cauliflower**, cut into florets

3 tablespoons **extra-virgin olive oil**, divided

½ teaspoon **fine sea salt**, divided

1 **yellow onion**, finely chopped (2 cups)

2 **celery ribs**, diced

3 **garlic cloves**, minced

1 tablespoon **fresh thyme leaves**

5 cups **vegetable stock**

1 cup cubed **Yukon Gold potato** (5.3 oz / 150g)

1 **dried bay leaf**

1½ cups shredded **sharp cheddar cheese** (6 oz / 170g), divided ❶

Freshly ground **black pepper**

1 tablespoon **white wine vinegar**

Chopped **fresh chives** or flat-leaf parsley leaves, for garnish

Even if this soup is just an excuse for you to eat cheese crisps, I highly encourage you to try it. Roasting the cauliflower until it's golden brown adds much more flavour than boiling does. Stirring in some sharp cheddar cheese doesn't hurt either. The cheese crisps are best eaten fresh. Just resist the temptation to polish them off before dinner!

---

1. **Preheat the oven:** Place an oven rack in the upper third of the oven and preheat to 425°F (220°C). Line a large baking sheet with parchment paper.

2. **Roast the cauliflower:** Scatter the cauliflower on the prepared baking sheet. Drizzle with 2 tablespoons of the olive oil and toss to coat. Sprinkle with ¼ teaspoon of the salt. Roast until lightly browned around the edges, 25 to 30 minutes. (Keep the oven on.)

3. **Meanwhile, start making the soup:** In a large Dutch oven or pot, heat the remaining 1 tablespoon olive oil over medium heat. Add the onion and cook, stirring occasionally, until soft and translucent, 3 to 4 minutes. Add the celery and cook, stirring occasionally, until the celery begins to soften, about 2 minutes. Add the garlic and thyme and cook, stirring constantly, until fragrant, about 1 minute.

4. **Continue and simmer:** Add the vegetable stock, potato, bay leaf, and the remaining ¼ teaspoon salt. Cover with the lid slightly ajar and bring to a boil over medium-high heat. Reduce the heat to medium-low and simmer until the potato is fork-tender, 10 to 15 minutes.

5. **Add the roasted cauliflower and simmer:** Transfer the roasted cauliflower to the pot (set aside the baking sheet with the parchment), cover with the lid slightly ajar, and simmer for 10 minutes to let the flavours meld.

6. **Meanwhile, bake the cheese crisps:** Divide ½ cup of the cheddar into 10 small circles on the parchment-lined baking sheet, leaving at least 1 inch (2.5 cm) between them. Sprinkle generously with pepper. Bake until golden brown all over, 5 to 8 minutes. Transfer to a rack or plate lined with paper towel.

7. **Finish the soup and serve:** Discard the bay leaf. Stir in the remaining 1 cup cheddar and the white wine vinegar. Transfer the soup to a high-speed blender, working in batches if needed, and blend until silky smooth. Season with more salt, if needed. Pour the soup into bowls. Garnish with chives and serve with the cheese crisps on the side.

VEGAN: Use your favourite meltable vegan cheddar cheese or omit. If making the cheese crisps, you may need to adjust bake time based on the brand of cheese.

---

❶ White cheddar cheese will yield a paler soup (like the one pictured). Orange cheddar won't change the taste, just the look.

ACTIVE TIME: 30 MINUTES • **TOTAL TIME:** 35 MINUTES • **SERVES** 4

THAI YELLOW COCONUT CURRY WITH LENTILS

2 tablespoons **grapeseed oil**, divided

1 **yellow onion**, thinly sliced (2 cups)

4 to 6 tablespoons **Thai yellow curry paste**, divided ❶

3 **garlic cloves**, minced

12 oz (340g) **baby potatoes**, halved

1 large **carrot**, peeled and thinly sliced on the diagonal

4 cups **vegetable stock**

1 can (14 fl oz / 398 ml) **full-fat coconut milk**

1 can (14 fl oz / 398 ml) **lentils**, drained and rinsed

1 tablespoon **tamari**

1 bunch **Swiss chard**, chopped (stems thinly sliced, if using) ❷

1 tablespoon **fresh lime juice**

This fragrant broth uses Thai yellow curry paste as a shortcut to flavour. Crisp carrots, soft potatoes, creamy coconut milk, and tender lentils make this a meal-worthy soup. I love the flavour of Swiss chard in this, but you could use kale instead. And if you can't track down yellow curry, don't worry. You can use red curry and bolster it with a few pantry spices. ❶

1. **Sauté the aromatics and curry paste:** In a large Dutch oven or pot, heat 1 tablespoon of the grapeseed oil over medium heat. Add the onion and cook, stirring occasionally, until golden brown around the edges, 8 to 10 minutes. Add the remaining 1 tablespoon grapeseed oil, 4 tablespoons of the curry paste, and garlic and cook, stirring constantly, for 1 minute.

2. **Add the vegetables and stock:** Add the potatoes, carrots, and vegetable stock to the pot. Stir to scrape up the brown bits from the bottom of the pot. Cover with the lid slightly ajar and bring to a boil over medium-high heat, then reduce the heat to medium and cook until the potatoes are fork-tender, 8 to 10 minutes.

3. **Season and simmer:** Reduce the heat to medium-low. Pour in the coconut milk, lentils, and tamari. Taste and adjust seasonings (now's the time to add extra curry paste, if needed). Simmer for 5 to 10 minutes to let the flavours meld. Stir in the Swiss chard and lime juice. Once the Swiss chard just begins to wilt, ladle the soup into bowls.

❶ Curry pastes vary significantly by brand. If you are using a milder brand (like Thai Kitchen), you'll likely need to use the upper range (6 tablespoons). Taste and add extra curry paste, if needed, in the final seasoning step. If you can't find yellow curry paste, use 4 tablespoons red curry paste + 1 teaspoon curry powder + ½ teaspoon ground cumin + ½ teaspoon ground coriander. Taste and add 1 to 2 tablespoons more red curry paste, if needed.

❷ I use both the chard leaves and stems, but you can just use the tender leaves if you prefer. If using the stems, slice them much thinner than the leaves, so they soften in the soup.

WILD RICE AND MUSHROOM STEW

1¼ cups (225g) dried **wild rice** ❶

3 tablespoons **butter**, divided

1 **yellow onion**, finely chopped (2 cups)

2 **carrots**, peeled and diced

2 **celery ribs**, diced

8 oz (225g) **cremini mushrooms**, sliced

8 oz (225g) **shiitake mushrooms**, diced

3 **garlic cloves**, minced

2 tablespoons **tamari**

1 tablespoon **fresh thyme leaves** (or 1 teaspoon dried thyme)

2 teaspoons **dried rubbed sage**

7 cups **vegetable stock**

0.7 oz (20g) **dried porcini mushrooms**

¼ cup **all-purpose flour**

2 oz (57g) finely grated **Parmesan cheese** (½ cup), more for garnish

1 bunch **curly kale** (10 oz / 283g), stemmed and thinly sliced

Fine sea salt

Freshly ground **black pepper**

Warm **crusty bread**, for serving (optional)

This hearty stew goes all-in on *mushrooms*. It has fresh cremini and shiitake mushrooms as well as dried porcini. There's sage, thyme, garlic, and Parmesan in the mix too. Wild rice takes a while to cook, but soaking it in hot water while you chop the vegetables gives it a head start. Once the soup is simmering on the stove, you can just walk away and let it do its thing. I highly recommend serving with crusty bread because this soup is made for dipping.

---

1. **Soak the rice:** In small heatproof bowl, cover the rice with boiling water (the amount of water doesn't matter as long as the rice is fully submerged). Let soak while you continue making the soup, at least 20 minutes.

2. **Meanwhile, start cooking the veg:** Melt 1 tablespoon of the butter in a large Dutch oven or pot over medium heat. Add the onion and cook, stirring occasionally, until soft and translucent, 3 to 4 minutes. Add the carrots and celery and cook, stirring frequently, until they begin to soften, about 2 minutes.

3. **Add the fresh mushrooms and herbs:** Add the cremini and shiitake mushrooms and cook, stirring occasionally, until they start to brown, 7 to 8 minutes. Add the garlic, tamari, thyme, and sage and cook, stirring frequently, until fragrant, 1 to 2 minutes.

4. **Meanwhile, blend the porcini:** In a high-speed blender, combine the vegetable stock and dried porcini. Blend until the mixture is smooth, about 30 seconds.

5. **Combine and simmer:** Add the remaining 2 tablespoons butter to the vegetable mixture and stir until the butter is melted. Sprinkle in the flour and toss to coat the vegetables evenly. Pour the contents of the blender into the pot. Drain the rice and add it to the pot. Stir to scrape up the brown bits from the bottom of the pot. Cover with the lid slightly ajar and bring to a boil over medium-high heat, then reduce the heat to medium-low and simmer, stirring occasionally, until the rice is tender, 40 to 50 minutes.

6. **Finish and serve:** Stir in the Parmesan and kale. Season with salt and pepper to taste. Ladle the soup into bowls. Garnish with more Parmesan. Serve with crusty bread, if using.

VEGAN: Replace the butter with vegan butter or extra-virgin olive oil. Use vegan Parmesan cheese or omit.

GLUTEN-FREE: Replace the flour with white rice flour. Use gluten-free bread or omit.

---

❶ This recipe calls for wild rice, not a "wild rice blend" (which mixes wild rice with other types of rice). To reduce cooking time by 10 minutes, soak the rice overnight in room-temperature water. Drain then use as directed.

ACTIVE TIME: 40 MINUTES • **TOTAL TIME:** 1 HOUR • **SERVES** 6

SMOKY JALAPEÑO CORN CHOWDER

6 **sweet corn cobs** ❶

3 tablespoons **butter**, divided

1¼ teaspoons **fine sea salt**, divided

1 **red onion**, chopped (2 cups)

3 **garlic cloves**, minced

1 to 2 **jalapeño peppers**, seeded and minced

1 tablespoon **fresh thyme leaves**

1½ teaspoons **smoked sweet paprika**

½ teaspoon freshly ground **black pepper**

1 lb (454g) **baby potatoes**, halved

⅓ cup **all-purpose flour**

6 cups **vegetable stock**

½ cup **whipping (35%) cream**

Fresh cilantro leaves, for garnish ❷

In the summer, our local markets are bursting with sweet corn. This recipe makes use of that fresh corn in a soup that manages to be cozy and satisfying, yet not overly heavy. I use my favourite chef's knife for shaving the kernels from the cobs, but you can use a smaller knife if that's easier for you. Some of the best bits are hiding close to the cob, so make sure to scrape the cobs with the back of the knife to help bring that flavour to the party.

---

1. **Cook the corn:** Using a knife, strip the corn kernels from the cobs. Then run the back of the knife down the cobs to scrape off any extra bits of corn (scoop up the corn milk). Melt 1 tablespoon of the butter in a large Dutch oven or pot over medium heat. Add the corn kernels (and corn milk) and ¼ teaspoon of the salt and cook, stirring occasionally, until the corn is tender and bright yellow, 6 to 8 minutes. Transfer the corn to a medium bowl.

2. **Cook the other vegetables and spices:** In the same pot, melt the remaining 2 tablespoons butter over medium heat. Add the red onion and cook, stirring frequently, until soft and translucent, 3 to 4 minutes. Add the garlic, jalapeño, thyme, smoked paprika, black pepper, and the remaining 1 teaspoon salt and cook, stirring constantly, until fragrant, 1 to 2 minutes.

3. **Simmer the chowder:** Scatter the potatoes and flour into the pot and toss to coat evenly. Pour in the vegetable stock and stir to incorporate the flour and scrape up the brown bits from the bottom of the pot. Cover with the lid slightly ajar and bring to a boil over medium-high heat, then reduce the heat to medium-low and simmer, until the potatoes are fork-tender, 12 to 15 minutes.

4. **Add the corn and blend:** Add the corn kernels to the chowder. Stir in the cream and gently simmer, uncovered, for 5 minutes. Transfer 3 cups of the soup to a blender. Pulse 1 or 2 times, just to break down the vegetables slightly. Return the mixture to the pot and stir to mix. Season with more salt and black pepper, if needed.

5. **Serve:** Ladle the chowder into bowls. Garnish with the cilantro.

VEGAN: Use vegan butter or olive oil. Instead of whipping cream, use a plain unsweetened barista-style dairy-free milk or creamer.

GLUTEN-FREE: Replace the flour with white rice flour.

---

❶ Corn starts to lose its sweetness as soon as it's picked. Buy local and in season if you can. Frozen corn kernels are your next best bet. Since it's picked and flash-frozen at its peak, frozen corn typically has more flavour than packaged corn cobs sold out of season. Six cobs of corn yield about 6 cups of kernels.

❷ If you're not a fan of cilantro, swap it for sliced scallions instead.

ACTIVE TIME: 25 MINUTES • **TOTAL TIME:** 45 MINUTES • **SERVES** 6

MINESTRONE SOUP WITH PESTO

3 tablespoons **extra-virgin olive oil**, divided

1 **yellow onion**, finely chopped (2 cups)

3 **carrots**, peeled and diced

3 **celery ribs**, diced

5 **garlic cloves**, minced

1 tablespoon **fresh thyme leaves** (or 1 teaspoon dried thyme)

2 teaspoons **dried oregano**

¾ teaspoon **fine sea salt**

½ teaspoon freshly ground **black pepper**

1 can (28 fl oz / 796 ml) **whole peeled tomatoes**

1 can (14 fl oz / 398 ml) **diced fire-roasted tomatoes**

4 cups **vegetable stock**

⅔ cup **roasted red peppers** from a jar, diced

1 can (28 fl oz / 796 ml) **kidney beans**, drained and rinsed

1½ cups dried **elbow macaroni** (7 oz / 200g)

4 cups lightly packed **baby spinach**

6 tablespoons **Fresh Basil Pesto** (page 290), Vegan Pesto (page 290), or store-bought

Finely grated **Parmesan cheese**, for garnish

This minestrone soup is all about layering flavours, while keeping cook time down. It's brimming with veggies, beans, fresh pesto, and noodles—but not soggy ones. Most noodle soups need to be eaten immediately, before the noodles swell to oblivion. In this recipe, the noodles are cooked separately to ensure they stay *just right*. This way, your second bowl will be just as delicious as the first. ❶ If you have extra pesto kicking around, spread it on lightly toasted bread for serving.

---

1. **Cook the vegetables and spices:** In a large Dutch oven or pot, heat 2 tablespoons of the olive oil over medium heat. Add the onion and cook, stirring frequently, until soft and translucent, 3 to 4 minutes. Add the carrots and celery and cook, stirring frequently, for 2 minutes to soften slightly. Add the garlic, thyme, oregano, salt, and pepper and cook, stirring constantly, until the garlic is fragrant, 1 to 2 minutes.

2. **Mix the soup and simmer:** Using your hands, crush the whole tomatoes, with their juices, into the pot. Add the fire-roasted tomatoes, vegetable stock, roasted red peppers, and kidney beans and stir to mix. Cover with the lid slightly ajar and bring the soup to a boil over medium-high heat, then reduce the heat to medium-low and simmer, until the carrots are fork-tender, about 20 minutes.

3. **Meanwhile, cook the pasta:** Bring a medium pot of salted water to a boil over high heat. Add the noodles and cook until al dente according to the package directions. Using a colander, drain the noodles, then drizzle with the remaining 1 tablespoon olive oil. Toss the noodles in the colander until they are evenly coated. (This will prevent the noodles from sticking.)

4. **Finish the soup:** Stir in the spinach and season with more salt, if needed. Divide the pasta among bowls, then ladle the hot soup over the noodles. Give each bowl of soup a quick stir to combine. Garnish with a spoonful of pesto and the Parmesan.

VEGAN: Use vegan Parmesan cheese or omit. **GLUTEN-FREE:** Use gluten-free pasta (elbow macaroni or small shells).

---

❶ If you have leftovers, store the noodles separately from the soup. Refrigerate for up to 3 days. To reheat, warm the soup in a pot over medium heat, then add the noodles in the last 30 seconds to quickly warm them.

SPICY MISO RAMEN

MISO RAMEN

2 tablespoons **grapeseed oil**

1 **yellow onion**, thinly sliced (2 cups)

5 **garlic cloves**, minced

1 tablespoon minced **fresh ginger**

6 cups **vegetable stock**

4 large **eggs**

5 tablespoons **white miso**

2 tablespoons **toasted sesame seeds**

1 tablespoon **toasted sesame oil**

1 tablespoon **sambal oelek**

1 teaspoon **rice vinegar**

10 oz (283g) dried **ramen noodles**

TOPPINGS (OPTIONAL)

Thinly sliced **smoked tofu**

Watercress or baby spinach

Thinly sliced **scallions**

Toasted sesame seeds

Red pepper flakes

When I make this soup for others, they're always surprised by how much flavour a homemade vegetarian ramen can have. The broth in some traditional ramen styles has a creamy, almost silky quality. Here, we cheat it with veggies. The onion, garlic, and ginger get blended with vegetable stock, miso paste, and toasted sesame seeds until smooth. The result is a creamy, salty, slightly spicy broth that's good to the last drop. Ramen noodles are best served immediately, so hold off cooking them until the end.

1. **Start the Miso Ramen:** In a large Dutch oven or pot, heat the grapeseed oil over medium heat. Add the onion and cook, stirring occasionally, until golden brown around the edges, 8 to 10 minutes. Add the garlic and ginger and cook, stirring constantly, until fragrant, 1 to 2 minutes. Pour in the vegetable stock. Cover with the lid slightly ajar and bring to a boil over medium-high heat, then reduce the heat to medium-low and simmer for 15 to 20 minutes to let the flavours infuse.

2. **Meanwhile, boil the eggs and set aside toppings:** Bring a medium saucepan of water to a boil over medium-high heat. Gently lower the eggs into the water. Adjust the heat, if needed, to maintain a gentle boil and cook the eggs for 6½ minutes (adjust timing based on your desired doneness; see page 21). Fill a small bowl with ice water and gently lower the eggs into the bowl to cool. Peel the eggs and set aside other toppings.

3. **Blend and season the soup:** Working in batches if needed, transfer the soup to a high-speed blender. Add the miso, sesame seeds, sesame oil, sambal oelek, and rice vinegar. Blend until smooth and creamy, 1 to 2 minutes. Pour the soup back into the pot, cover with the lid, and keep warm over low heat until ready to serve. ❶

4. **Cook the ramen noodles:** Bring a large pot of unsalted water to a boil over high heat. Add the noodles and cook according to the package directions. (Be careful not to overcook.) Drain the noodles.

5. **Assemble:** Divide the noodles among bowls, then ladle the soup overtop. Cut the eggs in half lengthwise. Garnish each bowl with 2 egg halves and toppings of choice.

VEGAN: Omit the eggs. **GLUTEN-FREE:** Use gluten-free ramen noodles.

❶ The soup can be made ahead to this point. Refrigerate, without the noodles and toppings, in an airtight container for up to 3 days. Cook the noodles fresh when you need them.

ACTIVE TIME: 25 MINUTES • **TOTAL TIME:** 1 HOUR • **SERVES** 6 TO 8

EASY VEGGIE CHILI

CHILI

1 **sweet onion**, quartered (10 oz / 283g)

2 **carrots**, peeled and roughly chopped

2 **celery ribs**, roughly chopped

2 tablespoons **extra-virgin olive oil**, divided

1 **sweet potato**, diced (2 cups)

4 **garlic cloves**, minced

2 tablespoons **tomato paste**

1 tablespoon **ground cumin**

2 teaspoons **ground coriander**

¾ teaspoon **smoked sweet paprika**

2 cans (28 fl oz / 796 ml each) **diced fire-roasted tomatoes**

1 can (19 fl oz / 540 ml) **lentils**, drained and rinsed

1 can (14 fl oz / 398 ml) **kidney beans**, drained and rinsed

⅔ cup **roasted red peppers** from a jar, diced

1 cup **vegetable stock**

3 tablespoons **tamari**

1 canned **chipotle pepper** in adobo, minced + 1 tablespoon **adobo sauce**

TOPPINGS (OPTIONAL)

Pitted, peeled, and chopped **avocado**

Diced **red onion**

Sour cream or plain **Greek yogurt**

Shredded **sharp cheddar cheese**

Chopped **fresh cilantro leaves**

I love to make this comforting chili during the winter months. Chipotle peppers in adobo sauce, fire-roasted tomatoes, and smoked paprika bring a lot of flavour with little effort. The food processor makes quick work of mincing, but you can do this first step by hand if you don't have one. This chili is perfect for making ahead—I usually keep some stashed away in the freezer. ❶ When it comes to toppings, more is better. It's fun to set out small bowls of toppings and let everyone garnish their own bowl.

1. **Start the Chili—mince the onion, carrots, and celery:** In a food processor, pulse the onion until finely minced. Transfer to a medium bowl. Add the carrots and celery to the food processor and pulse until finely minced—keep them in the food processor for now. (Alternatively, mince with a knife.)

2. **Cook the vegetables:** In a large Dutch oven or pot, heat 1 tablespoon of the olive oil over medium heat. Add the onion and cook, stirring frequently, until soft and translucent, 3 to 4 minutes. Add the carrots, celery, and sweet potato and cook, stirring occasionally, until the vegetables begin to soften, 6 to 8 minutes.

3. **Add the spices:** Add the remaining 1 tablespoon olive oil, garlic, tomato paste, cumin, coriander, and smoked paprika. Cook, stirring constantly, until fragrant, 1 to 2 minutes.

4. **Continue and simmer:** Add the tomatoes, lentils, kidney beans, roasted red peppers, vegetable stock, tamari, and chipotle pepper and adobo sauce. Stir to mix. Cover with a lid and simmer over medium-low heat, stirring occasionally, until the sweet potato is fork-tender, about 25 minutes. Remove the lid and simmer to thicken slightly, 5 to 10 minutes.

5. **Serve:** Ladle the chili into bowls. Garnish with toppings of your choice.

VEGAN: The chili itself is vegan, so just stick to vegan toppings and you're good to go.

❶ This recipe makes a lot of chili. Refrigerate leftovers in an airtight container for up to 3 days or freeze in freezer bags or freezer-safe containers for up to 3 months. If frozen, defrost in the fridge overnight and reheat on the stove.

ACTIVE TIME: 45 MINUTES • **TOTAL TIME:** 1 HOUR • **SERVES** 4

ROASTED BUTTERNUT SQUASH SOUP WITH BUTTERY SAGE CROUTONS

SOUP

5 cups **butternut squash** cut into ½-inch (1 cm) cubes ❶

1 **yellow onion**, chopped (2 cups)

1 **Granny Smith apple**, chopped ❷

2 tablespoons + 1 teaspoon **grapeseed oil**, divided

1 tablespoon **fresh thyme leaves**

1½ teaspoons minced **fresh sage leaves**

½ teaspoon **fine sea salt**

5 **unpeeled garlic cloves**

4 cups **vegetable stock**

1 can (14 fl oz / 398 ml) **cannellini beans**, drained and rinsed

1 tablespoon **tamari**

Freshly ground **black pepper**

CROUTONS

1½ cups torn **sourdough bread**

3 tablespoons **butter**

12 **fresh sage leaves**

Fine sea salt

This cozy soup practically cooks itself in the oven, which frees you up to make some delicious buttery croutons that are by no means run-of-the-mill. They're made from sourdough bread tossed in a sage-infused brown butter. Many high-speed blenders are capable of warming soup, so you can skip the step of warming the soup on the stovetop if your blender does this.

1. **Preheat the oven:** Place the oven racks in the upper and lower thirds of the oven and preheat to 450°F (230°C). Set aside 2 large baking sheets.

2. **Start the Soup—roast the veg:** Divide the butternut squash, onion, and apple between the 2 baking sheets. Drizzle each baking sheet with 1 tablespoon of grapeseed oil, then toss to coat. Evenly sprinkle with the thyme, sage, and salt. Place the garlic cloves on a small piece of foil and drizzle with the remaining 1 teaspoon grapeseed oil. Wrap the foil around the garlic and place it on one of the baking sheets. Roast until the butternut squash is fork-tender and brown around the edges, 30 to 35 minutes, swapping top and bottom positions halfway through.

3. **Meanwhile, start the Croutons—toast the bread:** Scatter the bread in a large dry skillet ❸ over medium heat. Toast, shaking the pan occasionally, until the bread is crisp on the outside, 6 to 8 minutes. Transfer the bread to a small bowl.

4. **Fry the sage:** Melt the butter in the same skillet over medium heat. Lay the sage leaves in a single layer and fry until they begin to crisp up, about 1 minute. Using a slotted spoon or fork, transfer the sage to a plate lined with paper towel to absorb excess oil. Sprinkle the sage with a pinch of salt.

5. **Brown the butter:** Continue to cook the butter over medium heat, swirling the pan frequently, until the butter is golden brown, 1 to 2 minutes. Scatter in the toasted bread, toss to coat, and cook, stirring frequently, until golden brown around the edges, 3 to 5 minutes. Remove from the heat.

6. **Finish the soup:** Working in batches if needed, transfer the roasted butternut squash, onion, and apple to a high-speed blender, making sure to scrape up the brown bits from the bottom of the baking sheets. Unwrap the garlic and squeeze the cloves out of their skin and into the blender. Add the vegetable stock, cannellini beans, and tamari. Blend until completely smooth. Transfer the soup to a pot and warm over low heat. (Or if your high-speed blender has a soup setting, heat the soup directly in the blender.) Season with salt and pepper to taste. Pour the soup into bowls and garnish with the sage leaves and croutons.

VEGAN: Use a vegan butter or skip the croutons. Depending on the brand, the butter may not brown, but it'll still taste delicious. I've had luck getting Miyoko's brand to brown.

GLUTEN-FREE: Use gluten-free sourdough or baguette or skip the croutons.

❶ About a 1¾- to 2-lb (794 to 907g) squash before trimming and peeling.

❷ Or another tart apple. I usually don't bother peeling the apple here, but you can if you prefer to.

❸ A light-coloured skillet will make it easier to see when the butter is browning.

ACTIVE TIME: 30 MINUTES • **TOTAL TIME:** 30 MINUTES • **SERVES** 4

SESAME AND SMOKED TOFU NOODLE SOUP

2 tablespoons **grapeseed oil**, divided

4 oz (113g) **shiitake mushrooms**, sliced (2 cups)

1 **carrot**, peeled and cut into matchsticks

1 teaspoon minced **fresh ginger**

3 **garlic cloves**, minced

3 cups chopped **baby bok choy**

2 tablespoons **tamari**

1 tablespoon + 1 teaspoon **toasted sesame oil**, divided, more for serving

1 teaspoon **sambal oelek**, more for serving (optional)

8 oz (225g) **smoked tofu**, cubed

6 cups **vegetable stock** ❶

1¾ cups dried **small shell pasta** (6 oz / 170g)

1 tablespoon **white miso**

1½ cups shredded **savoy cabbage**

2 **scallions**, thinly sliced

1 **lime**, cut into wedges

Whenever I had a cold as a kid, my mom would make her version of a chicken noodle soup. It always had a spoonful of miso paste stirred into it. And for some reason she always called it "macaroni soup," regardless what noodle went into it (usually shells). This light, nourishing soup is bolstered with ginger, garlic, and of course miso. The toppings are a vegetarian take on what I grew up with—but are delicious in their own right. Thankfully, Mom approves.

---

1. **Cook the veg:** In a large Dutch oven or pot, heat 1 tablespoon of the grapeseed oil over medium heat. Add the mushrooms and cook, stirring occasionally, until softened and golden at the edges, about 3 minutes. Add the remaining 1 tablespoon of grapeseed oil, the carrot, ginger, and garlic and cook, stirring constantly, for 1 minute. Add the bok choy and cook until bright green and tender, about 1 minute. Pour in the tamari, 1 tablespoon of the sesame oil, and the sambal oelek (if using) and toss to coat. Stir in the smoked tofu. Transfer the mixture to a medium bowl.

2. **Bring the broth to a boil:** Pour the vegetable stock into the pot. Cover with the lid slightly ajar and bring to a simmer over medium-high heat, then reduce the heat to low and keep warm until ready to serve.

3. **Meanwhile, cook the pasta:** Bring a medium pot of salted water to a boil over high heat. Add the pasta and cook until al dente according to the package directions. Using a colander, drain the pasta, then drizzle with the remaining 1 teaspoon sesame oil. Toss the pasta in the colander until evenly coated.

4. **Season the broth:** Whisk the miso into the soup until dissolved. Season with more tamari, if needed.

5. **Assemble:** Divide the pasta among bowls and top with the vegetable-tofu mixture and cabbage. Ladle the hot soup overtop. Garnish with the scallions and a squeeze of lime. Serve with extra lime wedges, sesame oil, and sambal oelek (if using) on the side.

GLUTEN-FREE: Use gluten-free small shells or elbow macaroni.

---

❶ The taste of the vegetable stock makes a big impact in this recipe. I recommend Better Than Bouillon Vegetable Base (page 25).

POTATO AND LENTIL STEW WITH CRISPY SHALLOTS

1 large **shallot**, thinly sliced into rounds (½ cup)

¼ cup **extra-virgin olive oil**

¾ teaspoon + pinch of **fine sea salt**, divided

1 **yellow onion**, finely chopped (2 cups)

2 **carrots**, peeled and diced

2 **celery ribs**, diced

1 tablespoon **tomato paste**

3 **garlic cloves**, minced

2 tablespoons **nutritional yeast**

1 tablespoon **fresh thyme leaves**, more for garnish

5 cups **vegetable stock**

1 lb (454g) **Yukon gold potatoes**, diced (3 cups)

¾ cup dried **brown lentils**, picked over, rinsed, and drained

1 tablespoon **fresh lemon juice**

Plain **Greek yogurt**, for garnish (optional)

This hearty soup is anything but boring. Fried shallots make for a tasty garnish—and they also steep extra flavour into the olive oil used for cooking. Warming the shallots and the olive oil together will help the shallots fry more evenly. Budget-friendly, easy to find, and fairly fast-cooking, dried brown lentils pair perfectly with potatoes in this tasty stew. Blending some of the soup at the end helps to thicken it. I transfer the soup to a blender container, but if you have an immersion blender, you can blend directly in the pot.

---

1. Fry the shallots: In a large Dutch oven or pot, combine the shallots and olive oil over medium heat. Cook the shallots, stirring occasionally, until crispy and golden brown, 8 to 10 minutes. Some pieces may cook faster than other, so using tongs, scoop out fried pieces as they finish and transfer to a plate. Sprinkle the hot shallots with a pinch of salt and set aside.

2. Start the soup: To the same pot, with the hot oil, add the onion and cook over medium heat, stirring occasionally, until soft and translucent, 3 to 4 minutes. Add the carrots, celery, tomato paste, and ¼ teaspoon of the salt and cook, stirring occasionally, until the vegetables begin to soften, about 3 minutes. Add the garlic, nutritional yeast, and thyme and cook, stirring constantly, until fragrant, 1 to 2 minutes.

3. Continue and simmer: Pour in the vegetable stock and stir to scrape up the brown bits from the bottom of the pot. Add the potatoes and lentils, cover with the lid slightly ajar, and bring to a boil over medium-high heat. Reduce the heat to medium-low and simmer until the potatoes and lentils are tender, 25 to 35 minutes.

4. Season and blend: Add the lemon juice and the remaining ½ teaspoon salt and stir to mix. Transfer 3 cups of the soup to a blender and pulse until almost smooth. Pour the blended mixture back into the pot and stir to mix. Season with more salt, if needed.

5. Serve: Ladle the soup into bowls. Top each bowl with a spoonful of the yogurt, if using. Sprinkle with the fried shallots and more thyme.

VEGAN: Replace the yogurt with vegan sour cream or omit.

ACTIVE TIME: 30 MINUTES • **TOTAL TIME:** 40 MINUTES • **SERVES** 6

NO CREAM OF BROCCOLI SOUP WITH GARLICKY BREADCRUMBS

GARLICKY BREADCRUMBS

1 tablespoon **extra-virgin olive oil**

1 **garlic clove**, minced

6 tablespoons **panko breadcrumbs**

1 teaspoon **lemon zest**

Fine sea salt

SOUP

1¼ lb (567g) **broccoli**

1 tablespoon **extra-virgin olive oil**

2 **leeks**, chopped (white, light, and dark green parts; 7 cups)

1 cup diced **Yukon Gold potato** (5.3 oz / 150g)

3 **garlic cloves**, minced

¾ teaspoon **fine sea salt**

¾ cup raw **cashews** ❷

6 cups **vegetable stock**

1 tablespoon **fresh lemon juice**

Crusty bread, for serving (optional)

This silky soup is undetectably dairy-free. It's also as zero-waste as you can get. Keep the potato skin on, use the broccoli florets *and* the stalks, and don't toss the dark green parts of the leek. You'll use it all! The hint of lemon really brightens this dish. ❶ Serve the garlicky lemon breadcrumbs on the side—and generously sprinkle them over the soup before digging in.

1. **Make the Garlicky Breadcrumbs:** In a large Dutch oven or pot, heat the olive oil over medium heat. Add the garlic and cook, stirring constantly, until fragrant, 1 to 2 minutes. Scatter in the panko and cook, stirring frequently, until golden brown, 3 to 5 minutes. Transfer the panko mixture to a small bowl. Stir in the lemon zest and salt to taste. Wipe out the pot and set aside.

2. **Start the Soup—prep the broccoli:** Separate the broccoli florets from the stalks. Roughly chop the florets and transfer to a medium bowl. Trim the end of the stalks, then roughly chop the stalks and transfer to a separate medium bowl. (The stalks take longer to cook than the florets, so they will be added separately.)

3. **Sauté the vegetables:** In the pot, heat the olive oil over medium heat. Add the leeks and potato and cook, stirring occasionally, until the leeks are bright green, 4 to 5 minutes. Add the broccoli stalks, garlic, and salt and cook, stirring frequently, until the broccoli is bright green, 2 to 3 minutes.

4. **Simmer the soup:** Add the cashews and vegetable stock. Cover with the lid slightly ajar and bring to a boil over medium-high heat, then reduce the heat to medium-low and simmer until the potatoes are fork-tender and the cashews are soft enough to squeeze between your fingers, about 10 minutes. Add the broccoli florets and simmer until bright green and fork-tender, 2 to 3 minutes. Stir in the lemon juice.

5. **Blend and serve:** Working in batches if needed, transfer the soup to a high-speed blender and blend until completely smooth. Season with more salt, if needed. Pour the soup into bowls and top with the breadcrumbs. Serve with crusty bread, if using.

GLUTEN-FREE: Use gluten-free panko breadcrumbs. Use gluten-free bread or omit.

❶ This recipe uses the whole lemon: zest it first (for the breadcrumbs), then proceed to squeeze the juice (for the soup). One lemon should be sufficient for both.

❷ If you don't have a high-speed blender, quick-soak the cashews at the start of this recipe. Place the cashews in a small heatproof bowl, cover with boiling water, and soak for 20 to 30 minutes, until soft, while you prep the soup. Drain, then use as directed.

SMOKY RED LENTIL SOUP

3 tablespoons **extra-virgin olive oil**, divided

1 **yellow onion**, finely chopped (2 cups)

2 **carrots**, peeled and diced

1 large **russet potato** (10 oz / 283g), peeled and cut into ½-inch (1 cm) cubes (2 cups)

4 **garlic cloves**, minced

2 tablespoons **smoked sweet paprika**, more for garnish

1 tablespoon **ground cumin**

2 teaspoons **ground coriander**

¼ teaspoon **red pepper flakes**

6 cups **vegetable stock**

1¼ cups dried **red lentils**, picked over, rinsed, and drained

⅔ cup **roasted red peppers** from a jar, diced

1 can (28 fl oz / 796 ml) **crushed** or **diced fire-roasted tomatoes** ❶

1 teaspoon **fine sea salt**

GARNISHES (OPTIONAL)

Plain **Greek yogurt**

Fresh cilantro leaves

This soup is perfect for those nights when I'm digging through the pantry to avoid a trip to the grocery store. Smoked paprika, fire-roasted tomatoes, and jarred roasted red peppers come together to create a subtle smoky flavour. It's a delicious combination that requires very little effort. Red lentils are known for their quick cooking time, but when cooked with acidic foods, they take longer to cook. This recipe cooks the lentils most of the way, then adds the tomatoes for a quick final simmer. This method allows the lentils to cook in the shortest amount of time.

---

1. **Cook the veg:** In a large Dutch oven or pot, heat 2 tablespoons of the olive oil over medium heat. Add the onion and cook, stirring occasionally, until soft and translucent, 3 to 4 minutes. Add the carrots and potato and cook, stirring occasionally, until the carrots are golden brown around the edges, 6 to 8 minutes.

2. **Add the garlic and spices:** Add the remaining 1 tablespoon olive oil, garlic, smoked paprika, cumin, coriander, and red pepper flakes. Cook, stirring constantly, until fragrant, 1 to 2 minutes.

3. **Combine and simmer:** Add the vegetable stock, red lentils, and roasted red peppers. Stir to combine. Cover with the lid slightly ajar and bring to a boil over medium-high heat. Reduce the heat to medium-low and simmer until the lentils are fully cooked and the potatoes are soft, about 15 minutes. Add the crushed tomatoes and salt, then bring to a simmer, uncovered, over medium heat and cook for 5 minutes. Season with more salt, if needed.

4. **Serve:** Ladle the soup into bowls. Garnish with the yogurt (if using), smoked paprika, and cilantro, if using.

VEGAN: Replace the Greek yogurt with vegan sour cream or omit.

---

❶ Fire-roasted tomatoes add a subtle smoky flavour. If you can't find fire-roasted tomatoes, use a can of whole peeled tomatoes and crush them with your hand as you add them and their juices to the pot.

VEGGIE WONTON SOUP

SOUP BROTH

3 quarts **vegetable stock**

3 **garlic cloves**, thinly sliced

2-inch (5 cm) piece of **fresh ginger**, quartered

Fine sea salt

White pepper

WONTONS

16 oz (454g) **wonton wrappers**

0.25 oz (7g) **dried porcini mushrooms** ❷

2 tablespoons **grapeseed oil**

7 oz (200g) **shiitake mushrooms**, minced (2⅔ cups)

1 cup crumbled **firm** or **medium-firm tofu**

3 **garlic cloves**, finely grated

2 teaspoons finely grated **fresh ginger**

3 tablespoons **tamari**

1 tablespoon **toasted sesame oil**

2 teaspoons **rice vinegar**

¼ teaspoon **fine sea salt**

4 **scallions**, thinly sliced

GARNISHES

2½ cups chopped **savoy** or **napa cabbage**

6 oz (170g) **snap peas**, thinly sliced

1 **carrot**, peeled and cut into matchsticks

Thinly sliced **scallions**

Toasted sesame oil

Growing up, everyone pitched in to make wontons. It's always a good time catching up with family while everyone works at the kitchen table. And there's nothing more rewarding than filling your belly with steaming hot wontons when you're done! I recommend tackling this recipe on a weekend, when you're not rushed for time. If you have helpers, double the batch. That way, you're guaranteed to have leftovers for the freezer (depending how hungry those helpers are!). The wontons freeze well and cook in minutes, making quick and easy dinners throughout the week. ❶

---

1. **Make the Soup Broth:** In a large Dutch oven or pot, combine the vegetable stock, garlic, and ginger. Cover with the lid slightly ajar and bring to a boil over medium-high heat. Once boiling, reduce the heat to low and simmer, covered, for at least 30 minutes.

2. **Start the Wontons—prep your station:** Set the unopened package of wonton wrappers on the counter to come up to room temperature. Fill a small bowl with cold water (for dipping your fingers). Set aside a damp kitchen towel (for covering the wonton package). Line a large baking sheet with parchment paper.

3. **Blend the dried porcini:** In a high-speed blender, grind the dried porcini mushrooms into a fine powder. Keep the lid on and let the powder settle.

4. **Cook the shiitake and tofu:** In a large nonstick or cast-iron skillet, heat the grapeseed oil over medium heat. Add the shiitake mushrooms and cook, stirring occasionally, until golden brown, 6 to 8 minutes. Add the tofu and, using a flexible spatula, break it up into smaller pieces. Cook, stirring frequently, until the tofu releases its moisture and begins to brown, 4 to 6 minutes.

5. **Mix the wonton filling:** Transfer the mushroom-tofu mixture to a large bowl. Add the garlic and ginger and stir well to mix. Add the porcini powder, tamari, sesame oil, rice vinegar, and salt. Stir well to mix, then fold in the scallions.

CONTINUED ON NEXT PAGE

VEGAN: Use vegan wonton wrappers.

---

❶ Wontons can be made in advance and frozen. To freeze wontons, cover the baking sheet of wontons with plastic wrap and transfer it to the freezer. Once the wontons are firm to the touch, transfer them to freezer bags or airtight containers and freeze for up to 3 months. (This method will ensure the wontons don't stick together.) Cook as directed.

❷ Dried porcini mushrooms provide an extra boost of deep, "meaty" flavour to these wontons. If you can't find them, use 0.5 ounce (14g) dried shiitake mushrooms instead. Dried shiitake has a milder flavour than porcini, which is why you need to use more.

CONTINUED FROM PREVIOUS PAGE

6. **Wrap the wontons (page 231):** Take a few wonton wrappers out of the package and drape the damp kitchen towel over the package to prevent the remaining wrappers from drying out. Dip your finger in the water and run it along all 4 edges of a wonton wrapper. Spoon about 1 teaspoon of the filling into the centre of the wrapper. Fold the wrapper in half on the diagonal to form a triangle. Press down around the filling to push out any air, then firmly squeeze or press the edges together. You can leave the wontons as triangles or go one step further by rolling, bringing the two bottom corners together, wetting the ends to moisten, then pinching to seal (see opposite page). Place the folded wonton on the prepared baking sheet. Repeat until all the wontons are made.

7. **Cook the wontons:** Season the soup with salt and white pepper to taste. Discard the ginger. Increase the heat to medium-high and bring the soup to a gentle boil. Drop the cabbage into the soup and cook until softened and bright green, 1 to 2 minutes. Scoop the cabbage into individual bowls. Working in batches so you don't overcrowd the pot, drop the wontons into the soup and cook until they are supple and float to the surface, 3 to 4 minutes. Ladle the wontons and soup into the bowls. Garnish with snap peas, carrot, scallions, and a drizzle of sesame oil.

SALADS

ACTIVE TIME: 25 MINUTES • **TOTAL TIME:** 25 MINUTES • **SERVES** 3

SANTA FE SALAD WITH CHIPOTLE LIME VINAIGRETTE

VINAIGRETTE

¼ cup **extra-virgin olive oil**

Zest of 1 **lime**

¼ cup **fresh lime juice**

1 canned **chipotle pepper** in adobo, minced + 1 tablespoon **adobo sauce**

1 tablespoon **honey**

¼ teaspoon **salt**

1 large **shallot**, thinly sliced (½ cup)

SALAD

1 tablespoon **grapeseed oil**

1½ cups **frozen corn kernels** ❶

¼ teaspoon **fine sea salt**

2 **garlic cloves**, grated

1 head **romaine lettuce**, torn into bite-size pieces

1 can (14 fl oz / 398 ml) **black beans**, drained and rinsed

1 **red bell pepper**, diced

1 cup thinly sliced **English cucumber**

3 **Medjool dates**, pitted and minced

1 **avocado**, peeled, pitted, and chopped

½ cup crumbled **feta cheese**

⅓ cup chopped **fresh cilantro leaves**

This colourful salad packs a punch of flavour. It has creamy avocado, sautéed corn, crisp veggies, protein-rich black beans, and tangy feta cheese. The zippy chipotle lime vinaigrette does double duty by pickling the shallots while you assemble the salad. And the dates bring an unexpected, but delicious, hint of something sweet.

1. **Make the Vinaigrette:** In a small bowl, combine the olive oil, lime zest, lime juice, chipotle pepper and adobo sauce, honey, and salt. Whisk until blended. Submerge the shallots in the vinaigrette to soften.

2. **Start the Salad—sauté the corn:** In a large skillet, heat the grapeseed oil over medium-high heat. Add the corn and salt and sauté, stirring occasionally, until golden brown around the edges, 4 to 6 minutes. Remove from the heat. Add the garlic and stir constantly, letting the residual heat warm the garlic until golden and fragrant, about 1 minute.

3. **Assemble:** In a large bowl, toss the lettuce with just enough vinaigrette to lightly coat. Transfer the dressed lettuce to a large serving platter. Top with the sautéed corn, black beans, bell pepper, cucumber, and dates. (Or combine these ingredients in the large bowl and toss.) Scatter the shallots over the toppings and drizzle with the rest of the vinaigrette. Garnish with the avocado, feta, and cilantro. Gently toss before serving.

VEGAN: Use a vegan feta or omit. Replace the honey with maple syrup.

❶ You can replace frozen corn with the kernels cut from 2 sweet corn cobs, when corn is in season.

ACTIVE TIME: 35 MINUTES • **TOTAL TIME:** 35 MINUTES • **SERVES** 4

CRISPY RICE SALAD WITH SMASHED CUCUMBERS

SPICY PICKLED RADISHES

⅓ cup **boiling water**

1 tablespoon **granulated sugar**

¼ teaspoon **fine sea salt**

⅓ cup **rice vinegar**

4 **radishes**, thinly sliced

2 **fresh red bird's eye chilies**, thinly sliced

RICE SALAD

4 cups **cooked jasmine rice** (page 302)

4 tablespoons **grapeseed oil**, divided

½ teaspoon **fine sea salt**

3 **mini cucumbers**

4 cups chopped **baby bok choy** ❶

2 tablespoons **tamari**

2 tablespoons **fresh lime juice**

⅓ cup lightly packed **Thai basil leaves** ❷

⅓ cup lightly packed **fresh cilantro leaves**

8 oz (225g) **smoked tofu**, cubed (optional)

½ cup **dry-roasted peanuts**

Lime wedges

Crispy rice is magical. Some people might get disappointed if the rice sticks to the bottom of the pot—but *that's* the good stuff. This recipe takes a slightly different route to maximize crispiness by using a nonstick pan to cook both sides of the rice until golden brown. It's then tossed with smashed cucumbers, fresh herbs, and a tangy lime dressing. Pickling the radishes with chili peppers makes them slightly spicy. If you want more heat, sprinkle some of the chilies onto your plate—or drizzle on some of the spicy pickling brine.

1. **Make the Spicy Pickled Radishes:** In a small heatproof bowl, whisk together the boiling water, sugar, and salt until the sugar and salt are dissolved. Stir in the rice vinegar, radishes, and chilies. Let sit for at least 10 minutes.

2. **Make the Rice Salad—crisp the rice:** In a large bowl, toss the rice, 1 tablespoon of the grapeseed oil, and salt to mix. In a large nonstick skillet, heat 2 tablespoons of the grapeseed oil over medium heat. Once the oil is hot, drop a couple of grains of rice into it. If it sizzles, it's good to go; if it doesn't, heat the oil longer. Scatter the rice into the pan (set aside the bowl) and cook, undisturbed, until golden brown on the bottom, 6 to 8 minutes. Using a flexible spatula, flip the rice in sections and cook, undisturbed, until the other side is golden brown, about 6 minutes. Remove from the heat.

3. **Meanwhile, smash the cucumbers:** Trim the ends off the cucumbers. Place the flat side of your knife over each cucumber and press down with the palm of your hand until the cucumber breaks open. Tear the cucumbers into bite-size pieces and transfer to the large bowl (no need to wipe it clean). Add the bok choy.

4. **Make the dressing:** Pour ⅓ cup of the pickling brine into a small bowl, using a fork to hold back the radishes and chilies. Stir in the tamari, lime juice, and the remaining 1 tablespoon grapeseed oil.

5. **Combine and serve:** Transfer the crispy rice to a large serving platter. Drizzle 2 tablespoons of the dressing over the cucumbers and bok choy, toss to coat, and scatter over the rice. Scoop the radish out of the pickling brine and scatter them over the dish. Top with the Thai basil, cilantro, smoked tofu (if using), and peanuts. Serve with lime wedges and a small bowl of the pickling brine and chilies for drizzling (if you like things spicy).

❶ Opt for Shanghai bok choy (pale green stalks) instead of regular bok choy (white stalks) if you have the choice. Either variety will work, but the Shanghai variety tends to have a milder, sweeter taste.

❷ Thai basil has purple stems and is not the same as sweet Italian basil. It can be found at well-stocked grocery stores and Asian grocery stores. If you can't find Thai basil, double up on cilantro.

ACTIVE TIME: 25 MINUTES • **TOTAL TIME:** 25 MINUTES • **SERVES** 2

CHICKPEA SALAD WITH CRISPY PITA

- 1 **pita**, torn into bite-size pieces
- 3 tablespoons **extra-virgin olive oil**, divided
- 3 teaspoons **za'atar**, divided
- ½ teaspoon + a pinch of **fine sea salt**, divided
- 1 large **shallot**, minced (½ cup)
- 3 **garlic cloves**, minced
- 1 can (14 fl oz / 398 ml) **chickpeas**, drained and rinsed
- ¼ teaspoon **red pepper flakes**
- 2 cups packed stemmed and thinly sliced **lacinato kale**
- ¼ cup **dried cranberries**
- 3 tablespoons **fresh lemon juice**
- ¼ cup loosely packed **fresh mint**, chopped
- 1 cup plain **Greek yogurt**
- ½ **English cucumber**, chopped
- 1 **watermelon radish** (or 2 or 3 red radishes), thinly sliced

This pretty chickpea salad comes together in a flash. Chickpeas are cooked with shallots, garlic, and lemony kale, then spooned over a bed of creamy yogurt. Crisp fresh veggies and toasted pita top it all off. Za'atar is one of the stars of the show here—it's a delicious spice blend of dried oregano, thyme, toasted sesame seeds, and other spices that adds a herby, nutty vibe to the whole meal. You can buy za'atar at your local grocery store, Middle Eastern grocery store, or if you're feeling adventurous, mix your own!

---

1. Toast the pita: Scatter the pita in a large dry skillet over medium heat and cook, stirring occasionally, until dried, 5 to 8 minutes. Drizzle in 1 tablespoon of the olive oil and toss to coat. Sprinkle with 1 teaspoon of the za'atar and a pinch of the salt and toss to coat. Cook, stirring frequently, until the spices are fragrant and the pita is crispy around the edges, 1 to 2 minutes. Transfer to a plate to cool.

2. Cook the rest: In the same skillet, heat the remaining 2 tablespoons olive oil over medium heat. Scatter in the shallot and cook, stirring frequently, until golden brown around the edges, about 2 minutes. Add the garlic, chickpeas, red pepper flakes, the remaining ½ teaspoon salt, and the remaining 2 teaspoons za'atar and cook, stirring frequently, until the chickpeas are hot, 3 to 4 minutes. Stir in the kale, cranberries, and lemon juice. Immediately remove the skillet from the heat and stir in the mint.

3. Assemble: Divide the chickpea and kale mixture among plates, along with the yogurt, cucumber, radishes, and toasted pita. Garnish the yogurt with extra olive oil and za'atar, if desired.

VEGAN: Replace the Greek yogurt with Vegan Tzatziki (page 293) or hummus. **GLUTEN-FREE:** Use gluten-free pita.

ACTIVE TIME: 40 MINUTES • **TOTAL TIME:** 40 MINUTES • **SERVES** 5

BROCCOLI SALAD WITH STICKY HARISSA SAUCE

6 **Medjool dates**, pitted and chopped

¼ cup **boiling water**

1 can (14 fl oz / 398 ml) **chickpeas**, drained, rinsed, and patted dry

8 tablespoons **extra-virgin olive oil**, divided

1 teaspoon **fine sea salt**, divided

2 lb (907g) **broccoli**

4 **garlic cloves**, thinly sliced

1 teaspoon **ground cumin**

1 teaspoon **ground coriander**

2 to 3 tablespoons **rose harissa paste** ❶

3 tablespoons **red wine vinegar**

¾ cup **unsalted roasted almonds**, roughly chopped

¾ cup crumbled **feta cheese** (3.5 oz / 100g)

¼ cup minced **fresh flat-leaf parsley leaves**

1 to 2 tablespoons **fresh lemon juice**

For most of my life I've avoided broccoli salads. The idea of chewing on big pieces of raw broccoli doesn't excite me. That all changed with *this* broccoli salad. This broccoli is coated in a sticky harissa sauce that's sweet, spicy, and fragrant. Half the broccoli gets roasted in the oven until golden brown, while the rest gets chopped into tiny pieces for a subtle bit of crunch. The combination is anything but boring. This sturdy salad gets better as it sits, so it's a great make-ahead dish.

---

1. **Preheat the oven:** Place the oven racks in the upper and lower thirds of the oven and preheat to 425°F (220°C). Line 2 large baking sheets with parchment paper.

2. **Make a date paste:** Add the dates and boiling water to a small heatproof bowl. Let sit for at least 10 minutes to soften. Use a fork to mash the dates into the water to form a rough paste.

3. **Meanwhile, roast the chickpeas:** Scatter the chickpeas on one of the prepared baking sheets. Drizzle with 1 tablespoon of the olive oil and toss to coat. Sprinkle with ¼ teaspoon of the salt. Roast on the upper rack until the chickpeas are crispy and golden brown, 20 to 30 minutes.

4. **Prep the broccoli (roasted and raw):** Trim and peel the broccoli stalks. Chop half of the broccoli into bite-size pieces and scatter on the second baking sheet. Drizzle with 1 tablespoon of the olive oil and toss to coat. Sprinkle with ¼ teaspoon of the salt. Roast on the lower rack until golden brown around the edges, 15 to 20 minutes. Meanwhile, mince the remaining raw broccoli into tiny pieces. Transfer the roasted and raw broccoli to a large bowl.

5. **Make the sauce:** In a small saucepan, combine the garlic and the remaining 6 tablespoons olive oil and heat over medium heat. When small bubbles rise to the surface, keep cooking, swirling the pan frequently, until the garlic just starts to turn golden around the edges, 4 to 5 minutes. Whisk in the cumin and coriander and remove from the heat. Scrape the date paste into the saucepan and whisk to combine. Whisk in the rose harissa, 1 tablespoon at a time, until you reach your desired spice level. Whisk in the remaining ½ teaspoon salt and red wine vinegar.

6. **Assemble:** Pour the sauce over the broccoli and toss to coat. Sprinkle the chickpeas, almonds, feta, and parsley over the salad. Gently toss to mix. Add lemon juice to taste and more salt, if needed.

VEGAN: Use vegan feta cheese or omit.

---

❶ Rose harissa contains some dried rose petals for extra flavour. You can use regular harissa instead. Harissa can be quite spicy—and spice levels vary by brand—so start small and add more to taste.

ACTIVE TIME: 45 MINUTES • **TOTAL TIME:** 45 MINUTES • **SERVES** 4

SEARED BRUSSELS SPROUTS CAESAR SALAD

Caesar salad is a classic—and easily one of the salads I crave most often. This version uses a lighter dressing that doesn't taste like a compromise. It's paired with homemade croutons, smoky chickpea crumble, and sautéed Brussels sprouts. You don't need to use a mandoline to shave razor-thin slices. A regular knife works just fine—the Brussels sprouts get cooked, so you don't have to be as precise.

SMOKY CHICKPEA CRUMBLE

1 can (14 fl oz / 398 ml) **chickpeas**, drained, rinsed, and patted dry

2 tablespoons **tomato paste**

1 tablespoon **extra-virgin olive oil**

1 tablespoon **tamari**

1 tablespoon **Worcestershire sauce** ❶

1 teaspoon **smoked sweet paprika**

½ teaspoon freshly ground **black pepper**

CROUTONS

2 cups cubed **sourdough bread** or baguette

1 tablespoon **extra-virgin olive oil**

¼ teaspoon **fine sea salt**

¼ teaspoon freshly ground **black pepper**

BRUSSELS SPROUTS

2 tablespoons **extra-virgin olive oil**

2 lb (907g) **Brussels sprouts**, trimmed and very thinly sliced lengthwise

¼ teaspoon **fine sea salt**, divided

FOR SERVING

Yogurt Caesar Dressing (page 294), Vegan Caesar Dressing (page 294) ❷, or store-bought

Finely grated **Parmesan cheese** (about ¼ cup)

Lemon wedges

1. Preheat the oven: Place the oven racks in the upper and lower thirds of the oven and preheat to 425°F (220°C). Line 2 large baking sheets with parchment paper.

2. Make the Smoky Chickpea Crumble: In a medium bowl, combine the chickpeas, tomato paste, olive oil, tamari, Worcestershire sauce, smoked paprika, and pepper. Use a potato masher or fork to mash the chickpeas until about half of them are smashed. Spread the mixture on one of the prepared baking sheets. Bake on the upper rack until the chickpeas are dry and brown around the edges, 25 to 30 minutes, flipping halfway through. Transfer to a plate to cool.

3. Meanwhile, make the Croutons: Scatter the bread on the second baking sheet. Drizzle with the olive oil and toss to coat. Sprinkle with the salt and pepper. Bake on the lower rack until the bread is golden brown, 5 to 8 minutes.

4. Cook the Brussels Sprouts ❸: In a large skillet, heat 1 tablespoon of the olive oil over medium-high heat. Add half of the sliced Brussels sprouts and sprinkle with ⅛ teaspoon of the salt. Sauté, stirring occasionally, until the Brussels sprouts are bright green and some of the edges are brown, about 4 minutes. Transfer to a large bowl. Repeat to cook the remaining Brussels sprouts with the remaining 1 tablespoon olive oil and the remaining ⅛ teaspoon salt.

5. Combine and serve: Toss the Brussels sprouts with enough dressing to coat to your liking. Sprinkle with the chickpea crumble, croutons, and Parmesan. Toss to combine. Taste and adjust seasoning with salt, pepper, and/or a squeeze of lemon, if needed. Divide the salad among bowls and serve with lemon wedges.

VEGAN: Use vegan Parmesan cheese or omit. **GLUTEN-FREE:** Use gluten-free bread or baguette.

❶ Worcestershire sauce is usually made with anchovies, but there are now a number of vegetarian-friendly options. Find them at well-stocked grocery stores or online.

❷ If making the Vegan Caesar Dressing (page 294), budget time to quick-soak the cashews before you begin.

❸ If you're planning to split this salad across two meals: Make everything except for the Brussels sprouts. The Caesar dressing and chickpea crumble can be stored in the fridge, and the croutons at room temperature. The next day, quickly reheat the chickpea crumble in the skillet, then cook the Brussels sprouts "to order."

ACTIVE TIME: 45 MINUTES • **TOTAL TIME:** 45 MINUTES • **SERVES** 4

GREEN GODDESS SALAD WITH EVERYTHING BAGEL CROUTONS

SALAD

1½ lb (680g) **fingerling potatoes** ❶

4 large **eggs**

1 tablespoon **butter**

1 **everything** or **sesame bagel**

2 tablespoons **extra-virgin olive oil**

1 bunch **radishes** (greens attached, optional) ❷

1½ cups **snap peas**, trimmed ❸

Flaky sea salt

1 large head **butter lettuce**, torn into bite-size pieces

2 **celery ribs**, thinly sliced

DRESSING

⅔ cup plain **Greek yogurt**

⅔ cup lightly packed **fresh flat-leaf parsley leaves**

2 tablespoons **fresh tarragon leaves**

2 tablespoons chopped **fresh chives**, more for garnish

2 tablespoons **extra-virgin olive oil**

2 tablespoons **fresh lemon juice**

1 tablespoon drained **capers**

½ teaspoon **fine sea salt**

½ teaspoon freshly ground **black pepper**

If you're looking for a pretty salad with substance, this is it. This salad is bursting with fresh herbs, seared veggies, crisp lettuce, and buttery everything-bagel croutons. The creamy, herby dressing is made with Greek yogurt instead of sour cream or mayonnaise. There are a few components, but most of it can be done while the potatoes are boiling. This makes a great do-ahead lunch—just store the dressing separately and drizzle it over the salad when you're ready to dig in.

1. **Start the Salad—boil the potatoes:** Add the potatoes to a large pot of salted water and cover with the lid slightly ajar. Bring to a boil over medium-high heat and cook the potatoes until fork-tender, 20 to 25 minutes. Drain the potatoes.

2. **Meanwhile, boil the eggs:** Bring a medium saucepan of water to a boil over medium-high heat. Gently lower the eggs into the water. Adjust the heat, if needed, to maintain a gentle boil and cook the eggs for 6½ minutes (adjust timing based on your desired doneness; see page 21). Fill a medium bowl with ice water and gently lower the eggs into the bowl to cool.

3. **Make the Dressing:** In a food processor or blender, combine the yogurt, parsley, tarragon, chives, olive oil, lemon juice, capers, salt, and pepper. Process until smooth and creamy.

4. **Continue the Salad—toast the bagel croutons:** Melt the butter in a large skillet over medium heat. Tear the bagel into bite-size pieces and scatter into the skillet. Cook, stirring occasionally, until golden brown, 3 to 5 minutes. Transfer to a large serving platter.

5. **Sear the potatoes, radishes, and snap peas:** Give the skillet a wipe, then return it to the stovetop and heat the olive oil over medium-high heat. Add the potatoes and radishes and sauté until golden brown, 5 to 8 minutes. Add the snap peas and sauté until charred in a few spots, 2 to 3 minutes. Sprinkle with the flaky salt to taste.

6. **Assemble:** In a large bowl, combine the lettuce and celery. Drizzle with just enough dressing to lightly coat, then toss to mix. Peel the eggs and cut in half lengthwise. On a serving platter, arrange the dressed greens, potatoes, radishes, snap peas, eggs, and bagel croutons. Garnish with chives and serve with the remaining dressing for drizzling.

GLUTEN-FREE: Use a gluten-free bagel or bread.

❶ Fingerling potatoes can be replaced with baby potatoes. If using baby potatoes, check them after 15 minutes, because they tend to cook faster.

❷ Radish greens are delicious seared, but you can trim them before cooking if you prefer.

❸ To trim the snap peas, remove the tips and the tough string that runs down the length of the pod.

ACTIVE TIME: 30 MINUTES • **TOTAL TIME:** 30 MINUTES • **SERVES** 3 TO 4

VIBRANT GREENS SALAD WITH SESAME LIME VINAIGRETTE

VEGETABLES

1 lb (454g) **asparagus**, trimmed

2 bunches **broccolini** (1 lb / 454g total), trimmed

8 oz (227g) **green beans**, trimmed

1 cup **snow peas**, trimmed ❶

1½ cups **frozen shelled edamame**

PAN-FRIED TOFU

1 tablespoon **grapeseed oil**

12 oz (340g) **extra-firm tofu**, patted dry and cut into ½-inch (1 cm) cubes

1 tablespoon **tamari**

1 tablespoon **sambal oelek** or Sriracha sauce

VINAIGRETTE

Zest of 1 **lime**

¼ cup **fresh lime juice**

3 tablespoons **grapeseed oil**

2 tablespoons **toasted sesame oil**

2 teaspoons **honey**

1 teaspoon finely grated **fresh ginger**

1 teaspoon **Dijon mustard**

½ teaspoon **fine sea salt**

4 cups shredded **napa** or **savoy cabbage**

1 tablespoon **toasted sesame seeds**, for garnish

This über-healthy salad is, quite literally, full of greens. The vegetables are quickly blanched, which keeps them crisp. They're then dressed with a vibrant lime and toasted sesame dressing. It's a great make-ahead salad because it's sturdy and won't wilt while it waits. The tofu is pan-fried and tossed with a splash of tamari and sambal oelek (Sriracha sauce works fine too). If you're not a fan of tofu, you can swap it for some poached eggs instead.

---

1. **Prepare your blanching station:** Bring a large pot of heavily salted water to a boil over high heat. Fill a large bowl with ice water. ❷ Set a colander over the sink. Line a large baking sheet with a kitchen towel.

2. **Blanch the Vegetables:** Once the water is boiling, add the asparagus and cook until tender, 2 to 3 minutes. Using tongs, transfer the asparagus to the ice bath for 30 seconds to stop the cooking. Transfer the asparagus to the colander, shake off excess water, then lay the asparagus on the kitchen towel to dry. Repeat with the remaining vegetables, one at a time, blanching the broccolini for 2 to 3 minutes, green beans for 2 to 3 minutes, snow peas for 30 seconds, and edamame for about 4 minutes, draining the edamame in the colander.

3. **Meanwhile, make the Pan-Fried Tofu:** In a large nonstick skillet, heat the grapeseed oil over medium heat. Add the tofu and cook, stirring occasionally, until golden brown on all sides, about 10 minutes. Add the tamari and sambal oelek. Toss to coat the tofu and cook, stirring frequently, until all the liquid has been absorbed by the tofu, 1 to 2 minutes. Remove from the heat.

4. **Make the Vinaigrette:** In a small bowl, whisk together the lime zest, lime juice, grapeseed oil, sesame oil, honey, ginger, Dijon mustard, and salt.

5. **Assemble:** Scatter the cabbage on a serving platter. Pour about one-quarter of the vinaigrette overtop. Using your hands, massage the dressing into the cabbage. Top with the blanched vegetables and drizzle with the remaining dressing. Top with the tofu and sprinkle with the sesame seeds.

VEGAN: Replace the honey with maple syrup.

---

❶ If you can't find snow peas, use snap peas and cook for slightly longer, 1 to 2 minutes total.

❷ Keep some extra ice on hand, because your ice bath might need a top-up after the first few vegetables—you want the water to stay ice cold.

ACTIVE TIME: 40 MINUTES • **TOTAL TIME:** 45 MINUTES • **SERVES** 4 TO 6

BARLEY SALAD WITH MUSHROOMS AND BURRATA

1¼ cups dried **pearled barley** ❶

4 cups **vegetable stock**

1 can (14 fl oz / 398 ml) **cannellini beans**, drained and rinsed

4 tablespoons **extra-virgin olive oil**, divided, more for drizzling

1 lb (454g) **mixed mushrooms** (shiitake, oyster, cremini), torn into bite-size pieces

2 tablespoons **butter**

2 cups thinly sliced **leeks** (white and light green parts)

5 **garlic cloves**, minced

1 tablespoon **fresh thyme leaves**

1 teaspoon **fine sea salt**

1 teaspoon freshly ground **black pepper**, more for garnish

1 bunch **curly kale** (10 oz / 283g), stemmed and thinly sliced

2 teaspoons **lemon zest**

2 tablespoons **fresh lemon juice**

8.8-oz (250g) **burrata cheese ball**, room temperature ❷

¼ cup chopped **fresh dill**

Flaky sea salt

Barley is one of the humblest ingredients, but it certainly shines in this salad. Toasting barley before cooking it is an easy way to intensify its nutty flavour. While the barley cooks, the rest of the dish comes together. The mushrooms are seared until golden brown, then sautéed with leeks and a garlic-infused butter. The burrata cheese brings decadence and creaminess. Once a ball of burrata is torn open, it's best eaten fresh—but that's not usually a problem. The rest of the salad keeps well for lunch the next day.

---

1. Toast and cook the barley: In a large dry Dutch oven or pot, cook the barley over medium heat, stirring frequently, until it smells nutty, 4 to 6 minutes. Pour in the vegetable stock. Cover with the lid slightly ajar and bring to a boil over high heat, then reduce the heat to medium-low and maintain a rolling simmer. Cook until the barley is tender, 20 to 30 minutes. Add the cannellini beans in the last 1 to 2 minutes of cooking, to warm the beans. Drain the bean and barley mixture in a colander.

2. Meanwhile, cook the mushrooms: In a large skillet, heat 2 tablespoons of the olive oil over medium-high heat. Once the oil is hot, add the mushrooms and cook, undisturbed, until lightly browned on the bottom, 3 to 4 minutes. Reduce the heat to medium and cook the mushrooms, stirring occasionally, until golden brown all over, 5 to 6 minutes.

3. Cook the rest of the vegetables: To the mushrooms, add the remaining 2 tablespoons olive oil, butter, leeks, garlic, thyme, salt, and pepper and cook, stirring frequently, until the leeks have softened, 3 to 5 minutes. Stir in the kale and cook until softened, 2 to 3 minutes. Add the barley and beans, lemon zest, and lemon juice. (If your skillet isn't large enough, combine everything in the pot instead.) Stir to mix.

4. Assemble: Transfer the mixture to a serving platter. Tear the burrata into bite-size pieces and scatter overtop, then drizzle with more olive oil. Garnish with the dill, pepper, and flaky salt.

VEGAN: Use vegan butter. Omit the burrata cheese and substitute with a crumbled vegan feta.

---

❶ Pearled (or pearl) barley is the most widely available variety. It cooks faster because the outer layers have been removed. If you wish to use pot barley, (hulled or whole grain; slightly darker in colour), budget for longer cooking time, 50 to 60 minutes total.

❷ Burrata is best at room temperature, so let it sit on the counter while you prepare this dish. If you can't find burrata, use a ball of fresh mozzarella.

ACTIVE TIME: 45 MINUTES • **TOTAL TIME:** 50 MINUTES • **SERVES** 4

KALE LENTIL SALAD WITH HALLOUMI

1 lb (454g) **sweet potatoes**, cut into ½-inch (1 cm) cubes (2 small potatoes)

5 tablespoons **extra-virgin olive** oil, divided

2 teaspoons **ground cumin**, divided

2 teaspoons **ground coriander**, divided

¾ teaspoon **fine sea salt**, divided

1 cup dried **black beluga lentils**, picked over, rinsed and drained ❶

8.8 oz (250g) **halloumi cheese**, cut into ½-inch (1 cm) cubes

1 medium **shallot**, minced (¼ cup)

⅓ cup **red wine vinegar**

¼ cup **fresh orange juice**

2 teaspoons **Dijon mustard**

½ teaspoon **smoked sweet paprika**

1 bunch **lacinato kale** (10 oz / 283g), stemmed and thinly sliced

⅓ cup minced **fresh flat-leaf parsley leaves**

1 medium **pomegranate**, seeded (1 cup) ❷

⅓ cup chopped **pistachios** or toasted pepitas

This lentil salad has cubes of golden-brown halloumi cheese, roasted sweet potatoes, fresh pomegranate seeds, and an orange-shallot-red-wine-vinegar dressing. It's punchy and herby in all the right ways. The cook times for lentils can vary significantly, so check for doneness early and often. You want the lentils to be tender but still firm enough to hold their shape.

---

1. **Preheat the oven:** Place the oven racks in the upper and lower thirds of the oven and preheat to 450°F (230°C). Set aside 2 large baking sheets.

2. **Roast the sweet potatoes:** Scatter the sweet potatoes on one of the baking sheets. Drizzle with 1 tablespoon of the olive oil and toss to coat. Sprinkle with 1 teaspoon of the cumin, 1 teaspoon of the coriander, and ¼ teaspoon of the salt, then toss to coat. Roast on the upper rack until fork-tender and golden brown around the edges, 25 to 30 minutes.

3. **Meanwhile, cook the lentils:** Add the lentils to a medium saucepan and add enough water to cover them by at least 3 inches (8 cm). Bring to a boil over high heat, then reduce the heat to medium-low and simmer the lentils until tender, 15 to 25 minutes. (Check frequently to avoid overcooking.) Drain the lentils and shake off excess water.

4. **At the same time, bake the halloumi:** Scatter the halloumi on the second baking sheet. Drizzle with 1 tablespoon of the olive oil and toss to coat. Bake on the lower rack until the halloumi is golden, 10 to 15 minutes, stirring halfway through.

5. **Meanwhile, make the dressing:** In a large serving bowl, whisk together the remaining 3 tablespoons olive oil, remaining 1 teaspoon cumin, remaining 1 teaspoon coriander, remaining ½ teaspoon salt, the shallot, red wine vinegar, orange juice, Dijon mustard, and smoked paprika until emulsified.

6. **Combine:** Add the kale to the bowl of dressing, and using your hands, massage the dressing into the leaves until fully coated. Add the lentils and toss to coat. Season with more salt, if needed. Scatter in the halloumi, sweet potatoes, parsley, and pomegranate seeds and gently toss to mix. Garnish with the pistachios.

VEGAN: Omit the halloumi. (If serving vegan(s) *and* non-vegan(s), just serve the halloumi on the side.)

---

❶ Black beluga lentils can be replaced with French green lentils (du Puy lentils), but budget for longer cooking time.

❷ To seed a pomegranate, I usually slice it in half crosswise, then submerge one half at a time in a bowl of cool water and use my fingers to dislodge the seeds. The pith will float to the top, the seeds will sink to the bottom, and any extra juice will be contained. In a pinch, you could use dried cranberries instead of pomegranate seeds.

ROASTED SWEET POTATOES WITH JALAPEÑO CILANTRO SLAW

SWEET POTATOES AND CHICKPEAS

1½ teaspoons **ground cumin**

1 teaspoon **chili powder**

½ teaspoon **ground coriander**

½ teaspoon **smoked sweet paprika**

½ teaspoon **fine sea salt**

1½ lb (680g) **sweet potatoes**, cut into ½-inch (1 cm) thick wedges (3 small potatoes)

3 tablespoons **extra-virgin olive oil**, divided

1 can (14 fl oz / 398 ml) **chickpeas**, drained, rinsed, and patted dry

SLAW

5 cups shredded **green cabbage**

¾ cup plain **Greek yogurt**

¼ cup **fresh lime juice**

2 tablespoons **extra-virgin olive oil**

2 **scallions**, roughly chopped

2 **jalapeño peppers**, seeds and ribs removed

1 bunch **fresh cilantro**

½ teaspoon **fine sea salt**

GARNISHES

⅓ cup **roasted pepitas** ❶

½ cup crumbled **feta cheese**

1 **avocado**, pitted, peeled, and thinly sliced

Ever order a salad just to feel good about also ordering fries? This salad has the best of both worlds. A flavourful spice blend doubles up as seasoning for roasted sweet potato wedges and crunchy chickpeas. The crunchy slaw is tossed in a creamy sauce flavoured with fresh herbs, lime, and jalapeño. Top it all off with roasted pepitas, feta cheese, and avocado and you've got one flavour-packed salad!

1. **Preheat the oven:** Place the oven racks in the upper and lower thirds of the oven and preheat to 425°F (220°C). Line 2 large baking sheets with parchment paper.

2. **Start the Sweet Potatoes and Chickpeas—combine the spices:** In a small bowl, stir together the cumin, chili powder, coriander, smoked paprika, and salt.

3. **Roast the sweet potatoes:** Scatter the sweet potatoes on one of the prepared baking sheets. Drizzle with 2 tablespoons of the olive oil and toss to coat. Sprinkle with about two-thirds of the spice blend and toss to coat. Evenly spread the sweet potatoes on the baking sheet and roast on the upper rack until golden brown, 35 to 40 minutes, flipping halfway through.

4. **Roast the chickpeas:** Scatter the chickpeas on the second baking sheet. Drizzle with the remaining 1 tablespoon olive oil and toss to coat. Sprinkle with the remaining spice blend (about one-third) and toss to coat. Roast on the lower rack until crisp and golden brown, 20 to 25 minutes.

5. **Meanwhile, make the Slaw:** Put the shredded cabbage in a large bowl. In a food processor, combine the yogurt, lime juice, olive oil, scallions, and jalapeños. Pulse until smooth and creamy. Add the cilantro (leaves and stems) and salt. Pulse until the cilantro is chopped into small but still visible pieces. Taste and adjust seasoning, if needed. Pour about two-thirds of the sauce over the cabbage and toss to coat.

6. **Assemble:** Divide the slaw among plates, then pile the roasted sweet potatoes and chickpeas on top. Drizzle with the remaining sauce. Top with pepitas, feta, and avocado.

❶ You can roast your own pepitas by tossing them in ½ teaspoon olive oil, then squeezing them onto one of the baking sheets for the final 5 minutes of roasting. Keep an eye on them, because they might be done sooner.

DESSERTS

JAMMY RASPBERRY STREUSEL BARS

CRUST AND TOPPING

2½ cups (325g) **all-purpose flour** ❶

½ cup (100g) **granulated sugar**

½ teaspoon (3g) **fine sea salt**

¾ cup (170g) + 2 tablespoons (28g) **unsalted butter**, melted, divided

1 teaspoon (5g) pure **vanilla extract**

⅓ cup (30g) **old-fashioned rolled oats**

2 tablespoons (25g) packed **dark brown sugar**

1 teaspoon (3g) **cinnamon**

RASPBERRY FILLING

6 cups (24 oz / 680g) **frozen raspberries**, divided

⅔ cup (133g) **granulated sugar**

⅓ cup (40g) **cornstarch** ❶

⅓ cup (80g) **cold water**

If you love berries, these bars are for you. They are unapologetically fruit-forward, with a thick layer of raspberry filling. Frozen raspberries are usually more affordable than a big bowl of the fresh stuff—and they are a better choice anyway when berries are out of season. The tender shortbread dough doubles as the crust *and* the base for the crumbly cinnamon streusel topping. These bars are delicious as is, but also great with a scoop of vanilla ice cream. A word of warning: they tend to disappear quickly!

---

1. **Preheat the oven:** Place an oven rack in the centre position and preheat to 350°F (180°C). Line a 9-inch (23 cm) square baking pan with parchment paper, allowing excess paper to hang over each side for easy removal.

2. **Start the Crust and Topping—make the shortbread crust:** In a medium bowl, whisk together the flour, granulated sugar, and salt. In a small bowl, whisk together ¾ cup of the melted butter and vanilla, then pour it over the flour mixture. Using a silicone spatula, stir until there is no more visible flour. (The dough will be crumbly, but it should hold together when pinched between your fingers.) Firmly pack a ⅓-cup measure with dough and set it aside for the streusel topping. Scatter the remaining dough into the prepared baking pan. (Set aside the bowl.) Using your fingers, press the dough into a firm, even layer. Prick the surface of the dough with a fork. Bake until the edges are a pale golden brown, 22 to 24 minutes. (The crust does not need to be fully cooled before filling.)

3. **Meanwhile, make the Raspberry Filling:** In a medium saucepan, combine 3 cups of the frozen raspberries with the granulated sugar. Bring to a boil over medium-high heat, then reduce the heat to medium and cook, stirring occasionally, until the mixture deepens in colour and reduces to the consistency of a loose jam that coats the back of a spoon, about 15 minutes. In a small bowl, whisk together the cornstarch and cold water until smooth. Pour the cornstarch mixture into the berry mixture and stir to mix. Cook, stirring frequently, until the filling thickens to a spreadable jam consistency and the colour darkens again, about 2 minutes. Gently fold in the remaining 3 cups frozen raspberries.

CONTINUED ON NEXT PAGE

VEGAN: Use vegan butter. **GLUTEN-FREE:** Use your favourite gluten-free 1-to-1 flour blend.

---

❶ Flour and cornstarch are prone to measurement errors (often too much is added). For best results, use a scale. Otherwise, measure using the spoon-and-level method (page 19).

CONTINUED FROM PREVIOUS PAGE

4. Continue the Crust and Topping—make the streusel topping: Crumble the reserved ⅓ cup dough back into the reserved bowl. Add the oats, brown sugar, and cinnamon and toss to mix. Drizzle in the remaining 2 tablespoons melted butter. Stir until the mixture starts to stick together. (If the mixture is dry, add a bit more melted butter until it sticks together.)

5. Assemble and bake: Spoon the raspberry filling evenly over the baked shortbread crust. Evenly sprinkle with the streusel topping. Bake until the streusel is golden brown and the raspberry filling is gently bubbling at the edges, about 30 minutes. Let cool completely in the pan, then lift and slice into bars. ❷

❷ Store bars in an airtight container and refrigerate for up to 3 days.

BROWN BUTTER CHOCOLATE WALNUT COOKIES

¾ cup (170g) + 1 to 3 tablespoons (up to 43g) **unsalted butter**

1 cup (120g) raw **walnuts** ❶

¾ cup (150g) packed **dark brown sugar**

½ cup (100g) **granulated sugar**

1 large **egg**, room temperature

1 large **egg yolk**, room temperature

1 tablespoon (15g) pure **vanilla extract**

2 cups (260g) **all-purpose flour** ❷

¾ teaspoon (5g) **fine sea salt**

½ teaspoon (3g) **baking soda**

½ teaspoon (1g) **cinnamon**

5.3 oz (150g) **semi-sweet chocolate**, chopped (1 cup)

Flaky sea salt, for garnish

These cookies are soft, chewy, and studded with dark chocolate and toasted walnuts. Nutty brown butter makes them even more irresistible! This recipe is quicker to make than a lot of other brown butter recipes, because you don't need to chill the butter until it's completely solid. Brown butter reduces as it cooks, and the amount of evaporation depends on the stove's temperature and the pot's surface area, so topping up the butter after browning produces reliable results every time. One bowl and no mixer required—it doesn't get much better than this!

---

1. **Preheat the oven:** Place the oven racks in the upper and lower thirds of the oven and preheat to 350°F (180°C). Line 2 large baking sheets with parchment paper.

2. **Make the brown butter (page 18):** Melt ¾ cup of the butter in a small saucepan over medium heat. Using a silicone spatula, stir frequently to scrape up the brown bits from the bottom of the pan. Once the butter begins to foam, 3 to 5 minutes in, cook, stirring constantly, until the butter is golden brown and smells nutty. (Pay close attention as it can burn very easily at this stage.) Immediately pour the brown butter into a liquid measuring cup.

3. **Top up the brown butter:** Whisk in the remaining butter, in small increments, until you have a total of ¾ cup (170g) melted butter. Let cool for at least 5 minutes.

4. **Toast the walnuts:** Scatter the walnuts on one of the prepared baking sheets. Bake on the upper rack until golden brown and fragrant, about 5 minutes. Roughly chop the nuts and set aside to cool.

5. **Mix the cookie dough:** In a large bowl, combine the brown sugar, granulated sugar, and the slightly cooled brown butter. Stir vigorously until the sugars are incorporated and the butter has cooled to room temperature, 1 to 2 minutes. Stir in the egg, egg yolk, and vanilla until completely smooth. Add the flour, salt, baking soda, and cinnamon. Stir until faint flour streaks remain, then fold in the chocolate and chopped walnuts just until incorporated. (Do not overmix.)

6. **Scoop and bake ❸:** Scoop 3-tablespoon portions of cookie dough (about the size of a golf ball) onto the prepared baking sheets, leaving 2 inches (5 cm) between them. Bake until the edges are golden but the centres are still slightly soft, 10 to 12 minutes, swapping top and bottom positions halfway through. While the cookies are still warm, sprinkle with flaky salt. Let the cookies cool on the baking sheet for 5 minutes, then transfer to a rack to cool completely.

GLUTEN-FREE: Use your favourite gluten-free 1-to-1 flour blend.

---

❶ Walnuts can be omitted or can be replaced with pecans.

❷ Flour is prone to measurement errors (often too much is added). For best results, use a scale. Otherwise, measure using the spoon-and-level method (page 19).

❸ Baked cookies can be stored in an airtight container at room temperature for up to 3 days. The cookies are best fresh, so you can also freeze the portioned dough in an airtight container or freezer bag and bake as directed from frozen. Frozen dough may take an extra 1 to 2 minutes to bake.

ACTIVE TIME: 20 MINUTES • TOTAL TIME: 30 MINUTES • MAKES ABOUT 24 KNOTS

CARDAMOM SUGAR KNOTS

1 batch **Quick Pizza Dough** (page 297) or 1 lb (454g) store-bought, room temperature ❶

6 tablespoons (75 g) **granulated sugar**

¾ teaspoon (2g) **ground cardamom** ❷

½ teaspoon (1g) **cinnamon**

3 tablespoons (43g) **unsalted butter**, melted

My husband, Anguel, and I will occasionally drive to pick up pizza. Almost every time, we're so hungry that we shamelessly eat it in the car before making it home to the dinner table. In addition to the pizza, we often order cinnamon sticks for dessert. They are cleverly—and not surprisingly—also made from pizza dough. These cardamom knots are our at-home version, perfect for homemade pizza nights. Once the knots are warm and puffy from the oven, they're brushed with melted butter and coated with cardamom and cinnamon sugar. Super simple to make and highly addictive. Consider yourself warned!

1. **Preheat the oven:** Place an oven rack in the centre position and preheat to 425°F (220°C). Line a large baking sheet with parchment paper.

2. **Shape and bake the knots (page 266):** Divide the dough into 2 equal portions. Loosely cover one portion of dough with a kitchen towel or plastic wrap to prevent it from drying out. On a lightly floured work surface, use a rolling pin to stretch the other half of the dough into a long rectangle (about 4 x 12 inches / 10 x 30 cm). Cut the rectangle into about 12 strips, each about 1 inch (2.5 cm) wide and 4 inches (10 cm) long. Knot each piece of dough, tucking the ends underneath. Place the dough knot on the prepared baking sheet. ❸ Repeat with the remaining pieces and other portion of dough. Bake until the edges of the knots are pale golden brown, but are still soft to the touch, 10 to 12 minutes.

3. **Meanwhile, make the spiced sugar:** In a small bowl, stir together the sugar, cardamom, and cinnamon.

4. **Coat the knots:** As soon as the knots emerge from the oven, brush them with the melted butter. Using a slotted spoon, dip the knots, one at a time, in the sugar mixture, then roll around until completely coated. Transfer the knots to a bowl or plate. These knots are best eaten while still warm.

VEGAN: Use vegan butter. **GLUTEN-FREE:** Use your favourite gluten-free pizza dough.

❶ If the pizza dough is refrigerated, let it sit on the counter to come up to room temperature before rolling.

❷ The cardamom can be replaced with more cinnamon (1¼ teaspoons cinnamon total), if you prefer.

❸ If you're using a half sheet pan (18 x 13 inches / 46 x 33 cm), it should fit 24 knots, with about 1 inch (2.5 cm) space between them. If your baking sheets are smaller, divide the knots evenly between 2 baking sheets and bake one sheet at a time. Cover the second baking sheet with a kitchen towel or plastic wrap to prevent the dough from drying out.

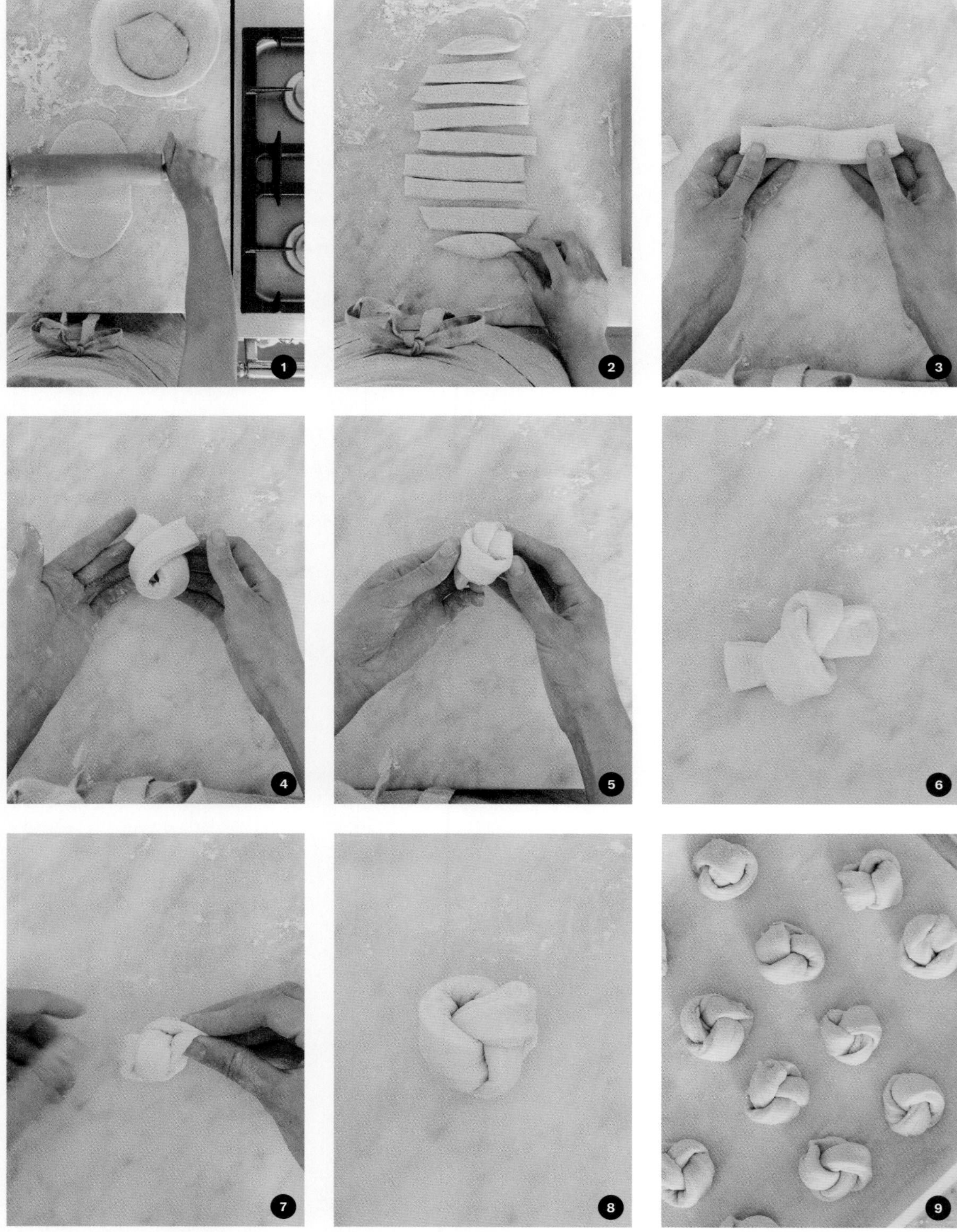
1
2
3
4
5
6
7
8
9

ACTIVE TIME: 20 MINUTES • **TOTAL TIME:** 45 MINUTES • **SERVES** 6

CHOCOLATE PUDDING WITH PRETZEL CRUMBLE

CHOCOLATE PUDDING

1 lb (454g) **silken** or **soft tofu**

3.5 oz (100g) **semi-sweet chocolate**, melted ❷

⅓ cup (107g) **maple syrup**

2 tablespoons (10g) **Dutch-process cocoa powder**

1 teaspoon (5g) pure **vanilla extract**

Pinch of **fine sea salt**

PRETZEL CRUMBLE

⅓ cup (30g) crushed **salted pretzels** ❸

2 tablespoons (25g) packed **dark brown sugar**

2 tablespoons (28g) **unsalted butter**, melted

¼ teaspoon **cinnamon**

Whipped cream, for serving (optional)

The simplicity (and deliciousness) of this dessert is the reason I make it often. The creamy chocolate pudding comes together in the blender. It can hang out in the fridge for hours (or days), which makes it perfect for instant snacks and desserts throughout the week. ❶ The pretzel crumble is both sweet and salty. It provides a crunchy contrast to the smooth pudding—just be careful not to eat it all before it's time to garnish!

1. **Preheat the oven:** Place an oven rack in the centre position and preheat to 350°F (180°C). Line a small baking sheet with parchment paper.

2. **Make the Chocolate Pudding:** In a high-speed blender, combine the tofu, melted chocolate, maple syrup, cocoa powder, vanilla, and salt. Blend for 45 seconds. Scrape down the sides, then blend until completely smooth, about 45 seconds more. Divide the mixture among 6 small ramekins or small bowls. Cover with plastic wrap and refrigerate until firm, at least 40 minutes.

3. **Meanwhile, make the Pretzel Crumble:** In a small bowl, combine the crushed pretzels, brown sugar, melted butter, and cinnamon and stir until well mixed. Spread the pretzel mixture on the prepared baking sheet and bake until golden brown and fragrant, 8 to 10 minutes, stirring halfway through. Let cool completely on the baking sheet.

4. **Assemble:** Just before serving, top the chilled chocolate pudding with whipped cream, if using. Generously sprinkle the pretzel crumble on top.

VEGAN: Use vegan butter and homemade or store-bought coconut whipped cream. **GLUTEN-FREE:** Use gluten-free pretzels.

❶ This is a great make-ahead dessert. Store the Chocolate Pudding, covered, in the fridge for up to 3 days. Store the Pretzel Crumble in an airtight container or resealable bag at room temperature for up to 3 days. Top the puddings with the pretzel crumble just before serving, so it stays crisp.

❷ Use your preferred method to melt the chocolate, typically either in a double boiler (chopped chocolate in a heatproof bowl over simmering water) or in a microwave (stirring in 30-second intervals, just until melted).

❸ You want a mix of small visible pieces (for texture) and fine pretzel "dust" (which will help the crumble bind). You can pulse the pretzels in a blender or food processor. Or put the pretzels in a sealed freezer bag and run a rolling pin over the pretzels to crush them.

ACTIVE TIME: 15 MINUTES • **TOTAL TIME:** 40 MINUTES • **SERVES** 6

WHIPPED YOGURT CREAM WITH BERRIES

4 cups (about 1¼ lb / 567g) **mixed fresh berries** ❶

½ cup (100g) **granulated sugar**, divided

1 teaspoon **lemon zest**, more for garnish

1 **vanilla bean**, split and seeds scraped, divided ❷

1 cup (230g) **whipping (35%) cream**

½ cup (120g) plain **full-fat Greek yogurt** or sour cream

½ cup (35g) crushed **gingersnap cookies** (optional)

Never underestimate the magic of whipped cream and berries! This understated dessert is one of my favourites to make—and eat—in the summer. Fresh berries are steeped with vanilla and lemon zest, then spooned over fluffy whipped cream with abandon. Adding Greek yogurt (or sour cream) to whipped cream gives it a refreshing tang. The crushed gingersnap cookies are optional, but highly recommended for a hit of spice and crunch.

---

1. **Macerate the berries:** In a medium bowl, combine the berries, ¼ cup of the sugar, lemon zest, and half of the vanilla seeds. Gently stir to combine. Let sit for at least 30 minutes to soften.

2. **Whip the cream:** In a separate medium bowl, combine the cream, yogurt, the remaining ¼ cup sugar, and the remaining half of the vanilla seeds. Using a handheld mixer fitted with the whisk attachment, whip the mixture until it holds medium-stiff peaks. (When the beaters are lifted, the tip of the peak should curl over just slightly but otherwise hold its shape.)

3. **Assemble:** Divide the whipped yogurt cream and the berries and their juices among bowls. Garnish with crushed gingersnaps (if using) and lemon zest. Serve immediately.

VEGAN: Omit the whipping cream and yogurt (skip step 2) and use homemade or store-bought coconut whipped cream instead.

GLUTEN-FREE: Use gluten-free gingersnaps or omit.

---

❶ Mix your favourites: raspberries, blueberries, strawberries, blackberries, etc. If using a larger berry like strawberries, first chop them into bite-size pieces.

❷ To scrape the seeds from a vanilla bean, slice the bean in half lengthwise. Use your fingertips to hold down the tip of the bean on the cutting board, and run the dull side of the knife down the pod to scrape out the seeds. Alternatively, you can use 1 tablespoon of vanilla bean paste or 2 teaspoons of pure vanilla extract.

ACTIVE TIME: 20 MINUTES • **TOTAL TIME:** 1 HOUR • **MAKES** 16 MUFFINS

BANANA CHOCOLATE MUFFINS

3 cups (390g) **all-purpose flour**

4 teaspoons (16g) **baking powder**

2 teaspoons (5g) **cinnamon**

½ teaspoon (3g) **fine sea salt**

1⅓ cups (320g) mashed **ripe banana** ❶

½ cup (110g) **grapeseed oil** ❷

2 large **eggs**, room temperature

1¼ cups (250g) firmly packed **dark brown sugar**

½ cup (120g) plain **full-fat Greek yogurt**, room temperature ❸

½ cup (120g) **whole milk**, room temperature

2 teaspoons (10g) pure **vanilla extract**

8 oz (227g) **semi-sweet chocolate**, chopped, or chocolate chips (1½ cups)

Turbinado or **demerara sugar**, for sprinkling (optional)

I think everyone should have a reliable muffin recipe they can whip up whenever the craving hits (which in our house is often). These tender muffins are flavoured with banana, cinnamon, vanilla, and chocolate. I've always loved buttermilk in baked goods, but I rarely have it at home. This recipe uses Greek yogurt to replicate buttermilk's tang (without requiring a trip to the store!). To encourage puffy muffin tops, I like to start the muffins at a high temperature, then reduce it for the rest of their bake time. Sprinkling coarse sugar on top is optional, but highly recommended for crunch.

---

1. **Preheat the oven:** Place an oven rack in the centre position and preheat to 425°F (220°C). Line a muffin tin with paper liners.

2. **Mix the dry ingredients:** In a large bowl, whisk together the flour, baking powder, cinnamon, and salt.

3. **Mix the wet ingredients:** In a medium bowl, whisk together the banana, grapeseed oil, eggs, brown sugar, yogurt, milk, and vanilla.

4. **Combine:** Add the wet ingredients to the dry ingredients. Use a stirring spoon to gently mix, stopping when there are only faint streaks of flour showing. Gently fold in the chocolate just until all the flour is incorporated. (Do not overmix.)

5. **Bake:** Scoop the batter into the muffin cups, filling the cups all the way to the top. Sprinkle with turbinado sugar, if using. Bake for 5 minutes, then reduce the oven temperature to 350°F (180°C) and bake until a tester inserted into the centre of a muffin comes out clean, 15 to 17 minutes. Let the muffins cool in the pan for 5 minutes, then transfer to a rack to cool completely. Increase the oven temperature to 425°F (220°C) and repeat to bake the remaining muffins. ❹

GLUTEN-FREE: Use your favourite gluten-free 1-to-1 flour blend.

---

❶ The riper the better! Black bananas are best, otherwise use bananas that at least have black and brown streaks. It usually takes 4 to 5 bananas to yield 1⅓ cups mashed.

❷ Or another neutral vegetable oil, such as canola. You can also use melted unsalted butter, but the muffins will be slightly less moist.

❸ Use full-fat Greek yogurt for the best flavour, but low-fat works as well.

❹ Store cooled muffins in an airtight container or resealable freezer bag at room temperature for up to 3 days or in the freezer for up to 3 months. If frozen, defrost on the counter before eating.

ACTIVE TIME: 30 MINUTES • **TOTAL TIME:** 1 HOUR 30 MINUTES • **SERVES** 6 TO 8

BOTTOMLESS APPLE CARAMEL PIE

1 lb (454g) **frozen puff pastry** (2 sheets), defrosted in fridge overnight

3½ lb (1.6kg) **Golden Delicious apples** ❶

2 tablespoons (30g) **fresh lemon juice**

½ cup (100g) packed **dark brown sugar**

3 tablespoons (43g) **unsalted butter**, melted

2 teaspoons (5g) **cinnamon**

2 teaspoons (10g) pure **vanilla extract**

½ teaspoons (3g) **fine sea salt**

⅓ cup (43g) **all-purpose flour**

1 large **egg**, whisked

Turbinado or **demerara sugar**, for sprinkling

Vanilla ice cream, for serving (optional)

This pie is bottomless—not in a fountain drink sense, but literally. It goes heavy on the fruit and skips the bottom crust in favour of a gooey caramel-like sauce. If you're serving this with vanilla ice cream (and why wouldn't you?!), the sauce can be drizzled right over top. Puff pastry is a good cheat for getting a flaky, golden-brown crust with minimal hassle. Don't be intimidated by a lattice-top pie: cutting extra-large strips makes it really easy (page 279). The lattice will look quite wide before baking, but it will shrink slightly in the oven.

---

1. Preheat the oven: Place an oven rack in the centre position and preheat to 375°F (190°C). Set aside a 9-inch (23 cm) deep-dish pie plate. Line a large baking sheet with parchment paper.

2. Cut the puff pastry: Unroll the puff pastry onto a lightly floured work surface. Lightly dust a rolling pin, then gently roll the pastry to smooth any creases, and if needed, gently stretch each sheet so that it measures at least 8 x 10 inches (20 x 25 cm). ❷ Use a sharp knife to cut 6 strips, each 2½ inches (7 cm) wide and 10 inches (25 cm) long. Transfer the strips to the prepared baking sheet and place in the fridge to keep cool while you prepare the filling. (Save excess puff pastry for another use.)

3. Prep the filling: Peel the apples and slice into ¼-inch (5 mm) thick wedges. In a large bowl, toss the apples with the lemon juice. Add the brown sugar, melted butter, cinnamon, vanilla, and salt and toss to mix. Sprinkle in the flour and toss to coat evenly.

4. Assemble (page 279): Transfer the apples and all their juices to the pie plate. Remove the puff pastry strips from the fridge. Arrange 3 strips of pastry across the pie dish, leaving even spacing between them. At one side of the pie dish, lay a fourth strip diagonally across the other strips. Weave it over and under to create a lattice effect (see page 279). Repeat with the remaining 2 strips, spaced evenly across the pie.

CONTINUED ON NEXT PAGE

VEGAN: Use vegan puff pastry and butter. Use a plain unsweetened barista-style dairy-free milk or creamer for lightly brushing on top of the pastry. Serve with vegan vanilla ice cream, if using.

---

❶ If you can't find Golden Delicious, then I recommend Braeburn or Honeycrisp. These are my favourites after lots of testing. But ultimately, this is your pie, so use what you want.

❷ If your puff pastry came as one large single sheet (rather than two smaller sheets), ensure it measures at least 15 x 10 inches (38 x 25 cm), or use the rolling pin to stretch it, if needed, before cutting into strips.

CONTINUED FROM PREVIOUS PAGE

5. Trim and brush the pie: Using scissors, trim the overhanging strips to ½ inch (1 cm). Use a large spoon to tuck the edges of the pastry strips down between the apples and the sides of the pie plate. Using a pastry brush, lightly brush the egg over the lattice. Sprinkle lightly with the turbinado sugar. If you have the time to spare, freeze the pie for 15 minutes before baking to help reduce shrinkage in the puff pastry.

6. Bake: Place the pie plate on the parchment-lined baking sheet to catch any juices that bubble over. Bake until the pastry is puffed and golden brown and the apples are soft when poked with a knife, 50 to 60 minutes. Serve with vanilla ice cream, if using. [3]

[3] Puff pastry is best when fresh from the oven. If you have leftover pie, reheat in the oven at 250°F (120°C) until warmed through.

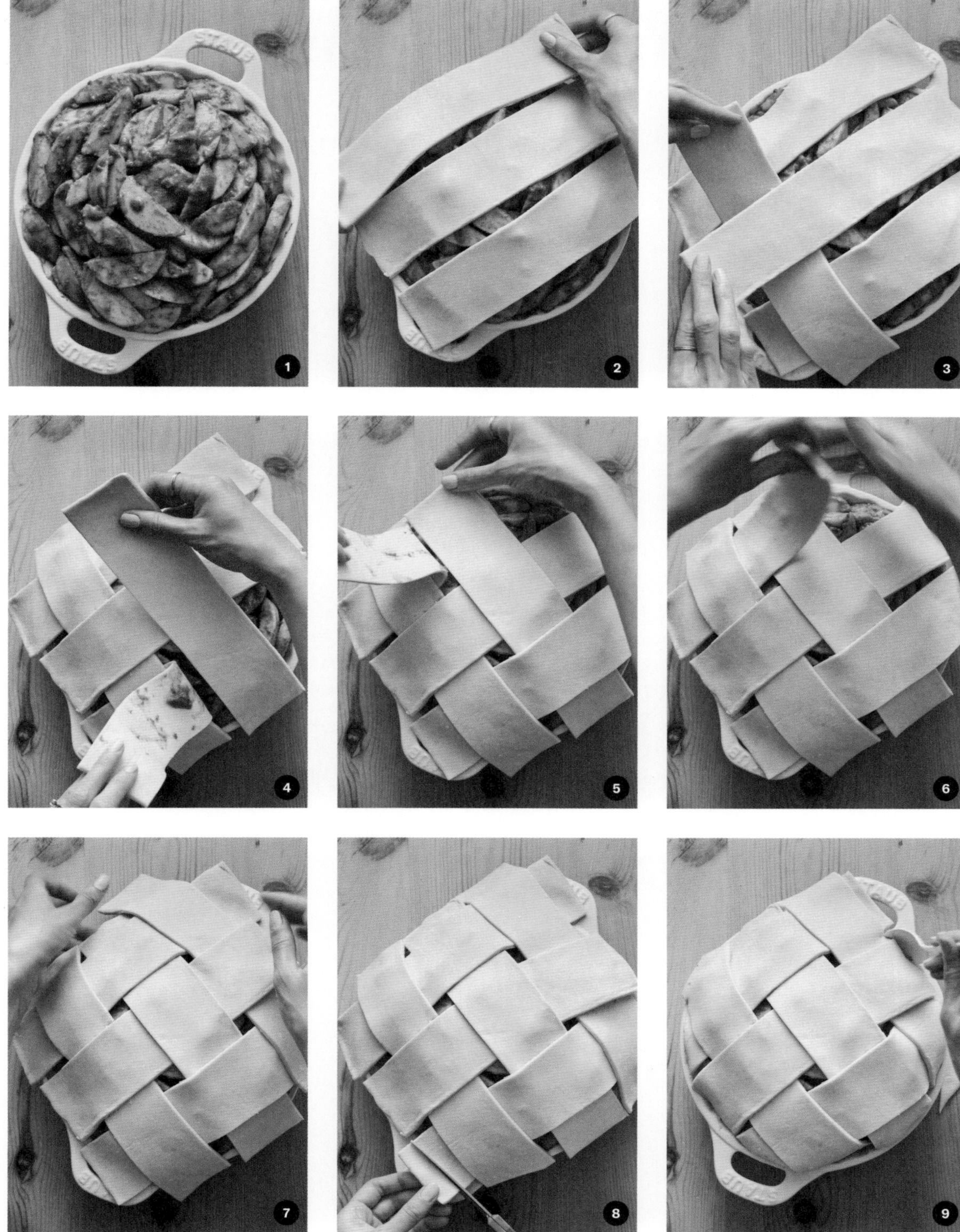

1
2
3
4
5
6
7
8
9

FLOURLESS CHOCOLATE CRACKLE COOKIES

1 cup (140g) raw **hazelnuts**

2½ cups (285g) **icing sugar**

¾ cup (63g) **Dutch-process cocoa powder**

¾ teaspoon (5g) **fine sea salt**

3 large **egg whites**, room temperature

2 teaspoons (10g) pure **vanilla extract**

5.3 oz (150g) **semi-sweet chocolate**, chopped (1 cup)

Chocolate lovers rejoice—these cookies are for you. They're soft and fudgy, with pockets of melted chocolate and toasted hazelnuts inside. If hazelnuts aren't your thing, swap them for pecans instead. The crackly, almost meringue-like exterior comes from the egg whites. The batter will seem very runny at first. Keep mixing, because it will thicken slightly. If you don't have a kitchen scale, fluff up ingredients like icing sugar and cocoa powder before measuring, then use the spoon-and-level method (page 19).

---

1. **Preheat the oven:** Place the oven racks in the upper and lower thirds of the oven and preheat to 350°F (180°C). Line 2 large baking sheets with parchment paper.

2. **Prep the hazelnuts:** Place the hazelnuts on one of the prepared baking sheets and bake on the upper rack until lightly toasted, 8 to 10 minutes, shaking the pan halfway through. Wrap the nuts in a clean kitchen towel and let steam for 5 minutes. Using your hands, rub the wrapped nuts to loosen as much of the skins as you can (it's okay if not all the skin comes off). Transfer the skinned nuts to a cutting board and roughly chop. Let cool.

3. **Meanwhile, mix the dough:** In a large bowl, whisk together the icing sugar, cocoa powder, and salt to remove lumps, about 1 minute. Add the egg whites and vanilla and whisk until the batter thickens slightly to resemble a smooth, glossy cake batter. Stir in the cooled hazelnuts and the chocolate.

4. **Scoop and bake:** Scoop 2-tablespoon portions of cookie dough (about the size of a ping-pong ball) onto the prepared baking sheets, leaving 2 inches (5 cm) between them. (You should have 18 balls.) Bake until the edges of the cookies are set and the tops are wrinkled, 8 to 10 minutes, swapping top and bottom positions halfway through. ❶ Let the cookies cool on the baking sheet for 10 minutes, then use a flexible spatula to carefully transfer them to a rack to cool completely. ❷

---

❶ If you love perfectly round cookies, you can use the edge of a flexible spatula to gently shape the cookie edges when they are hot from the oven.

❷ Store baked cookies in an airtight container at room temperature for up to 3 days.

ACTIVE TIME: 20 MINUTES • **TOTAL TIME:** 45 MINUTES • **SERVES** 5 TO 6

BUTTERSCOTCH BANANA DUTCH BABY PANCAKE

DUTCH BABY

3 large **eggs**

⅔ cup (87g) **all-purpose flour**

⅔ cup (151g) **whole milk**

1 tablespoon (13g) **granulated sugar**

1 teaspoon (5g) pure **vanilla extract**

½ teaspoon (1g) **cinnamon**

2 tablespoons (28g) **unsalted butter**

BUTTERSCOTCH SAUCE

3 tablespoons (38g) packed **dark brown sugar**

3 tablespoons (43g) **whipping (35%) cream**

2 tablespoons (28g) **unsalted butter**

2 teaspoons (10g) pure **vanilla extract**

Pinch of **fine sea salt**

FOR SERVING

Icing sugar, for dusting

Sliced **bananas**

Chopped **pecans** [1]

Whipped cream (optional)

The Dutch baby was the first recipe I learned in home economics. If a room full of high-schoolers could pull it off, so can you! This version goes over the top in the best way possible. It's drizzled with a stunningly simple butterscotch sauce and topped with fresh bananas and pecans. Letting the batter rest and come up to room temperature—while the oven heats—helps the pancake puff up in the oven.

---

1. **Preheat the oven and skillet:** Place an oven rack in the centre position and set a 10-inch (25 cm) cast-iron skillet on the rack. Preheat the oven to 425°F (220°C).

2. **Start the Dutch Baby—mix the batter:** In a blender, combine the eggs, flour, milk, granulated sugar, vanilla, and cinnamon. Blend until smooth and frothy, about 45 seconds. Set the container of batter aside to rest for at least 10 minutes so it comes up to room temperature.

3. **Pour the batter into the hot skillet and bake:** When the oven is heated, use oven mitts to carefully remove the hot skillet. Add the butter to the skillet and, using a pastry brush, thoroughly coat the bottom and sides of the skillet with the melted butter. Quickly pour the batter into the hot skillet and bake until the pancake is puffy and golden brown in the middle, 18 to 22 minutes.

4. **Meanwhile, make the Butterscotch Sauce:** In a small saucepan, whisk together the brown sugar, cream, and butter. Cook over medium heat until the sauce is bubbling. Once bubbling, cook, whisking occasionally, until the sauce thickens enough to coat the back of a spoon, 5 to 7 minutes. Whisk in the vanilla and salt. Remove from the heat. The sauce will continue to thicken as it cools.

5. **Assemble:** Dust the top of the pancake with the icing sugar. Top with sliced bananas, pecans, and butterscotch sauce. Slice into wedges and serve warm, with a dollop of whipped cream, if using.

GLUTEN-FREE: Use your favourite gluten-free 1-to-1 flour blend.

---

[1] You can toast the pecans first for extra flavour: Put the whole pecans in the skillet to toast while the oven preheats. Once fragrant, remove the pecans from the oven, let cool, and then chop. (Make sure to return the empty skillet to the oven, so it continues to heat.)

ACTIVE TIME: 15 MINUTES • **TOTAL TIME:** 5 HOURS 15 MINUTES (WITH FREEZE TIME) • **MAKES** 8 CUPS (2 L)

S'MORES NO-CHURN ICE CREAM

2 cups (200g) **mini marshmallows** ❶

2½ cups (568g) **whipping (35%) cream**

1 can (10 fl oz / 300 ml) **sweetened condensed milk**

4 teaspoons (20g) pure **vanilla extract**

1 teaspoon (6g) **fine sea salt**

1 cup (70g) crushed **graham crackers** ❷

3.6 oz (100g) **bittersweet chocolate**, finely chopped (⅔ cup)

This is campfire s'mores in a scoop. The ice cream is packed with marshmallows, graham crackers, and chocolate. The texture is extremely creamy, which is surprising given you don't need an ice-cream maker. I prefer to use a resealable freezer-safe glass container to store homemade ice cream. If you don't have one, you can use a loaf pan instead; cover it tightly with a layer of plastic wrap and then a layer of foil to keep out air. For the best texture and flavour, eat your homemade ice cream within 2 weeks (*if it lasts that long!*).

---

1. **Toast the marshmallows:** Spread the marshmallows on an unlined baking sheet. If you have a kitchen torch, use it to toast the marshmallows until golden brown. Otherwise, place an oven rack in the centre position and set the oven to broil. Broil the marshmallows until golden brown, 15 to 60 seconds (watch carefully, as they can burn quickly). Let the marshmallows cool completely on the baking sheet before lifting them with a flexible spatula. ❸

2. **Whip the cream:** In a medium bowl, and using a handheld mixer, whip the cream until it holds medium-stiff peaks. (When the beaters are lifted, the tip of the peak should curl over just slightly but otherwise hold its shape.)

3. **Combine:** In a large bowl, stir together the condensed milk, vanilla, and salt. Using a silicone spatula, gently fold the whipped cream into the condensed milk. Set aside 2 to 3 tablespoons of the marshmallows, graham crackers, and chocolate for garnish; sprinkle the rest into the ice cream mixture. Gently fold until incorporated.

4. **Assemble and freeze:** Spoon the ice cream mixture into an 8-cup (2 L) freezer-safe container with a lid (or a 9 x 5-inch / 2 L loaf pan). Sprinkle the reserved graham crackers, chocolate, and marshmallows on top. Cover tightly and freeze until solid, 5 to 6 hours (maybe longer, depending on your freezer).

GLUTEN-FREE: Use gluten-free graham crackers.

---

❶ Most marshmallows are made with gelatin, so they are not vegetarian/vegan. Check the labels if needed—brands like Dandies make vegan marshmallows. If using non-vegan marshmallows, which weigh less, use 2 cups (90g).

❷ To quickly crush graham crackers, place them in a resealable bag and use your fingers (or a rolling pin) to break them into small pieces. You could also use a food processor.

❸ If using the broiler method, some of the marshmallows might stick to the baking sheet (especially if using non-vegan marshmallows). Just scoop them up and add them to the ice cream—they'll still contribute mashmallowy flavour and texture. Don't use parchment paper, which can burn under the broiler.

SAUCES &
EXTRAS

ACTIVE TIME: 5 MINUTES • **TOTAL TIME:** 35 MINUTES • **MAKES** ABOUT 2 CUPS

QUICK PICKLED RED ONIONS

⅔ cup **boiling water**

1 tablespoon **granulated** or **cane sugar**

1 teaspoon **fine sea salt**

⅔ cup **apple cider vinegar**

1 **red onion**, thinly sliced ❷

Whatever you're eating, it's probably better with pickled red onions. They are amazingly versatile. You can use pickled red onions in sandwiches, salads, pizzas, bowls, and tacos. Always keep a jar in the fridge—you won't regret it. To keep things simple, this recipe skips the stovetop: just boil the water in the kettle and combine everything in a mason jar. Quick-pickling is a short-term preservation technique, so quick pickled onions are best used within a couple of weeks, but they'll probably be long gone by then!

---

1. **Prep the jar:** Run warm water over a 4-cup (1 L) mason jar to warm the glass. ❶

2. **Combine:** Pour the boiling water into the mason jar. Add the sugar and salt, then stir until dissolved. Pour in the apple cider vinegar and add the sliced red onion. Use a spoon to press the onions down into the liquid. If the onions are not fully submerged, add equal parts of additional water and apple cider vinegar to cover.

3. **Marinate:** The pickled red onions are best enjoyed when soft and light pink. You can enjoy them after 30 minutes of soaking, but they'll get better over time. Let sit on the counter for 1 hour to cool, seal with the lid, and refrigerate for up to 2 weeks.

---

❶ While mason jars are intended to hold hot liquid, sudden temperature changes can occasionally damage the glass. Warming the glass before adding boiling water will help prevent cracking.

❷ You can quickly slice the red onions using a mandoline, but a sharp chef's knife works too. If you're planning to eat the pickled onions on the day you make them, try to slice the onion as thinly as possible so it pickles faster.

FRESH BASIL PESTO

ACTIVE TIME: 10 MINUTES • **TOTAL TIME:** 15 MINUTES • **MAKES** ABOUT ½ CUP

2 tablespoons **pine nuts**

1 **garlic clove**

1 cup packed **fresh basil leaves** (1.5 oz / 43g)

1 oz (28g) finely grated **Parmesan cheese** (¼ cup)

1 tablespoon **fresh lemon juice**

¼ teaspoon **fine sea salt**

3 to 4 tablespoons **extra-virgin olive oil**

❶ Use the pesto immediately or transfer it to a small airtight container and refrigerate for up to 3 days or freeze for up to 3 months. To further prevent the pesto from turning brown, place a piece of plastic wrap directly on the surface before sealing with a lid.

Pesto is best when it is homemade. Although there are some decent store-bought options, most are disappointing. When fresh basil is in season, do yourself a favour and make a big batch. Extra pesto can be tucked away in the freezer. A squeeze of fresh lemon juice not only adds refreshing acidity, but it also helps prevent the basil from turning brown. You can use the food processor to quickly grate the Parmesan cheese (see page 14).

1. **Toast the pine nuts:** In a small dry skillet over medium heat, toast the pine nuts, stirring frequently, until golden brown and fragrant, 3 to 6 minutes. Transfer the pine nuts to a food processor and let cool.

2. **Mix the pesto:** Add the garlic to the food processor and pulse until finely minced. Add the basil, Parmesan, lemon juice, and salt and pulse until finely minced. Scrape down the sides as needed. With the motor running, drizzle in the olive oil until a smooth paste forms, pausing to scrape down the sides as needed. Season with more salt, if needed. ❶

VEGAN PESTO

ACTIVE TIME: 10 MINUTES • **TOTAL TIME:** 15 MINUTES • **MAKES** ABOUT ½ CUP

2 tablespoons **pine nuts**

1 **garlic clove**

1 cup packed **fresh basil leaves** (1.5 oz / 43g)

4 teaspoons **fresh lemon juice**

2 teaspoons **white miso**

¼ teaspoon **fine sea salt**

3 to 4 tablespoons **extra-virgin olive oil**

❶ Use the pesto immediately or transfer it to a small airtight container and refrigerate for up to 3 days or freeze for up to 3 months. To further prevent the pesto from turning brown, place a piece of plastic wrap directly on the surface before sealing with a lid.

This cheese-free pesto sauce is delicious. Rather than relying on a vegan cheese substitute (such as dairy-free Parmesan cheese or nutritional yeast), I prefer to use miso. The miso provides a subtle boost of umami, while still letting the fresh basil flavour shine through. I use this pesto in pastas, sandwiches, pizzas—and pretty much a million other things.

1. **Toast the pine nuts:** In a small dry skillet over medium heat, toast the pine nuts, stirring frequently, until golden brown and fragrant, 3 to 6 minutes. Transfer the pine nuts to a food processor and let cool.

2. **Mix the pesto:** Add the garlic to the food processor and pulse until finely minced. Add the basil, lemon juice, miso, and salt and pulse until finely minced. Scrape down the sides as needed. With the motor running, drizzle in the olive oil until a smooth paste forms, pausing to scrape down the sides as needed. Season with more salt, if needed. ❶

vegan pesto
fresh basil pesto

vegan
tzatziki
tzatziki

TZATZIKI

ACTIVE TIME: 10 MINUTES • **TOTAL TIME:** 10 MINUTES • **MAKES** ABOUT 1½ CUPS

½ **English cucumber**
1 cup plain **Greek yogurt**
2 tablespoons chopped **fresh dill**
1 tablespoon **fresh lemon juice**
¼ teaspoon **garlic powder**
¼ to ½ teaspoon **fine sea salt**
Freshly ground **black pepper**

➊ Use the tzatziki immediately or transfer it to an airtight container and refrigerate for up to 3 days.

I don't like to play favourites (okay, I guess I kind of do!), but tzatziki holds a special place in my heart. It's creamy, fresh, and made with some of my favourite things, like dill, lemon, and Greek yogurt. Tzatziki is delicious for dipping falafel into, scooping up with veggies, and spooning into sandwiches. I find a nut milk bag most convenient for draining the cucumber (it's easy to clean and can be reused), but you can also use cheesecloth or a clean kitchen towel. Take the time to squeeze out as much moisture from the cucumber as you can, so it doesn't water down the sauce.

---

1. Grate and drain the cucumber: Grate the cucumber on the large holes of a box grater. Transfer the cucumber to a nut milk bag (or cheesecloth or a thin kitchen towel, gathering the corners to form a small sack). Twist the bag over the sink to squeeze out as much liquid as possible.

2. Mix the tzatziki: Transfer the cucumber to a medium bowl. Add the yogurt, dill, lemon juice, and garlic powder and whisk until combined. Season with ¼ teaspoon of the salt and pepper to taste. Add the remaining ¼ teaspoon salt, if needed. ➊

VEGAN TZATZIKI

ACTIVE TIME: 10 MINUTES • **TOTAL TIME:** 40 MINUTES (INCLUDING SOAKING) • **MAKES** ABOUT 1½ CUPS

¾ cup raw **cashews**
½ **English cucumber**
¼ cup **fresh lemon juice**
⅓ cup **cold water**
2 tablespoons chopped **fresh dill**
½ teaspoon **fine sea salt**
¼ teaspoon **garlic powder**
Freshly ground **black pepper**

➊ Use the tzatziki immediately or transfer it to an airtight container and refrigerate for up to 3 days.

I often make this vegan version when serving a crowd, and no one ever suspects it's dairy-free. Make sure the cashews are blended completely smooth before adding the rest of the ingredients. If you have a wide blender container, you may want to double the recipe so there's more volume at the base of the container for the blades to spin effectively. This tzatziki is super yummy, so you'll probably appreciate having extra on hand anyway.

---

1. Quick-soak the cashews: Place the cashews in a small heatproof bowl. Add enough boiling water to cover the cashews. Let soak for at least 30 minutes to soften. Drain.

2. Grate and drain the cucumber: Grate the cucumber on the large holes of a box grater. Transfer the cucumber to a nut milk bag (or cheesecloth or a thin kitchen towel, gathering the corners to form a small sack). Twist the bag over the sink to squeeze out as much liquid as possible.

3. Blend the cashew base: In a high-speed blender, combine the drained cashews, lemon juice, and water. Blend until smooth and creamy, about 2 minutes, scraping down the sides often.

4. Mix the tzatziki: Transfer the cashew mixture to a medium bowl. Add the cucumber, dill, salt, and garlic powder and whisk until combined. Season with pepper to taste, and more salt, if needed. ➊

YOGURT CAESAR DRESSING

ACTIVE TIME: 5 MINUTES • **TOTAL TIME:** 5 MINUTES • **MAKES** ABOUT ¾ CUP

½ cup plain **Greek yogurt** ❶

0.5 oz (14g) finely grated **Parmesan cheese** (2 tablespoons)

1 or 2 **garlic cloves**, finely grated

2 tablespoons **fresh lemon juice**

2 teaspoons drained and chopped **capers**

1 teaspoon **Dijon mustard**

½ teaspoon **fine sea salt**

½ teaspoon freshly ground **black pepper**

❶ Full-fat Greek yogurt is recommended for the best flavour, but low-fat works as well.
❷ Use the dressing immediately or transfer it to an airtight container and refrigerate for up to 3 days.

This creamy Caesar dressing puts a lighter spin on the classic. It uses Greek yogurt as the base instead of egg yolks and oil. Don't worry, there's still plenty of tasty Parmesan cheese, garlic, and lemon! Capers bring a briny element since we're not using anchovies. Use this dressing in the Seared Brussels Sprouts Caesar Salad (page 245), in sandwiches and wraps, or as a dip with fresh veggies.

1. **Mix the dressing:** In a small bowl, whisk the yogurt, Parmesan, garlic, lemon juice, capers, Dijon mustard, salt, and pepper until smooth. Add more salt, if needed. ❷

VEGAN CAESAR DRESSING

ACTIVE TIME: 5 MINUTES • **TOTAL TIME:** 35 MINUTES (INCLUDING SOAKING) • **MAKES** ABOUT ⅔ CUP

⅓ cup raw **cashews**

¼ cup **water**

2 tablespoons **extra-virgin olive oil**

1½ teaspoons **Dijon mustard**

2 **garlic cloves**, finely grated

1 teaspoon **lemon zest**

2 tablespoons **fresh lemon juice**

2 teaspoons drained and chopped **capers**

½ teaspoon **fine sea salt**

½ teaspoon freshly ground **black pepper**

❶ If your blender has a wide container, you may want to double the recipe so there's more dressing for the blender to process. This way, the blades run more smoothly.
❷ Use the dressing immediately or transfer it to an airtight container and refrigerate for up to 3 days.

This is my go-to dairy-free Caesar dressing. Garlic and lemon zest help mute the natural sweetness of the creamy cashews. This dressing doesn't need, or even call for grated vegan Parmesan cheese, but you could sprinkle some in if you'd like. If you prefer things on the salty side, you may want to add an extra pinch of salt at the end. Let your taste buds be your guide. This is your dressing, after all.

1. **Quick-soak the cashews:** Place the cashews in a small heatproof bowl. Add enough boiling water to cover the cashews. Let soak for at least 30 minutes to soften. Drain.

2. **Blend ❶:** In a high-speed blender, combine the drained cashews, water, olive oil, and Dijon mustard. Blend for 1 minute. Scrape down the sides, then blend again until completely smooth, about 1 minute more.

3. **Mix the dressing:** Transfer the contents of the blender into a small bowl. Add the garlic, lemon zest, lemon juice, capers, salt, and pepper and whisk until smooth. Add more salt, if needed. ❷

vegan
caesar
dressing
yogurt
caesar
dressing

QUICK PIZZA DOUGH

2 cups **all-purpose flour** (260g)

1 teaspoon **instant (quick-rise) yeast** (4g) ❶

¾ teaspoon **fine sea salt** (5g)

¾ to 1 cup **warm water** (170g to 236g) ❷

Extra-virgin olive oil, for the bowl

This super-simple dough comes together in no time. It's so easy that it makes it hard to justify buying store-bought dough. Use this for the Mediterranean Pesto Pizza (page 117), Flatbread with Orange Arugula Salad (page 48), Cheesy Mushroom Calzones (page 190), and even for dessert (Cardamom Sugar Knots, page 265). When you're using the dough in a recipe, if it feels resistant when you're shaping or rolling it, simply let it rest for 5 to 10 minutes. This will give the gluten a chance to relax, making the dough easier to stretch.

1. **Mix the dough:** In a large bowl, stir together the flour, yeast, and salt. Create a well in the centre. Pour ¾ cup of the warm water into the well and use a flexible stirring spoon to mix until a shaggy dough forms. If the dough is too dry, mix in more water, 1 tablespoon at a time. Use your hand to roll the dough around in the bowl to incorporate any remaining bits of flour.

2. **Knead the dough:** Transfer the dough to a lightly floured work surface. Knead until the dough is a smooth ball and slowly springs back when poked with a finger, 2 to 4 minutes.

3. **Let the dough rise:** Lightly grease a large bowl with olive oil. Transfer the dough to the bowl and roll it around to lightly coat on all sides. Cover the bowl with plastic wrap or a clean kitchen towel. Let sit in a warm place until the dough has doubled in size, about 30 minutes. ❸

❶ Yeast has an expiry date, so check the package to make sure it's still active.

❷ The water should ideally be 120°F (50°C), which feels like warm bath water. Since the yeast is mixed with flour first, it can take hotter water than when it's proofed the traditional way, directly in warm water. But avoid water that is above 130°F (55°C), which will start to kill the yeast.

❸ Use immediately or cover the bowl tightly with plastic wrap and refrigerate for up to 24 hours. Let the dough come up to room temperature (covered) before rolling or stretching it.

ACTIVE TIME: 5 MINUTES • **TOTAL TIME:** 5 MINUTES • **MAKES** ABOUT 1 CUP

EVERYDAY GUACAMOLE

2 ripe **avocados**

1 to 2 tablespoons **fresh lime juice**

3 to 4 tablespoons chopped **fresh cilantro leaves**

¼ teaspoon **ground cumin** (optional)

Fine sea salt

This isn't a fancy guacamole, but it is the version I make almost weekly. Treat this as a loose "recipe" and adjust it to your tastes. Feel free to add chopped tomatoes, onions, or whatever else gets you excited.

1. **Prep the avocados:** Cut the avocados in half, remove the pit, and scoop out the flesh into a medium bowl. Use a fork to mash the avocado to desired consistency.

2. **Mix the guacamole:** Stir in the lime juice, cilantro, cumin (if using), and salt. Taste and adjust seasoning, if needed. ❶

❶ Use the guacamole immediately or place a piece of plastic wrap directly on the surface (to prevent browning) and refrigerate for up to 1 day.

ACTIVE TIME: 20 MINUTES • **TOTAL TIME:** 35 MINUTES • **MAKES** ABOUT 5 CUPS

GARLIC MASHED POTATOES

2½ lb (1.125kg) **Yukon Gold potatoes**, peeled and quartered ❶

½ cup **whole milk**

6 tablespoons softened **unsalted butter**

1 oz (28g) grated **Parmesan cheese** (¼ cup)

1 teaspoon **garlic powder**

Fine sea salt (about ½ teaspoon)

FOR GARNISH (OPTIONAL)

Melted **unsalted butter**

Chopped **fresh chives**

My dad always makes his "famous" mashed potatoes at family get-togethers. It involves plenty of butter and raiding the spice cabinet for garlic powder. I know some people turn their nose up at garlic powder, but I think there's a place for it. It's a quick way to add mellow garlic flavour. If you happen to have some slow-roasted garlic, you could add it instead. Treat this recipe as a guide, but feel free to heavily modify, as I've done. If it was up to my dad, he'd go ahead and add a lot more butter.

---

1. **Boil the potatoes:** Add the potatoes to a large pot of water, cover with the lid slightly ajar, and boil over high heat until tender when poked with a fork, 12 to 15 minutes. Drain the potatoes in a colander and let sit for 1 minute to release excess water.

2. **Rice or mash the potatoes:** Using a potato ricer, press the warm potatoes back into the pot. (Alternatively, you can mash the warm potatoes in the pot with a potato masher.) Using a silicone spatula, stir in the milk, butter, Parmesan, garlic powder, and salt to taste. Cover with a lid and keep warm over low heat until ready to serve. ❷ Garnish with the melted butter and chopped chives, if using.

Vegan: Use vegan butter and plain unsweetened barista-style dairy-free milk or creamer. Use vegan Parmesan cheese.

---

❶ Peeling the potatoes will result in a smoother, creamier mash. But Yukon Gold potatoes have such a thin skin that you can skip peeling, if you'd like.

❷ If the mashed potatoes have been sitting for a while, loosen them before serving with a splash of milk.

COOKING RICE

To say that rice is important to the Asian side of my family is no doubt an understatement. When I left home for college, my parting gift was a small rice cooker. So, for the longest time, the idea of cooking rice on the stove once terrified me. And it's no wonder! Have you read the back of a rice package? It seems like every bag of rice recommends a different rice-to-water ratio, even when it's referring to the same type of rice. How confusing!

I went through many bags of rice to find the method and ratios that I think are *almost* good enough to replace my rice cooker. If you eat rice on a near-daily basis or want to keep rice warm for a while, you'll probably still appreciate a rice cooker. In my opinion, it makes better brown rice than on the stovetop (just being honest!). But these methods and ratios are reliable enough that you don't exactly *need* a rice cooker. I use a Dutch oven for cooking rice because the heavy lid prevents the steam from escaping from the pot, and the heavy pot keeps rice warm until serving. But any medium pot with a heavy lid will also work. (Bonus points if it's glass, so you can see the rice in the pot without removing the lid.)

For best results, measure the water at eye level, in a liquid measuring cup set on a flat surface.

JASMINE RICE

ACTIVE TIME: 5 MINUTES • **TOTAL TIME:** 30 MINUTES • **MAKES** ABOUT 4 CUPS

1⅓ cups **jasmine rice**

1⅔ cups **water**

1. **Rinse the rice:** Rinse the rice in a sieve under cold running water, while swishing the rice with your fingertips, until the water runs mostly clear, about 1 minute. Shake the sieve to remove excess water (too much water will throw off your ratios, so drain well).

2. **Cook the rice:** Add the rice and water to a Dutch oven or medium pot and bring to a boil over high heat. Once the water is boiling, immediately cover with the lid, reduce the heat to medium-low and simmer for 15 minutes. Tilt the pot and quickly peek under the lid to confirm the water has been absorbed. (If not, continue to cook for 2 or 3 minutes more.) Remove from the heat.

3. **Steam the rice:** Keep the lid on the pot and let the rice steam for another 10 minutes. Fluff the rice with a fork or rice paddle.

MEDIUM-GRAIN AND LONG-GRAIN WHITE RICE

ACTIVE TIME: 5 MINUTES • **TOTAL TIME:** 30 MINUTES • **MAKES** ABOUT 4 CUPS

1⅓ cups **medium-grain** or **long-grain white rice**

2 cups **water**

1. **Rinse the rice:** Rinse the rice in a sieve under cold running water, while swishing the rice with your fingertips, until the water runs mostly clear, about 1 minute. Shake the sieve to remove excess water (too much water will throw off your ratios, so strain well).

2. **Cook the rice:** Transfer the rice to a Dutch oven or medium pot, cover with the water, and bring to a boil, uncovered, over high heat. Once the water is boiling, immediately cover with the lid, reduce the heat to low, and simmer for 15 minutes. Tilt the pot and quickly peek under the lid to confirm the water has been absorbed. If not, continue to cook for 2 or 3 minutes more. Remove from the heat.

3. **Steam the rice:** Keep the lid on the pot and let the rice steam for another 10 minutes. Fluff the rice with a fork or rice paddle.

SHORT-GRAIN BROWN RICE

ACTIVE TIME: 5 MINUTES • **TOTAL TIME:** 45 MINUTES • **MAKES** ABOUT 4 CUPS

10 cups **water**

1⅓ cups **short-grain brown rice**

1. **Bring the water to a boil:** In a Dutch oven or large pot with the lid slightly ajar, bring the water to a boil over medium-high heat.

2. **Cook the rice ("pasta method"):** Add the rice to the boiling water and cook, uncovered, maintaining a rolling boil over medium-high heat, until the rice is cooked through, about 30 minutes. As the rice boils, there should be plenty of water in the pot so the grains are moving around freely while cooking. If not, top up with more water.

3. **Drain and steam:** Quickly drain the rice in a sieve and shake off excess water. Return the rice to the pot, cover with the lid, and let steam for 10 minutes. Fluff the rice with a fork or rice paddle.

ACKNOWLEDGEMENTS

This book couldn't have happened without the many marvellous people who provided much-needed encouragement and hours of hard work to bring this project to life.

To my love, Anguel. Working with your spouse every day isn't easy. Working with your spouse, writing a book, *and* living in the middle of renovations is near impossible. But we did it. Thank you for your near-endless optimism, for your beautiful photography, and for cleaning up the kitchen (every, single, night). This book is as much yours as it is mine.

To my family, thank you for always supporting my dreams—and for not blinking an eye when I decided that I'd like my day job to involve eating, cooking, and fluffing food. I took a winding path to get to food as a career, and all the while, you knew I'd end up back here. Mom: Thank you for always lending your discerning palate (and for your brutal honesty), for being a dishwasher extraordinaire, and for your enthusiasm for shopping for "hero" produce. Dad: Thank you for eating your way through this entire book (at least twice), for giving the best advice, and for always making me laugh. Melissa: I feel so lucky to have a stepmom and a friend in you; thank you for always lending your ears. Sean: My forever littlish brother and built-in bestie for life, thank you for always making me laugh, for providing five-star tech support, and for being up for any adventure we throw your way. Popo (Grandma Lee): Even though you can't read this, we all know you understand English far better than you let on . . . thank you for passing on your love of eating all things wontons, noodles, and rice. Grandma Beaudoin: Thank you for being the first baker in my life. And to the rest of my family, thank you for your support and enthusiasm; I feel so lucky to have you.

To all the recipe testers, thank you for investing so much time and care into cooking and perfecting these recipes: Andrea Rush, Claire Wong, Shawn Johnstone, Alexa Hubley, Sean Beaudoin, Nora Lee, Emily Carlson, Kimberly Cheung, Sophie Mackenzie, Anna Thompson, Anna Schlagintweit, Erica Purcell, Jessica Soucy, Ryan Cutting, Heather Arnold, and Jeremy and Erynn Tucker. Much of this book was developed during the COVID-19 pandemic, and it brought special challenges of both sourcing ingredients and connecting in person, so thank you for getting creative. Andrea and Claire: Thank you for letting me watch you cook through recipes LIVE ON VIDEO. It was so fun, so helpful—and I'm sorry to make you eat food while I watched.

To my editor, Andrea Magyar, thank you for reaching out years ago, for patiently waiting while I built up the courage to do my own book, and for your unwavering support and encouragement throughout this process. Thank you for always being there to answer all my questions (I know there were a lot); I am so grateful to have done this together. To the team at Penguin Random House Canada, including the book's designer, Kate Sinclair, thank you for all the energy and enthusiasm you put into this, and to Shaun Oakey for being a copy editor extraordinaire.

To Molly Reeder, thank you for believing in this project and for contributing such stunning illustrations. You are a creative force, and I am so grateful to have your art in this book (and in my real-life kitchen!).

To my friends, thank you for understanding when Anguel and I disappeared for weeks (months?! years?!) to meet deadlines. Shawn and Alexa: We are beyond blessed to have friends like you. Thank you for supporting us throughout this entire process—detailed testing notes, photo review sessions, and the emergency tofu shipment. Alexa: Thank you for both editing *and* making some of the beautiful ceramics used in photographing this book—what can't you do?! Sophie: Thank you for answering all my ridiculous questions, and for not missing a beat when we go from discussing cat treats to the semantics of blending soup. Gab: Thank you for putting up with the incessant cookbook talk, for being so understanding of my schedule when booking your own shoots, and for introducing me to the food styling world in the first place.

And last but not least, to the readers of *Evergreen Kitchen* (evergreenkitchen.ca). What started as a silly project to share vegetarian recipes has grown into something much more fulfilling than Anguel and I ever imagined. Thank you to our readers, our brand partners, and anyone else who has—in any way—been a part of our little corner of the internet. We are eternally grateful. You made this book possible.

INDEX

A

acorn squash: Miso Ginger Glazed Squash, 54
Actually Good Fried Rice, 121
almond butter: Spicy Almond Sauce, 76
almonds
- Broccoli Salad with Sticky Harissa Sauce, 242
- Hot Honey Roasted Carrots and Lentils, 40
- Pesto Grain Bowls with Jammy Eggs, 143

apples
- Bottomless Apple Caramel Pie, 277–278
- Roasted Butternut Squash Soup with Buttery Sage Croutons, 219
- Savoury Cheddar Apple Hand Pies, 137–138

artichokes: Spinach and Artichoke Pasta, 87
arugula: Flatbread with Orange Arugula Salad, 48
asparagus
- Asparagus, Pea, and Whipped Feta Tart, 43
- Coconut Green Curry Pasta, 99
- Vibrant Greens Salad with Sesame Lime Vinaigrette, 249

avocados
- Everyday Guacamole, 298
- Roasted Sweet Potatoes with Jalapeño Cilantro Slaw, 254
- Santa Fe Salad with Chipotle Lime Vinaigrette, 235
- Veggie Sushi with Sriracha Mayo, 185–186

B

baked goods *see also* breads; pies and tarts
- Banana Chocolate Muffins, 274
- Brown Butter Chocolate Walnut Cookies, 262
- Cardamom Sugar Knots, 265
- Cheesy Mushroom Calzones, 190
- Flourless Chocolate Crackle Cookies, 280
- Jammy Raspberry Streusel Bars, 259–260

Baked Rice Pilaf with Feta and Roasted Tomatoes, 39
balsamic vinegar
- Balsamic Vegetable and Goat Cheese Sandwiches, 197
- Roasted Vegetables with Balsamic Glaze, 57

bananas
- Banana Chocolate Muffins, 274
- Butterscotch Banana Dutch Baby Pancake, 283

Barbecue Pulled Mushroom Sandwiches, 109
Barley Salad with Mushrooms and Burrata, 250
Bars, Jammy Raspberry Streusel, 259–260
basil
- Basil Oil, 147
- Fresh Basil Pesto, 290
- Vegan Pesto, 290

basil, Thai: Thai Basil and Lime Vinaigrette, 168
beans *see* butter beans; cannellini beans; chickpeas; green beans; kidney beans; navy beans; pinto beans
bell peppers
- Coconut Green Curry Pasta, 99
- Ginger Soy Soba Salad with Spicy Peanut Sauce, 95
- Grilled Halloumi Skewers with Thai Basil and Lime Vinaigrette, 168
- Grilled Vegetables, 197
- Harissa-Roasted Vegetables with Couscous, 62
- Lemon and Dill Orzo Salad, 83
- Mediterranean Pesto Pizza, 117
- Santa Fe Salad with Chipotle Lime Vinaigrette, 235
- Sheet-Pan Veggie Fajitas, 61
- Veggie Pad Thai, 88

berries
- Jammy Raspberry Streusel Bars, 259–260
- Whipped Yogurt Cream with Berries, 271

Bibimbap with Crispy Rice, 144
black beans
- Frico-Style Quesadillas, 194
- Santa Fe Salad with Chipotle Lime Vinaigrette, 235
- Sheet-Pan Veggie Fajitas, 61
- Sweet Potato Black Bean Burgers with Chipotle Mayo, 177

Blistered Tomatoes and Whipped Ricotta Toasts, 193

bok choy, baby
Crispy Rice Salad with Smashed Cucumbers, 236
Sesame and Smoked Tofu Noodle Soup, 220
Bottomless Apple Caramel Pie, 277–278
bowls
Bibimbap with Crispy Rice, 144
Burrito Bowls with Smoky Sofritas, 161
Charred Sweet Potatoes with Tomato Chili Jam, 148
Falafel Bowls, 154
Orange Ginger and Sesame Meatballs, 162
Peanut-Glazed Tofu Rice Bowls, 157
Pesto Grain Bowls with Jammy Eggs, 143
Polenta with Roasted Tomatoes and Basil Oil, 147
Shortcut Brothy Beans, 151
Smashed Potatoes and Roasted Cauliflower Bowls, 158
Braised Vegetables with Parmesan Croutons, 66
breads *see also* baked goods; croutons; toasts
Cheesy Bread, 201
Flatbreads, 48
Garlic Bread, 103–104
Garlicky Breadcrumbs, 224
Quick Pizza Dough, 297
broccoli
Broccoli Salad with Sticky Harissa Sauce, 242
Curry Vegetable Fritters, 178
No Cream of Broccoli Soup with Garlicky Breadcrumbs, 224
broccolini
Firecracker Tofu with Broccolini and Chili Garlic Oil, 47
Vibrant Greens Salad with Sesame Lime Vinaigrette, 249
Brown Butter Chocolate Walnut Cookies, 262
Brussels sprouts
Coconut Green Curry Pasta, 99
Roasted Vegetables with Balsamic Glaze, 57
Seared Brussels Sprouts Caesar Salad, 245
Buffalo-Sauced Cauliflower with Ranch Celery Salad, 133–134
Burgers, Sweet Potato Black Bean, with Chipotle Mayo, 177
burrata cheese: Barley Salad with Mushrooms and Burrata, 250
Burrito Bowls with Smoky Sofritas, 161
butter beans: Shortcut Brothy Beans, 151
butternut squash
Roasted Butternut Squash Pasta with Toasted Hazelnuts, 96
Roasted Butternut Squash Soup with Buttery Sage Croutons, 219
Butterscotch Banana Dutch Baby Pancake, 283
Butterscotch Sauce, 283
Buttery Sage Croutons, 219

C

cabbage
Barbecue Pulled Mushroom Sandwiches, 109
Braised Vegetables with Parmesan Croutons, 66
Crispy Veggie Potstickers, 129
Miso Ginger Glazed Squash, 54
Quick Pickled Cabbage, 154
Roasted Sweet Potatoes with Jalapeño Cilantro Slaw, 254
Sheet-Pan Veggie Fajitas, 61
Calzones, Cheesy Mushroom, 190
cannellini beans
Baked Rice Pilaf with Feta and Roasted Tomatoes, 39
Barley Salad with Mushrooms and Burrata, 250
Braised Vegetables with Parmesan Croutons, 66
Creamy White Beans, 133–134
Crispy Eggplant Roll-Ups, 58
Roasted Butternut Squash Soup with Buttery Sage Croutons, 219
Caprese Pesto Panini, 182
caramel: Bottomless Apple Caramel Pie, 277–278
Caramelized Onions, 126
Cardamom Sugar Knots, 265
carrots
Actually Good Fried Rice, 121
Bibimbap with Crispy Rice, 144
Braised Vegetables with Parmesan Croutons, 66
Coconut Green Curry Pasta, 99
Crispy Veggie Potstickers, 129
Curry Vegetable Fritters, 178
Hot Honey Roasted Carrots and Lentils, 40
Peanut-Glazed Tofu Rice Bowls, 157
Quick Pickled Carrots, 171
Roasted Vegetables with Balsamic Glaze, 57
Shepherd's Pie, 118
Vegetable Bourguignon, 122
Veggie Skillet Pot Pie, 106
Veggie Wonton Soup, 229–230
cashews
No Cream of Broccoli Soup with Garlicky Breadcrumbs, 224
Roasted Butternut Squash Pasta with Toasted Hazelnuts, 96
Seared Mushroom and Creamy Garlic Pasta, 79
Vegan Caesar Dressing, 294
Vegan Tzatziki, 293
cauliflower
Buffalo-Sauced Cauliflower with Ranch Celery Salad, 133–134
Healthier Macaroni and Cheese, 113
Roasted Cauliflower, Smashed Olive, and Lemon Pasta, 91
Silky Cauliflower Soup with Cheese and Pepper Crisps, 202
Smashed Potatoes and Roasted Cauliflower Bowls, 158

celery
Actually Good Fried Rice, 121
Braised Vegetables with Parmesan Croutons, 66
Celery Salad, 133–134
Green Goddess Salad with Everything Bagel Croutons, 246
Shepherd's Pie, 118
Vegetable Bourguignon, 122
Charred Sweet Potatoes with Tomato Chili Jam, 148
cheddar cheese
Cheesy Bread, 201
Cheesy Chipotle Quinoa Bake, 44
Cheesy Mushroom Calzones, 190
Frico-Style Quesadillas, 194
Healthier Macaroni and Cheese, 113
Pesto and Greens Frittata, 65
Savoury Cheddar Apple Hand Pies, 137–138
Silky Cauliflower Soup with Cheese and Pepper Crisps, 202
cheeses *see also specific cheeses*
Creamy Goat Cheese, 48
Ricotta Cream, 65
chickpeas
Broccoli Salad with Sticky Harissa Sauce, 242
Charred Sweet Potatoes with Tomato Chili Jam, 148
Chickpea Salad with Crispy Pita, 239
Falafel Bowls, 154
Harissa-Roasted Vegetables with Couscous, 62
Hot Honey Roasted Carrots and Lentils, 40
Pesto Pantry Pasta, 71
Roasted Sweet Potatoes with Jalapeño Cilantro Slaw, 254
Roasted Vegetables with Balsamic Glaze, 57
Smoky Chickpea Crumble, 245
Chili, Easy Veggie, 216
chipotle peppers in adobo
Cheesy Chipotle Quinoa Bake, 44
Chipotle Lime Vinaigrette, 235
Chipotle Mayo, 177
Chipotle Mushroom Tacos with Pineapple Jalapeño Salsa, 174
chocolate
Banana Chocolate Muffins, 274
Brown Butter Chocolate Walnut Cookies, 262
Chocolate Pudding with Pretzel Crumble, 268
Flourless Chocolate Crackle Cookies, 280
S'Mores No-Churn Ice Cream, 284
Chowder, Smoky Jalapeño Corn, 209
cilantro
Everyday Guacamole, 298
Herb Sauce, 158
Jalapeño Cilantro Slaw, 254
coconut milk
Coconut Green Curry Pasta, 99
Lemongrass Coconut Rice with Roasted Eggplant, 51
Thai Yellow Coconut Curry with Lentils, 205
condiments *see* dips and spreads
cookies
Brown Butter Chocolate Walnut, 262
Flourless Chocolate Crackle, 280
corn
Cheesy Chipotle Quinoa Bake, 44
Santa Fe Salad with Chipotle Lime Vinaigrette, 235
Smoky Jalapeño Corn Chowder, 209
cornmeal: Polenta with Roasted Tomatoes and Basil Oil, 147
cottage cheese: Crispy Eggplant Roll-Ups, 58
couscous: Harissa-Roasted Vegetables with Couscous, 62
cranberries, dried: Chickpea Salad with Crispy Pita, 239
Creamy Goat Cheese, 48
Creamy Roasted Red Pepper Pasta, 80
Creamy White Beans, 133–134
cremini mushrooms *see* mushrooms, cremini
Crispy Cauliflower, 133–134
Crispy Eggplant Roll-Ups, 58
Crispy Rice Salad with Smashed Cucumbers, 236
Crispy Tofu Banh Mi, 171–172
Crispy Veggie Potstickers, 129
croutons *see also* breads
Buttery Sage Croutons, 219
Croutons, 245
Green Goddess Salad with Everything Bagel Croutons, 246
cucumbers
Bibimbap with Crispy Rice, 144
Chickpea Salad with Crispy Pita, 239
Crispy Rice Salad with Smashed Cucumbers, 236
Lemon and Dill Orzo Salad, 83
Tzatziki, 293
Vegan Tzatziki, 293
Veggie Sushi with Sriracha Mayo, 185–186
curry paste
Coconut Green Curry Pasta, 99
Thai Yellow Coconut Curry with Lentils, 205
curry powder: Curry Vegetable Fritters, 178

D

dates, Medjool
Broccoli Salad with Sticky Harissa Sauce, 242
Date Barbecue Sauce, 109
Santa Fe Salad with Chipotle Lime Vinaigrette, 235
desserts
Banana Chocolate Muffins, 274
Bottomless Apple Caramel Pie, 277–278
Brown Butter Chocolate Walnut Cookies, 262
Butterscotch Banana Dutch Baby Pancake, 283
Cardamom Sugar Knots, 265

Chocolate Pudding with Pretzel Crumble, 268
Flourless Chocolate Crackle Cookies, 280
Jammy Raspberry Streusel Bars, 259–260
S'Mores No-Churn Ice Cream, 284
Whipped Yogurt Cream with Berries, 271
dill
Lemon and Dill Orzo Salad, 83
Tartar Sauce, 125
Tzatziki, 293
Vegan Tzatziki, 293
dips and spreads *see also* sauces
Chipotle Mayo, 177
Dipping Sauce, 129
Everyday Guacamole, 298
Garlic Mayo, 126
Garlic Yogurt, 167
Goat Cheese Spread, 197
Red Pepper Spread, 189
Tomato Chili Jam, 148
Yogurt Dip, 62
Dough, Quick Pizza, 297
dressings and vinaigrettes
Chipotle Lime Vinaigrette, 235
Lemon Vinaigrette, 83
Sesame Lime Vinaigrette, 249
Thai Basil and Lime Vinaigrette, 168
Vegan Caesar Dressing, 294
Yogurt Caesar Dressing, 294
dumplings
Crispy Veggie Potstickers, 129
Wontons, 229–230

E

Easy Veggie Chili, 216
edamame
Peanut-Glazed Tofu Rice Bowls, 157
Vibrant Greens Salad with Sesame Lime Vinaigrette, 249
eggplants
Crispy Eggplant Roll-Ups, 58
Lemongrass Coconut Rice with Roasted Eggplant, 51
Meatless Meatballs with Garlic Bread, 103–104
eggs
Pesto and Greens Frittata, 65
Pesto Grain Bowls with Jammy Eggs, 143
Everyday Guacamole, 298

F

Fajitas, Sheet-Pan Veggie, 61
Falafel Bowls, 154
farro: Pesto Grain Bowls with Jammy Eggs, 143
feta cheese
Asparagus, Pea, and Whipped Feta Tart, 43
Baked Rice Pilaf with Feta and Roasted Tomatoes, 39
Broccoli Salad with Sticky Harissa Sauce, 242
Lemon and Dill Orzo Salad, 83
Mediterranean Pesto Pizza, 117
Pesto Grain Bowls with Jammy Eggs, 143
Smashed Potatoes and Roasted Cauliflower Bowls, 158
Firecracker Tofu with Broccolini and Chili Garlic Oil, 47
Flatbread with Orange Arugula Salad, 48
Flourless Chocolate Crackle Cookies, 280
Fresh Basil Pesto, 290
Frico-Style Quesadillas, 194
Fried Rice, Actually Good, 121
Frittata, Pesto and Greens, 65
fritters
Curry Vegetable, 178
Pea, and Fries with Tartar Sauce, 125

G

garlic
Firecracker Tofu with Broccolini and Chili Garlic Oil, 47
Garlic Bread, 103–104
Garlic Mashed Potatoes, 301
Garlic Mayo, 126
Garlic Yogurt, 167
Garlicky Breadcrumbs, 224
Seared Mushroom and Creamy Garlic Pasta, 79
Vegan Caesar Dressing, 294
Yogurt Caesar Dressing, 294
ginger
Ginger Scallion Oil, 51
Ginger Soy Soba Salad with Spicy Peanut Sauce, 95
Miso Ginger Glazed Squash, 54
Orange Ginger and Sesame Meatballs, 162
Veggie Wonton Soup, 229–230
goat cheese
Creamy Goat Cheese, 48
Goat Cheese Spread, 197
Mushroom and Goat Cheese Toasts, 181
gochujang: Bibimbap with Crispy Rice, 144
Gouda Mushroom Melts, Smoky, 126
grains *see also* rice
Barley Salad with Mushrooms and Burrata, 250
Bibimbap with Crispy Rice, 144
Harissa-Roasted Vegetables with Couscous, 62
Pesto Grain Bowls with Jammy Eggs, 143
green beans: Vibrant Greens Salad with Sesame Lime Vinaigrette, 249
Green Goddess Salad with Everything Bagel Croutons, 246
Grilled Halloumi Skewers with Thai Basil and Lime Vinaigrette, 168
Grilled Vegetables, 197
Guacamole, Everyday, 298

H

halloumi cheese
Grilled Halloumi Skewers with Thai Basil and Lime Vinaigrette, 168
Harissa-Roasted Vegetables with Couscous, 62

Kale Lentil Salad with Halloumi, 253
Seared Halloumi Sandwiches with Roasted Red Pepper Spread, 189
Hand Pies, Savoury Cheddar Apple, 137–138
harissa paste
Broccoli Salad with Sticky Harissa Sauce, 242
Harissa-Roasted Vegetables with Couscous, 62
hazelnuts
Flourless Chocolate Crackle Cookies, 280
Roasted Butternut Squash Pasta with Toasted Hazelnuts, 96
Healthier Macaroni and Cheese, 113
Herb Sauce, 158, 189
Hot Honey Roasted Carrots and Lentils, 40
hummus: Smashed Potatoes and Roasted Cauliflower Bowls, 158

I

Ice Cream, S'Mores No-Churn, 284

J

jalapeño peppers
Jalapeño Cilantro Slaw, 254
Pineapple Salsa, 174
Smoky Jalapeño Corn Chowder, 209
Jam, Tomato Chili, 148
Jammy Raspberry Streusel Bars, 259–260
Jasmine Rice, 302

K

kale
Barley Salad with Mushrooms and Burrata, 250
Cheesy Mushroom Calzones, 190
Chickpea Salad with Crispy Pita, 239
Kale Lentil Salad with Halloumi, 253
Pesto Pantry Pasta, 71
Roasted Cauliflower, Smashed Olive, and Lemon Pasta, 91
Wild Rice and Mushroom Stew, 206
kidney beans
Easy Veggie Chili, 216
Minestrone Soup with Pesto, 210

L

Lemongrass Coconut Rice with Roasted Eggplant, 51
lemons
Lemon and Dill Orzo Salad, 83
Lemon Vinaigrette, 83
Roasted Cauliflower, Smashed Olive, and Lemon Pasta, 91
lentils
Easy Veggie Chili, 216
Hot Honey Roasted Carrots and Lentils, 40
Kale Lentil Salad with Halloumi, 253
Potato and Lentil Stew with Crispy Shallots, 223
Shepherd's Pie, 118
Smoky Red Lentil Soup, 226
Thai Yellow Coconut Curry with Lentils, 205
limes
Chipotle Lime Vinaigrette, 235
Everyday Guacamole, 298
Sesame Lime Vinaigrette, 249
Sriracha Lime Sauce, 171
Thai Basil and Lime Vinaigrette, 168

M

macaroni
Healthier Macaroni and Cheese, 113
Minestrone Soup with Pesto, 210
mangoes: Peanut-Glazed Tofu Rice Bowls, 157
Marinade, Balsamic, 197
mayonnaise
Chipotle Mayo, 177
Garlic Mayo, 126
Veggie Sushi with Sriracha Mayo, 185–186
meatballs
Meatless, with Garlic Bread, 103–104
Orange Ginger and Sesame, 162
Mediterranean Pesto Pizza, 117
Medium-Grain and Long-Grain Rice, 303
Minestrone Soup with Pesto, 210
miso
Miso Brown Butter Pasta, 92
Miso Ginger Glazed Squash, 54
Spicy Miso Ramen, 213
mozzarella cheese
Caprese Pesto Panini, 182
Cheesy Mushroom Calzones, 190
Mediterranean Pesto Pizza, 117
Pea Fritters and Fries with Tartar Sauce, 125
Muffins, Banana Chocolate, 274
mushrooms, cremini
Cheesy Mushroom Calzones, 190
Crispy Veggie Potstickers, 129
Grilled Halloumi Skewers with Thai Basil and Lime Vinaigrette, 168
Meatless Meatballs with Garlic Bread, 103–104
Mushroom Stroganoff, 72
Vegetable Bourguignon, 122
Veggie Skillet Pot Pie, 106
Wild Rice and Mushroom Stew, 206
mushrooms, mixed
Barley Salad with Mushrooms and Burrata, 250
Mushroom and Goat Cheese Toasts, 181
Seared Mushroom and Creamy Garlic Pasta, 79
mushrooms, oyster
Chipotle Mushroom Tacos with Pineapple Jalapeño Salsa, 174
Shawarma-Spiced Mushroom Pita, 167
mushrooms, porcini
Veggie Wonton Soup, 229–230
Wild Rice and Mushroom Stew, 206

mushrooms, portobello: Smoky Gouda Mushroom Melts, 126
mushrooms, shiitake
Sesame and Smoked Tofu Noodle Soup, 220
Vegetable Ragu, 114
Veggie Wonton Soup, 229–230
Wild Rice and Mushroom Stew, 206
mushrooms, trumpet: Barbecue Pulled Mushroom Sandwiches, 109

N

navy beans
Miso Ginger Glazed Squash, 54
Polenta with Roasted Tomatoes and Basil Oil, 147
Veggie Skillet Pot Pie, 106
No Cream of Broccoli Soup with Garlicky Breadcrumbs, 224
noodle dishes *see also* pastas
Ginger Soy Soba Salad with Spicy Peanut Sauce, 95
Mushroom Stroganoff, 72
Sesame and Smoked Tofu Noodle Soup, 220
Spicy Miso Ramen, 213
Spicy Sesame Almond Noodles, 76
Veggie Pad Thai, 88
nuts *see* almonds; cashews; hazelnuts; peanuts/peanut butter; pecans; pistachios; walnuts

O

oats: Jammy Raspberry Streusel Bars, 259–260
oils
Basil, 147
Ginger Scallion, 51
olives
Lemon and Dill Orzo Salad, 83
Mediterranean Pesto Pizza, 117
Roasted Cauliflower, Smashed Olive, and Lemon Pasta, 91
one-pot bakes
Baked Rice Pilaf with Feta and Roasted Tomatoes, 39
Braised Vegetables with Parmesan Croutons, 66
Cheesy Chipotle Quinoa Bake, 44
Lemongrass Coconut Rice with Roasted Eggplant, 51
onions
Caramelized Onions, 126
Quick Pickled Red Onions, 289
oranges
Flatbread with Orange Arugula Salad, 48
Orange Ginger and Sesame Meatballs, 162
orzo: Lemon and Dill Orzo Salad, 83
oyster mushrooms *see* mushrooms, oyster

P

Pad Thai, Veggie, 88
Pancake, Butterscotch Banana Dutch Baby, 283
Pan-Fried Tofu, 249
Panini, Caprese Pesto, 182
Parmesan cheese
Baked Rice Pilaf with Feta and Roasted Tomatoes, 39
Braised Vegetables with Parmesan Croutons, 66
Cheesy Mushroom Calzones, 190
Creamy Roasted Red Pepper Pasta, 80
Crispy Eggplant Roll-Ups, 58
Flatbread with Orange Arugula Salad, 48
Fresh Basil Pesto, 290
Garlic Mashed Potatoes, 301
Healthier Macaroni and Cheese, 113
Miso Brown Butter Pasta, 92
Mushroom Stroganoff, 72
Pesto Pantry Pasta, 71
Polenta, 147
Roasted Cauliflower, Smashed Olive, and Lemon Pasta, 91
Seared Mushroom and Creamy Garlic Pasta, 79
Spinach, Pea, and Pesto Pasta, 75
Spinach and Artichoke Pasta, 87
Vegetable Ragu, 114
Wild Rice and Mushroom Stew, 206
Yogurt Caesar Dressing, 294
parsley, flat-leaf
Falafel Bowls, 154
Green Goddess Salad with Everything Bagel Croutons, 246
Herb Sauce, 158, 189
parsnips: Roasted Vegetables with Balsamic Glaze, 57
pastas *see also* noodle dishes
Coconut Green Curry Pasta, 99
Creamy Roasted Red Pepper Pasta, 80
Healthier Macaroni and Cheese, 113
Lemon and Dill Orzo Salad, 83
Miso Brown Butter Pasta, 92
Mushroom Stroganoff, 72
Pesto Pantry Pasta, 71
Roasted Butternut Squash Pasta with Toasted Hazelnuts, 96
Roasted Cauliflower, Smashed Olive, and Lemon Pasta, 91
Seared Mushroom and Creamy Garlic Pasta, 79
Spinach, Pea, and Pesto Pasta, 75
Spinach and Artichoke Pasta, 87
Vegetable Ragu, 114
pastries *see* pies and tarts
Pea Fritters and Fries with Tartar Sauce, 125
peanuts/peanut butter
Crispy Rice Salad with Smashed Cucumbers, 236
Ginger Soy Soba Salad with Spicy Peanut Sauce, 95
Peanut-Glazed Tofu Rice Bowls, 157
Veggie Pad Thai, 88
peas
Actually Good Fried Rice, 121
Asparagus, Pea, and Whipped Feta Tart, 43
Green Goddess Salad with

Everything Bagel Croutons, 246
Pea Fritters and Fries with Tartar Sauce, 125
Savoury Cheddar Apple Hand Pies, 137–138
Shepherd's Pie, 118
Spicy Sesame Almond Noodles, 76
Spinach, Pea, and Pesto Pasta, 75
Veggie Skillet Pot Pie, 106
Veggie Wonton Soup, 229–230
Vibrant Greens Salad with Sesame Lime Vinaigrette, 249
pecans: Butterscotch Banana Dutch Baby Pancake, 283
pepitas
Roasted Sweet Potatoes with Jalapeño Cilantro Slaw, 254
Sweet Potato Black Bean Burgers with Chipotle Mayo, 177
peppers *see* bell peppers; chipotle peppers in adobo; jalapeño peppers; red peppers, roasted
pesto
Caprese Pesto Panini, 182
Fresh Basil Pesto, 290
Mediterranean Pesto Pizza, 117
Minestrone Soup with Pesto, 210
Pesto and Greens Frittata, 65
Pesto Grain Bowls with Jammy Eggs, 143
Pesto Pantry Pasta, 71
Spinach, Pea, and Pesto Pasta, 75
Vegan Pesto, 290
pickles *see* quick pickles
pies and tarts *see also* baked goods
Asparagus, Pea, and Whipped Feta Tart, 43
Bottomless Apple Caramel Pie, 277–278
Savoury Cheddar Apple Hand Pies, 137–138
Shepherd's Pie, 118
Veggie Skillet Pot Pie, 106
pine nuts
Fresh Basil Pesto, 290
Vegan Pesto, 290
Pineapple Salsa, 174
pinto beans
Burrito Bowls with Smoky Sofritas, 161
Cheesy Chipotle Quinoa Bake, 44
Frico-Style Quesadillas, 194
pistachios
Kale Lentil Salad with Halloumi, 253
Smashed Potatoes and Roasted Cauliflower Bowls, 158
pitas
Chickpea Salad with Crispy Pita, 239
Shawarma-Spiced Mushroom Pita, 167
pizzas
Cheesy Mushroom Calzones, 190
Mediterranean Pesto Pizza, 117
Quick Pizza Dough, 297
Polenta with Roasted Tomatoes and Basil Oil, 147
pomegranates: Kale Lentil Salad with Halloumi, 253
porcini mushrooms *see* mushrooms, porcini
portobello mushrooms *see* mushrooms, portobello
Pot Pie, Veggie Skillet, 106
potatoes
Curry Vegetable Fritters, 178
Garlic Mashed Potatoes, 301
Green Goddess Salad with Everything Bagel Croutons, 246
No Cream of Broccoli Soup with Garlicky Breadcrumbs, 224
Pea Fritters and Fries with Tartar Sauce, 125
Potato and Lentil Stew with Crispy Shallots, 223
Savoury Cheddar Apple Hand Pies, 137–138
Silky Cauliflower Soup with Cheese and Pepper Crisps, 202
Smashed Potatoes and Roasted Cauliflower Bowls, 158
Smoky Jalapeño Corn Chowder, 209
Smoky Red Lentil Soup, 226
Thai Yellow Coconut Curry with Lentils, 205
Veggie Skillet Pot Pie, 106
potatoes, sweet *see* sweet potatoes
Potstickers, Crispy Veggie, 129
Pudding, Chocolate, with Pretzel Crumble, 268
puff pastry
Asparagus, Pea, and Whipped Feta Tart, 43
Bottomless Apple Caramel Pie, 277–278
Savoury Cheddar Apple Hand Pies, 137–138
Veggie Skillet Pot Pie, 106
pumpkin seeds *see* pepitas

Q

Quesadillas, Frico-Style, 194
quick pickles
Quick Pickled Cabbage, 154
Quick Pickled Carrots, 171
Quick Pickled Red Onions, 289
Quick Pickled Shallots, 51
Spicy Pickled Radishes, 236
quinoa
Cheesy Chipotle Quinoa Bake, 44
Pea Fritters and Fries with Tartar Sauce, 125

R

radishes
Chickpea Salad with Crispy Pita, 239
Green Goddess Salad with Everything Bagel Croutons, 246
Spicy Pickled Radishes, 236
Ragu, Vegetable, 114
ramen noodles
Spicy Miso Ramen, 213
Spicy Sesame Almond Noodles, 76
raspberries: Jammy Raspberry Streusel Bars, 259–260
red peppers, roasted
Creamy Roasted Red Pepper Pasta, 80

Easy Veggie Chili, 216
Pesto Pantry Pasta, 71
Red Pepper Spread, 189
Smoky Red Lentil Soup, 226
rice *see also* grains
Actually Good Fried Rice, 121
Baked Rice Pilaf with Feta and Roasted Tomatoes, 39
Bibimbap with Crispy Rice, 144
Charred Sweet Potatoes with Tomato Chili Jam, 148
Crispy Rice Salad with Smashed Cucumbers, 236
how to cook, 302
Jasmine Rice, 302
Lemongrass Coconut Rice with Roasted Eggplant, 51
Medium-Grain and Long-Grain Rice, 303
Orange Ginger and Sesame Meatballs, 162
Peanut-Glazed Tofu Rice Bowls, 157
Short-Grain Brown Rice, 303
Sweet Potato Black Bean Burgers with Chipotle Mayo, 177
Veggie Sushi with Sriracha Mayo, 185–186
Wild Rice and Mushroom Stew, 206
ricotta cheese
Blistered Tomatoes and Whipped Ricotta Toasts, 193
Ricotta Cream, 65
Roasted Butternut Squash Pasta with Toasted Hazelnuts, 96
Roasted Butternut Squash Soup with Buttery Sage Croutons, 219
Roasted Cauliflower, Smashed Olive, and Lemon Pasta, 91
Roasted Mushrooms, 126
Roasted Sweet Potatoes with Jalapeño Cilantro Slaw, 254
Roasted Tomato Soup with Cheesy Bread, 201
Roasted Vegetables with Balsamic Glaze, 57

S

sage leaves: Buttery Sage Croutons, 219
salads
Barley Salad with Mushrooms and Burrata, 250
Broccoli Salad with Sticky Harissa Sauce, 242
Celery Salad, 133–134
Chickpea Salad with Crispy Pita, 239
Crispy Rice Salad with Smashed Cucumbers, 236
Flatbread with Orange Arugula Salad, 48
Ginger Soy Soba Salad with Spicy Peanut Sauce, 95
Green Goddess Salad with Everything Bagel Croutons, 246
Kale Lentil Salad with Halloumi, 253
Lemon and Dill Orzo Salad, 83
Roasted Sweet Potatoes with Jalapeño Cilantro Slaw, 254
Santa Fe Salad with Chipotle Lime Vinaigrette, 235
Seared Brussels Sprouts Caesar Salad, 245
Vibrant Greens Salad with Sesame Lime Vinaigrette, 249
Salsa, Pineapple, 174
sandwiches
Balsamic Vegetable and Goat Cheese Sandwiches, 197
Barbecue Pulled Mushroom Sandwiches, 109
Blistered Tomatoes and Whipped Ricotta Toasts, 193
Caprese Pesto Panini, 182
Crispy Tofu Banh Mi, 171–172
Mushroom and Goat Cheese Toasts, 181
Seared Halloumi Sandwiches with Roasted Red Pepper Spread, 189
Shawarma-Spiced Mushroom Pita, 167
Smoky Gouda Mushroom Melts, 126
Santa Fe Salad with Chipotle Lime Vinaigrette, 235
sauces *see also* dips and spreads
Balsamic Marinade, 197
Basil Oil, 147
Buffalo Sauce, 133–134
Butterscotch Sauce, 283
Date Barbecue Sauce, 109
Dipping Sauce, 129
Fresh Basil Pesto, 290
Herb Sauce, 158, 189
Hot Honey, 40
Miso Ginger Glaze, 54
Peanut Butter Sauce, 157
Peanut Sauce, 95
Pineapple Salsa, 174
Spicy Almond Sauce, 76
Sriracha Lime Sauce, 171
Tartar Sauce, 125
Tzatziki, 293
Vegan Pesto, 290
Vegan Tzatziki, 293
Savoury Cheddar Apple Hand Pies, 137–138
scallions: Ginger Scallion Oil, 51
Seared Brussels Sprouts Caesar Salad, 245
Seared Halloumi Sandwiches with Roasted Red Pepper Spread, 189
Seared Mushroom and Creamy Garlic Pasta, 79
seeds *see* pepitas; pine nuts; sesame seeds
sesame oil: Sesame and Smoked Tofu Noodle Soup, 220
sesame seeds
Orange Ginger and Sesame Meatballs, 162
Sesame Lime Vinaigrette, 249
Spicy Sesame Almond Noodles, 76
shallots
Potato and Lentil Stew with Crispy Shallots, 223
Quick Pickled Shallots, 51

Shawarma-Spiced Mushroom Pita, 167
sheet-pan bakes
- Firecracker Tofu with Broccolini and Chili Garlic Oil, 47
- Harissa-Roasted Vegetables with Couscous, 62
- Hot Honey Roasted Carrots and Lentils, 40
- Lemongrass Coconut Rice with Roasted Eggplant, 51
- Miso Ginger Glazed Squash, 54
- Roasted Vegetables with Balsamic Glaze, 57
- Sheet-Pan Veggie Fajitas, 61

Shepherd's Pie, 118
shiitake mushrooms *see* mushrooms, shiitake
Shortcut Brothy Beans, 151
Short-Grain Brown Rice, 303
Silky Cauliflower Soup with Cheese and Pepper Crisps, 202
Skewers, Grilled Halloumi, with Thai Basil and Lime Vinaigrette, 168
Skillet Pot Pie, Veggie, 106
Slaw, Jalapeño Cilantro, 254
Smashed Potatoes and Roasted Cauliflower Bowls, 158
Smoky Chickpea Crumble, 245
Smoky Gouda Mushroom Melts, 126
Smoky Jalapeño Corn Chowder, 209
Smoky Red Lentil Soup, 226
S'Mores No-Churn Ice Cream, 284
Soba Salad, Ginger Soy, with Spicy Peanut Sauce, 95
soups and stews
- Easy Veggie Chili, 216
- Minestrone Soup with Pesto, 210
- No Cream of Broccoli Soup with Garlicky Breadcrumbs, 224
- Potato and Lentil Stew with Crispy Shallots, 223
- Roasted Butternut Squash Soup with Buttery Sage Croutons, 219
- Roasted Tomato Soup with Cheesy Bread, 201
- Sesame and Smoked Tofu Noodle Soup, 220
- Silky Cauliflower Soup with Cheese and Pepper Crisps, 202
- Smoky Jalapeño Corn Chowder, 209
- Smoky Red Lentil Soup, 226
- Spicy Miso Ramen, 213
- Thai Yellow Coconut Curry with Lentils, 205
- Veggie Wonton Soup, 229–230
- Wild Rice and Mushroom Stew, 206

spice blends: Fajita Seasoning, 61
Spicy Almond Sauce, 76
Spicy Miso Ramen, 213
Spicy Pickled Radishes, 236
Spicy Sesame Almond Noodles, 76
spinach
- Baked Rice Pilaf with Feta and Roasted Tomatoes, 39
- Bibimbap with Crispy Rice, 144
- Caprese Pesto Panini, 182
- Frico-Style Quesadillas, 194
- Lemon and Dill Orzo Salad, 83
- Minestrone Soup with Pesto, 210
- Pea Fritters and Fries with Tartar Sauce, 125
- Pesto and Greens Frittata, 65
- Pesto Grain Bowls with Jammy Eggs, 143
- Spicy Sesame Almond Noodles, 76
- Spinach, Pea, and Pesto Pasta, 75
- Spinach and Artichoke Pasta, 87

spreads *see* dips and spreads
squash
- Miso Ginger Glazed Squash, 54
- Roasted Butternut Squash Pasta with Toasted Hazelnuts, 96
- Roasted Butternut Squash Soup with Buttery Sage Croutons, 219

Sriracha sauce
- Sriracha Lime Sauce, 171
- Veggie Sushi with Sriracha Mayo, 185–186

stews *see* soups and stews
Sushi, Veggie, with Sriracha Mayo, 185–186
sweet potatoes
- Charred Sweet Potatoes with Tomato Chili Jam, 148
- Easy Veggie Chili, 216
- Frico-Style Quesadillas, 194
- Kale Lentil Salad with Halloumi, 253
- Roasted Sweet Potatoes with Jalapeño Cilantro Slaw, 254
- Sweet Potato Black Bean Burgers with Chipotle Mayo, 177
- Veggie Sushi with Sriracha Mayo, 185–186

Swiss chard
- Shortcut Brothy Beans, 151
- Thai Yellow Coconut Curry with Lentils, 205

T

Tacos, Chipotle Mushroom, with Pineapple Jalapeño Salsa, 174
Tartar Sauce, 125
tarts *see* pies and tarts
Thai Yellow Coconut Curry with Lentils, 205
toasts *see also* breads
- Blistered Tomatoes and Whipped Ricotta Toasts, 193
- Mushroom and Goat Cheese Toasts, 181

tofu
- Burrito Bowls with Smoky Sofritas, 161
- Crispy Tofu Banh Mi, 171–172
- Firecracker Tofu with Broccolini and Chili Garlic Oil, 47
- Lemongrass Coconut Rice with Roasted Eggplant, 51
- Orange Ginger and Sesame Meatballs, 162
- Pan-Fried Tofu, 249
- Peanut-Glazed Tofu Rice Bowls, 157
- Veggie Pad Thai, 88
- Veggie Wonton Soup, 229–230

tofu, silken: Chocolate Pudding with Pretzel Crumble, 268

tofu, smoked
Crispy Rice Salad with Smashed Cucumbers, 236
Ginger Soy Soba Salad with Spicy Peanut Sauce, 95
Sesame and Smoked Tofu Noodle Soup, 220
tomatoes
Baked Rice Pilaf with Feta and Roasted Tomatoes, 39
Blistered Tomatoes and Whipped Ricotta Toasts, 193
Braised Vegetables with Parmesan Croutons, 66
Caprese Pesto Panini, 182
Date Barbecue Sauce, 109
Minestrone Soup with Pesto, 210
Polenta with Roasted Tomatoes and Basil Oil, 147
Tomato Chili Jam, 148
tomatoes, fire-roasted
Burrito Bowls with Smoky Sofritas, 161
Cheesy Chipotle Quinoa Bake, 44
Easy Veggie Chili, 216
Roasted Tomato Soup with Cheesy Bread, 201
Smoky Red Lentil Soup, 226
Vegetable Ragu, 114
tomatoes, sun-dried
Creamy Roasted Red Pepper Pasta, 80
Mediterranean Pesto Pizza, 117
Pesto and Greens Frittata, 65
Pesto Pantry Pasta, 71
tortillas
Chipotle Mushroom Tacos with Pineapple Jalapeño Salsa, 174
Frico-Style Quesadillas, 194
Sheet-Pan Veggie Fajitas, 61
trumpet mushrooms *see* mushrooms, trumpet
Tzatziki, 293

V

Vegan Caesar Dressing, 294
Vegan Pesto, 290
Vegan Tzatziki, 293
Vegetable Bourguignon, 122
Vegetable Ragu, 114
Veggie Pad Thai, 88
Veggie Skillet Pot Pie, 106
Veggie Sushi with Sriracha Mayo, 185–186
Veggie Wonton Soup, 229–230
Vibrant Greens Salad with Sesame Lime Vinaigrette, 249
vinaigrettes *see* dressings and vinaigrettes

W

walnuts
Blistered Tomatoes and Whipped Ricotta Toasts, 193
Brown Butter Chocolate Walnut Cookies, 262
Red Pepper Spread, 189
Shepherd's Pie, 118
Whipped Yogurt Cream with Berries, 271
Wild Rice and Mushroom Stew, 206
Wontons, 229–230

Y

yogurt, Greek
Banana Chocolate Muffins, 274
Celery Salad, 133–134
Chickpea Salad with Crispy Pita, 239
Garlic Yogurt, 167
Green Goddess Salad with Everything Bagel Croutons, 246
Jalapeño Cilantro Slaw, 254
Tartar Sauce, 125
Tzatziki, 293
Whipped Yogurt Cream with Berries, 271
Yogurt Caesar Dressing, 294
Yogurt Dip, 62

Z

zucchini
Grilled Halloumi Skewers with Thai Basil and Lime Vinaigrette, 168
Grilled Vegetables, 197
Harissa-Roasted Vegetables with Couscous, 62